BEYOND PUBLIC EDUCATION

Myron Lieberman

PRAEGER

PRAEGER SPECIAL STUDIES • PRAEGER SCIENTIFIC

New York • Philadelphia • Eastbourne, UK
Toronto • Hong Kong • Tokyo • Sydney

Library of Congress Cataloging-in-Publication Data

Lieberman, Myron, 1919-
 Beyond public education.

 Includes index.
 1. Public schools — United States. 2. Education
— United States — Aims and objectives. 3. School
management and organization — United States.
I. Title.
LA217 L53   1986   379.73   85-25571
ISBN 0-275-92039-9 (alk. paper)
     0-275-92631-1

Library of Congress Catalog Card Number: 85-25571
ISBN: 0-275-92039-9

First published in 1986 (cl. and pbk.)

Praeger Publishers, 521 Fifth Avenue, New York, NY 10175
A division of Greenwood Press, Inc.

Printed in the United States of America

∞

The paper used in this book complies with the Permanent
Paper Standard issued by the National Information Standards
Organization (Z39.48-1984).

10 9 8 7 6 5 4 3

For Grace Lieberman

FOREWORD

Of all the institutions in American society that are essential to its survival and growth, the schools play the major role. They are the basis for transmitting both a sense of history and a sense of the future. They transmit facts and they must teach students to think. They transmit the values, hopes, and aspirations of our culture and provide the basis for lives of work and creativity necessary to maintain our economic prosperity.

Unfortunately, our schools have become institutionalized bureaucracies with little flexibility and, very often, few choices to change how they deal with delivering effective, less costly education. I have advocated for many years that an essential step in improving the educational system in our K-12 schools is to have business operating schools for local school districts. The combined business experience of general management, financial awareness, and orientation toward achieving reasonable objectives causes people in profit-seeking enterprises to deal with problems in a different fashion. The incentives of business people are set differently and rewards are passed out to managers and professional personnel based upon achieving measurable goals. Today's public education system does not have in it a means for establishing goals that will lead to high-quality, cost-effective education for all our children.

When I was first made aware of Dr. Lieberman's book, I was gratified to find a leading educator who shared these views. So when Dr. Lieberman asked me if I would write a few words as a preface to his important work, I readily agreed. I subscribe wholeheartedly to the reforms he suggests.

Schools *can* be changed. Tools exist today to help teachers do the kind of job that is required in the final years of the twentieth century to improve dramatically basic literacy. We know good schools can exist without use of technology through efforts of dedicated professional teachers. The fact is, however, that there simply is not enough money to hire all the qualified teachers necessary (even if available) to supply the quality of education that all of America's children deserve. The only way this can be done, and provide important changes in the process within the classroom and overall improvement in the

v

total school, is through the increased use of educational technology, such as computer-based education systems and programs.

The educational reform movement notwithstanding, only the management of schools by business can generate the new technology and the increased utilization of existing technology that will lead to higher quality and more cost-effective education. Furthermore, operating schools as for-profit businesses will increasingly insure that students will be evaluated in quantifiable terms. In this way, parents and communities, as well as the students themselves, will have a better understanding of what the students have learned and what remains to be done. Such an outcome is critically needed, and Dr. Lieberman's book points the way to its achievement.

I hope people will read Dr. Lieberman's work with care. This book is destined to become the focus of a national debate on changing the basic ways we deliver education to our children.

William C. Norris
Chairman, Control Data Corporation;
Member, Task Force on Education
for Economic Growth
Education Commission of the States

Preface

In my opinion, the argument of this book is supported by extensive data. Nevertheless, in an effort to accommodate readers who wish only to follow the overall argument while avoiding a mass of detail, I have not cited all the sources and data that support the argument. Furthermore, I have not tried to be precise where precision would be irrelevant. For example, it can hardly matter whether 72 or 73 percent of the nation's teachers are unionized. What is important is that teachers are a heavily unionized group; the short-term fluctuations do not affect the validity of any point in the discussion. In cases of this kind, I have used precise figures where they were readily available, but have made no special effort to locate and use such figures when they are essentially irrelevant to the argument.

Similarly, the discussion does not always cite sources where the data cited are a matter of common knowledge, or of common professional knowledge. For instance, I have not documented the fact that most school boards have staggered terms, or that most state aid is based upon average daily attendance. Again, where the sources for such statements were readily available, they have been cited, but I have not tried to document the obvious or the widely known.

Of course, readers can decide for themselves whether I have evaded substantiation of a controversial statement or whether a statement is acceptable by reasonable persons without additional documentation. Needless to say, if data or sources have been omitted where they were essential, I am responsible for the omission.

Two major reform reports were released after this manuscript was completed. One is *A Nation Prepared: Teachers for the 21st Century:* The Report of the Task Force on Teaching as a Profession of the Carnegie Forum on Education and the Economy. Unlike other reform reports, *A Nation Prepared* devotes some attention to teacher unions and the governance structure of education. It also acknowledges the futility of trying to raise all teacher salaries and the importance of market factors and incentives in teacher compensation. Although both the NEA and AFT approved this report at their 1986 conventions, its recommendations are so unrealistic and so undesirable that the report does not justify any change in my negative conclusions about the impact of the educational reform movement.

The other major report which was unavailable in time to be considered here is *The 1991 Report on Education*, a report prepared by seven educational task forces of the National Governors Association.

ACKNOWLEDGMENTS

I am indebted to several persons and organizations for assistance in writing this book. Annette Kirk graciously shared some valuable insights as a member of the National Commission on Excellence in Education, and I am also indebted to Russell Kirk for specific suggestions and words of encouragement. I would also like to express my appreciation to Bruce Cooper of Fordham University; Milton Friedman of the Hoover Institution; Donald E. Frey of Wake Forest University; Kim Colby of the Christian Legal Society; Lawrence Uzzell, Scripps Howard Newspapers; Walter M. Bruning, President, United School Services of America; Charles Lavaroni, the first president of the National Independent Private Schools Association and Education Director, Kittredge School, San Francisco; Gerald F. Ludden, Director, Dorris-Eaton School, Walnut Creek, California; Mary T. Carey and Clare Carey Willard, Co-Directors, The Carey School, San Mateo, California; Patrick A. O'Donnell, President, Discovery Center School, San Francisco; Dr. Glen E. Robinson, Executive Director, Educational Research Service; and the New Jersey School Boards Association.

A special note of appreciation is due Ohio University, especially Dean of Education Allen Myers and Dr. Fred B. Dressel, chairman of the Division of Applied Behavioral Sciences and Educational Leadership. It should be emphasized, however, that the positions set forth in this book are solely my responsibility and cannot fairly be ascribed to anyone else.

CONTENTS

LIST OF FIGURES
AND TABLES

1

INTRODUCTION:
WHAT THIS BOOK IS ABOUT

In recent years, educational reform has become a growth industry in the United States. Government agencies, foundations, political leaders, professional organizations, legislative bodies, media—all have bought into it. A growing avalanche of reports, studies, surveys, recommendations, and policy statements tell us what's wrong with education and what to do about it. Whoever adds to this avalanche deservedly faces a critical threshold question: What do you have to say that has not already been said, ad nauseam if not ad infinitum?

What I have to say can be summarized as follows:

1. Public education is experiencing an irreversible decline as a prestigious, influential social institution in our society. The statistics about public education, in terms of students enrolled, teachers employed, and dollars expended, will continue to be impressive. Even so, public education will continue to lose parental/student respect and support; a smaller proportion of the highly talented will seek careers in public education; and public schools will be increasingly irrelevant to the intellectual and moral development of young people.

2. Despite an unprecedented amount of public attention devoted to the subject since 1980, public education was not undergoing any significant reform as of the fall of 1985. Such "educational reform" as has been achieved is a media event—that is, the media attention it has received is much greater than any changes that have taken place. As much as anything, media gullibility obscures the political, educational, and intellectual bankruptcy of the education reform movement.

1

3. For the most part, the recent educational reform movement has focused upon the academic deficiencies of public education. As a result, it has overlooked concerns and problems in vocational education and in such nonacademic areas as patriotism, religion, work habits, sex, dress, language, crime, drug use, and alcoholism. When these concerns and problems are taken into account, it is clear that dissatisfaction with public education, as well as its vulnerability to alternative systems of education, have been widely underestimated.

4. The major obstacles to educational reform include, but are not limited to, the governance structure of education, teacher unions and the vulnerability of reforms to the bargaining process, tenure laws, the insulation of education from market and competitive forces, higher education, and a pervasive leadership gap. To be achievable, reform proposals must include a strategy for dealing with these obstacles, and with others that adversely affect vested interests in the status quo. Unfortunately, the current reform movement does not even recognize their existence, let alone have a strategy for dealing with them. Partly for this reason, it will fail as dismally as other reform movements in the past have failed.

5. In public schools, the process of education will improve only in response to (a) changes in its governance structure, that is, the way education is organized, financed, and controlled; and/or (b) the expansion of nonpublic education. Both of these conditions will create and strengthen interests opposed to public education. By the time public schools accept basic educational reform, or have it forced upon them, private schools or private enterprise will educate a larger proportion of our youth. They will also command more support and more influence than they do at the present time. Consequently, it will no longer be possible to restore the prestige and influence of public schools or their "market share."

6. Tuition tax credits and vouchers (hereinafter, "family choice proposals" or "tuition tax credits/vouchers") constitute the most significant proposals to improve the process of education through changes in its governance structure. Such proposals are intended to strengthen parental or family choice by making private schools a more economically attractive option for more parents. For the most part, therefore, tuition tax credits and vouchers are not intended to strengthen public education but to provide feasible alternatives to it.

Arguably, tuition tax credits/vouchers could improve public education as well as provide alternatives to it. At this time, what seems clear is that the specifics of any tuition tax credit/voucher legislation will largely determine its effects upon public schools. As matters stand, the specifics are likely to differ from state to state with varying results on every important issue associated with the legislation. Although this book supports tuition tax credits/vouchers, it also asserts that their effects on both private and public schools are not certain and will depend primarily upon the legislative specifics.

7. Regardless of the fate of tuition tax credits/vouchers, private profit-making schools (hereinafter called "entrepreneurial schools") will be the most effective way to achieve significant improvement in elementary and secondary education. Although not argued in great detail, this position is frequently related to the discussion of public school reform. The discussion also devotes some attention to the reasons why nonprofit private schools are unlikely to bring about basic educational improvement. In my view, private enterprise must go beyond selling goods and services to public and nonprofit elementary and secondary schools; school districts, schools, and programs within schools must be operated privately for profit on a much larger scale in order to bring about widespread educational improvement. It is also my view that privatizing education this way will make it more responsive as well as more equitable. The evidence supporting these conclusions may not be overwhelming, but realistic assessments of conventional approaches to reform strongly suggest the urgency of careful consideration of the alternatives.

THE AUDIENCE: TO WHOM IS THE MESSAGE ADDRESSED?

This is a book about educational policy and practice. Understandably, it is intended for policymakers and policy administrators at all levels of education: school boards, school administrators, leaders in teacher unions and unions of nonteaching employees, professional and commercial organizations that deal with schools, foundation officials, and so on.

Nevertheless, for two reasons, parents of school-age children are a major audience. One of my major objectives is to help parents reject cosmetic changes in education that leave the status quo essentially unchanged. My analysis is intended to explain how and why parent participation in school affairs is usually futile and what must be done to make it effective.

Parents are a major audience for another and perhaps more important reason. Ordinarily, policymakers need a certain measure of public understanding and support in order to enact and implement basic policy changes. Parents obviously constitute a potentially important base of support for educational reform. Even parents who are unable to become active participants in school affairs can help to achieve reform, merely by supporting elected policymakers who are on the right track. Needless to say, this observation is also applicable to the vast number of citizens who do not have school-age children but who do have, or may have, a strong interest in school affairs. In the long run, the issues will not be resolved merely by the interest groups employed in education.

At the present time, almost one-fourth of our population is involved full-time in education as students, teachers, or other employees. Simply because of the numbers and resources involved, most persons without any direct relationship to education nevertheless have a stake or an interest in its effectiveness. For example, many citizens who are not parents of school-age children are nevertheless deeply concerned about the ways public schools relate to teenage sex, pregnancy, abortion, alcohol, drug abuse, and other social issues. Inasmuch as the analysis devotes considerable attention to these issues, it should be of interest to this group. Another primary audience is the teaching profession, a group with which the author has been closely associated for over 35 years.

Although this book is devoted primarily to public education, it raises issues of the utmost importance to private schools. Indeed, as the discussion emphasizes, we are at the threshold of an era of intensified competition and controversy between public and nonpublic schools. Be that as it may, my argument is that the relationships between public and private schools will be absolutely critical in the years ahead.

Some target audiences are small numerically but critical strategically. Media personnel with responsibilities for news and/or editorial comment about education are especially important. I would also categorize leaders of big business in the same way. Regardless of whether their companies are currently active in education markets, our leading corporate managers can play a vital role in achieving educational reform. As a matter of fact, I regard this group as potentially more important to our educational future than our leadership in government or higher education.

THE NEED FOR EDUCATIONAL REFORM

Why is educational reform needed? One reason is that educational achievement has declined significantly in the past 20 years. As we shall see, there is considerable controversy over who or what is responsible for our educational decline. There is also considerable controversy over what should be done to remedy the situation. There is, however, relatively little controversy over the fact of decline. For this reason, it is not necessary to present elaborate arguments on the subject. Instead, I shall simply cite some of the evidence that has persuaded many citizens that educational achievement in the United States has declined in recent years. The evidence to be cited is from the highly publicized report to the nation and the U.S. Secretary of Education by the National Commission on Excellence in Education. Established by the secretary of education on August 5, 1981, the commission was charged with several responsibilities, including:

> (1) To review and synthesize the data and scholarly literature on the quality of learning and teaching in the nation's schools, colleges, and universities, both public and private, with special concern for the educational experience of teen-age youth;
> (2) To examine and to compare and contrast the curricula, standards, and expectations of the educational system of several advanced countries with those of the United States. . . .[1]

The commission's report, released on April 26, 1983, was entitled *A Nation At Risk: The Imperative for Educational Reform*. In explaining why educational deterioration rendered the United States "a nation at risk," and why educational reform was "imperative," the commission cited a wide variety of data. Because the data cited by the commission are so extensive and the fact of educational deterioration is widely accepted, readers are referred to the full commission report for its extemely negative conclusions about the quality of education in the United States. It may be helpful, however, to list the kinds of data on which the commission relied to reach its conclusions.

1. International comparisons that showed that on 19 academic tests, American students were never first or second, and ranked last seven times among industrialized nations.
2. A substantial amount of illiteracy, especially among minority youth.
3. Lower achievement scores on standardized tests than in 1957.
4. A "virtually unbroken decline" from 1963 to 1981 in the scores on college aptitude tests.
5. A dramatic decline in the number and proportion of students demonstrating superior achievement on the Scholastic Aptitude Tests.

6. An enormous increase in remedial courses; for example, one-fourth of all the mathematics courses in public four-year colleges are remedial courses. Additionally, the data showed that our armed forces were being forced to sponsor extensive remedial work to make up for the educational deficiencies of their recruits.
7. Substantial increases in the proportion of high school students taking programs of study lacking any central purpose or defensible academic core.
8. Lower expectations of students, as revealed by declines in homework required, grade inflation occurring simultaneously with declines in achievement, elimination or reduction of basic academic subjects as requirements for graduation, a tremendous increase in elective courses and tendency for students to elect the least demanding personal development courses instead of defensible academic ones, and declines in standards for college admissions.
9. A teaching profession recruited largely from less able college students, and an absolute shortage of teachers in such critical areas as physics, chemistry, and mathematics.[2]

As the commission itself pointed out, the facts it cited are only illustrative. Even so, they demonstrate the magnitude of the problems confronting U.S. education. On this issue, the commission report is in agreement with other recent reports on U.S. education. Without exception, they assert that the deficiencies in our education require nationwide or at least large-scale improvement. Otherwise, they will be inadequate. This important point requires some elaboration.

Institutional versus Ad Hoc Reform

Whatever one's view of the quality of education in the United States, no one seriously disputes that some school districts are better than others. In some, much less attention is paid to fundamentals, such as reading, even though the need is as great or greater than in adjacent school districts that do emphasize it. The same antisocial pupil behavior and sloppy work habits that are tolerated in some districts are not in others. The quality of teacher evaluation is often indefensible, for no valid reason or excuse. To contend that improvement is impossible in these situations would be unrealistic, and no such contention is made in this book.

Even so, such improvement, important as it may be to particular school districts, is not an improvement in public education as a social institution. It is simply an ad hoc improvement that may well be offset by a change for the worse somewhere else, or even in the same district at a later time. An analogy may help to illustrate this important point.

A college football team is losing constantly. Despite reasonably good talent, its play is ragged: fumbles, interceptions, penalties, bonehead strategy, and low morale characterize its play. Finally, a new coach is hired and things improve immediately. Not only the won/loss record but the level of play goes up appreciably. Beyond any doubt, we can say that the quality of football has improved at this fortunate institution of higher education.

Can we also say that the quality of intercollegiate football per se has improved? Not really. Perhaps our new coach left an institution that replaced him with an incompetent coach. As a result, its teams, which formerly performed very well, now perform very poorly. At any given time, coaches are being hired and fired. The changes often affect the fortunes of individual institutions, but they do not raise the overall quality of the game.

Throughout this analysis, I assert that certain reforms cannot be adopted on a national basis. By "national basis," I do not mean that the reforms have to be adopted in every state or every school district. I mean only that the reforms have to be institutionalized, that is, become permanently established on a large scale. My argument is cognizant of the fact that the reforms may have already been adopted in some school districts. The issue, however, is their generalizability, not their ad hoc existence. Thus the fact that some school districts employ a competent staff does not mean that all districts can do so; the pool of competent teachers is simply not large enough. Theoretically, the size of the pool can be increased—for example, by increasing teacher salaries. Practically, no improvement in teacher salaries that has even a remote chance of being adopted will increase the pool of competent teachers to any significant extent.

The Educational Reform Movement

Efforts to reform or improve public education are not new; in fact, they have existed as long as the public schools themselves. From time to time, however, the attention devoted to educational reform has varied a great deal. In recent years, and especially since 1981, an unprecedented amount of time and effort and resources have been devoted to educational reform. From 1981 ro 1983, several prestigious task forces, study groups, educational commissions, and other advisory groups have issued reform proposals. These proposals typically outline major deficiencies in public education and set forth policies and programs intended to remedy these deficiencies. In referring to the "reform movement," therefore, I am referring to the reform proposals or reform documents listed in Appendix A. Although Appendix A does not include every reform proposal made in recent years, it clearly includes the most prestigious proposals and/or the ones that have received the most attention in the media as well as in professional journals and conferences.

In addition to the documents listed in Appendix A, the phrase "reform movement" is intended to denote the following activities:

- The legislation introduced in Congress and the various state legislatures to implement reform proposals.
- The activities on reform issues by national educational organizations. These include but are not limited to the activities of the National Education Association, American Federation of Teachers, American Association of School Administrators, National School Boards Association, National Association of Secondary School Principals, and the National Association of Elementary School Principals.
- A vast number of national, regional, state, and local conventions, meetings, conferences, symposia, and other events devoted to recommendations in the reform proposals.
- Attention in the media to the need for educational reform and recent proposals to bring it about.

As with any social movement, the educational reform movement cannot be defined precisely. Undoubtedly, one could easily justify changes in any definition or in its application to specific persons or documents. Nevertheless, I believe that the preceding comments accurately reflect what most people mean by "the educational reform movement."

AN OVERVIEW OF THE ARGUMENT

Given the large number and variety of educational reform proposals, it was not feasible to analyze each and every one in this book. Instead, I have analyzed in depth certain issues that are demonstrably critical to meaningful reform. Some of these issues have received a great deal of publicity; others have received none. My analysis is intended to illustrate the obstacles confronting reform that have been ignored by the reform movement. Readers who agree that I have identified some basic oversights in conventional school reform are unlikely to require additional reasons for its futility. Readers not convinced are not likely to be persuaded by additional examples along the same lines.

Chapter 2, therefore, begins my analysis of conventional school reform. This chapter discusses a problem that is universally ignored by the reform movement, to wit, the role of teacher unions in the reform process. Chapter 3 analyzes some financial issues pertaining to reform, especially the issues related to teacher salaries. In this chapter I shall argue that overpayment of some teachers is as serious a problem as underpayment of others, and that as a practical matter, these problems can and should be treated jointly. In Chapter 4, the focus is on teacher tenure; it is my contention that public schools are unable effectively to fire teachers either for programmatic reasons or for incompetence. In addition to explaining why job security for teachers has gotten out of hand, the chapter suggests a much different approach to teacher tenure. This approach would emphasize buyouts instead of litigation as the normal way to resolve tenure cases. Because this approach could be implemented by bargaining as well as by legislation, it is potentially one of the few reforms that could be introduced within a relatively short period of time.

Chapter 5 addresses the archaic and inefficient decisionmaking structure of American education, an issue that is completely ignored by the reform movement.

Chapter 6 is then devoted to the role of public education in non-academic areas, such as teenage sex and use of alcohol and drugs. The main point is to show the widespread public dissatisfaction with school performance in these areas; such dissatisfaction, regardless of its validity, is an important strategic fact. Individuals who differ on the reasons for their dissatisfaction with public schools may nevertheless agree on the remedial actions that are needed.

Chapters 2-6 include several brief discussions of how and why entrepreneurial schools would avoid the problems that public schools cannot overcome. In other words, I have tried to relate the suggested remedy to a specific diagnosis of the problems. The analysis can only be suggestive for at least two important reasons. First, the discussion does not cover all the major problems of education—no effort is made here to show how entrepreneurial schools can remedy problems that are not discussed. Second, there is little discussion of the unique problems that may characterize entrepreneurial but not public schools. The latter issue is discussed in Chapter 9, the only chapter devoted primarily to entrepreneurial schools.

In Chapter 7 the analysis turns to what is perhaps the most depressing fact about the contemporary reform movement: the absence of educational and political leadership that recognizes the basic obstacles to improving public education. This, as much as anything, leads to the most pessimistic conclusions about the prospects for reform in public education. This chapter also answers one of the most perplexing questions about our educational situation. How would so many presumably well-informed conscientious educational and lay leaders produce such a large number of unrealistic and even harmful proposals to reform education? Here, the analysis relies heavily upon the observations of a task force participant who recognized and sought to explain the futilitarian nature of the reform proposals.

Having presented these conclusions and the prima facie case that supports them, the discussion turns in Chapter 8 to two potentially significant reforms that are ignored by the education reform movement: tuition tax credits and vouchers. As previously noted, my conclusion is that tuition tax credits/vouchers have the potential to be either helpful or harmful to education; the specifics of the legislation implementing them will be the decisive factor that determines the direction of their effects. Unlike their proponents, who see only beneficial consequences, and opponents who see only harmful consequences, I foresee some desirable and some undesirable consequences, as well as a great deal of uncertainty over what the consequences will be. Regardless, and despite intense opposition from the public education lobby, the position advocated here is that tuition tax credits and vouchers should be tried despite their limitations and uncertainties.

Chapter 9 concludes the analysis with a more detailed description of the pros and cons of private, profit-making schools. Such schools (K-12) already exist, but very little is known about them.[3] The analysis includes a scenario that illustrates how entrepreneurial schools might have an enormous impact upon education within a relatively short period of time. Perhaps inconsistently, entrepreneurial schools are presented as a suggestion worth exploring as a prediction. One can say, however, that the research and development on the subject justify both the suggestion and the prediction. Furthermore, as the analysis makes clear, entrepreneurial schools are consistent with the growing trend to utilize private enterprise to carry out public policy.[4]

The Burden of Proof

As Appendix A shows, the reform proposals were sponsored by the best-known, most prestigious leaders of U.S. education. For example, the chairman of the National Commission on Excellence in Education was the president of the University of California; the president of Yale University was one of the other three presidents of institutions of higher education included among the commissioners. Similarly, the author of the Carnegie Foundation report on secondary education, Ernest L. Boyer, is a former U.S. Commissioner of Education. Previously, Dr. Boyer had been chancellor of the State University of New York, perhaps the most powerful state educational leadership position in the United States. At the time the report was published, Dr. Boyer was president of the Carnegie Foundation for the Advancement of Teaching, a major philanthropic foundation active in the field of education. In addition, the list of advisers and consultants for this report alone reads like a Who's Who in education.

The reform proposals, especially *A Nation At Risk* and *High School*, have received an extraordinary amount of publicity. Over 3 million copies of *A Nation At Risk* have been distributed by the U.S. Government Printing Office or through full reprints in various publications. It has been the subject of regional and national meetings sponsored by the Department of Education, and has served as the basis of President Reagan's educational policies; additionally, it has been on the agenda of thousands of educational conferences and the end is nowhere in sight.

High School, the reform report sponsored by the Carnegie Foundation, was widely disseminated after its initial publication in 1983.[5] By June 1983 the Carnegie Foundation had sold 25,000 hardcover copies and 140 copies of a film version of the book. The other reform proposals have also received extensive publicity and discussion. Several enjoy both prestigious professional and nonprofessional sponsorship: university presidents, business leaders, scientists, teachers, community leaders, deans, and so on. Nevertheless, these proposals are useless as guides to reform. Indeed, by diverting attention away from the underlying obstacles to reform, they are worse than useless.

The reader may be thinking: Are you saying that all of these educational and political leaders, scholars, public officials, business leaders, school administrators, professors, and teachers are wrong and you are right? Yes, that is the *raison d'être* for this book, presumptuous as it seems to put it this way. Let me hasten to point out, however, that one does not need any extraordinary intellectual capacity to understand the futility of the reform movement. Nor is it difficult to understand why so many political and educational leaders believe, or at least say, that basic reform is achievable within a few years. On the contrary, any reasonably intelligent person can understand these developments. In this connection, it should be noted that the vast majority of the reforms being bandied about today have been around for a long time. In fact, perhaps their most notable characteristic is their banality. Whatever their merits, they are not fresh remedies for a sick institution.

For example, virtually all of the reform proposals that discuss teacher education assert that it overemphasizes courses in teaching methods. Be this as it may, at least ten well-known books on education since 1949 have asserted that teacher training devotes too much time to pedagogy (methods or "how to teach" courses) and insufficient time to the subject taught.[6]

It would be laboring the obvious to cite the additional publications that have made the same point in the past 20 years. If we are not to be naive about it, we must ask the question: What reason is there to believe that current proposals to deemphasize methods courses will fare better today than they have in the past? Not one of the contemporary reform proposals raises, let alone answers, this question. Similarly, their failure to raise the same question with respect to other reforms that have been recommended for several decades suggests that the burden of proof should not be on those who doubt whether these reforms can be achieved. It should be on those who advocate them, to explain why they are achievable now when they have not been achievable for decades, or even generations.

In considering the prospects for reform, we should note that new and imposing obstacles stand in the way of several reforms that have been urged for several decades. This is especially pertinent to reforms that would require a higher level of public financial support. For example, the proportion of our population with children in school is declining and will continue to decline well into the twenty-first century. In 1983 the median age of our population was 30.9, and there were more than twice as many persons under 18 than over 65. Sometime in the twenty-first century, the median age will be over 40, and there will be more persons over 65 than under 18. Public expenditures for education are bound to be adversely affected by these demographic changes. For example, elderly recipients of federal assistance receive about ten times as much per recipient as child beneficiaries of such assistance.

More importantly, the politics of the issues involved are changing. Public opinion polls show clearly that parents and younger citizens are more willing to be taxed for education than the elderly. For instance, a 1983 Gallup Poll revealed that citizens under 50 were evenly divided on whether they would support increased taxes for education; those over 50, however, were opposed to increased taxes for education by a 62 to 28 margin.[7] Furthermore, because of increased resort to contraceptive measures, children are increasingly viewed as the result of a private decision whose costs should be borne by those who make the decision, that is, the parents. The 1984 elections indicated in several ways that the elderly are already a more potent political force than the education lobby; inasmuch as the proportion of the elderly will increase for several decades, we can expect popular support for education spending to decline even more in the future.[8]

Similarly, proposals to attract more able persons into the teaching profession now encounter new obstacles. In the not-so-distant past, teaching was the major career choice for many women of talent and ability. As a result of the feminist movement, however, opportunities for women in more attractive occupations have increased dramatically. Inasmuch as teaching is still a predominantly female occupation, its competitive position is bound to be adversely affected by women's liberation. Able women who would have become teachers are going into law, medicine, business, and many other fields that were not as hospitable to women in the past. Similarly, able black persons of both sexes are not restricted to education as they were in the past.

Efforts to increase defense spending and the tax reduction movement are also stronger today than they were 10 or 20 years ago. Thus insofar as reform is equated with, or depends upon, increased spending for public education, there is no prima facie reason to believe proposed reforms are more likely to be implemented today than in the past. Even the argument that many years of neglect have brought us to the point where reform is imperative is not very persuasive. It is doubtful whether there is more concern about educational reform today than there was after the Soviet Union launched the first man in space in 1957. No one event triggered more soul-searching about U.S. education; indeed, the National Defense Education Act of 1958 was a direct consequence of this event. It was also an important cause of the tremendous national interest in the Conant study, which was published in 1959.[9] Nevertheless, although the Conant study advocated several reforms currently being proposed, it was followed by the educational decline noted by the contemporary reform movement. Significantly, none raises any hard questions about this fact.

Despite upbeat rhetoric from President Reagan, former Secretary of Education Terrel H. Bell, and a host of other political and educational leaders, there is much less to the reform movement than meets the eye. Although educational deterioration is real enough (in fact, it has been seriously understated), the educational reform movement is a media event. That is, educational reform is taking place in newspaper articles and television broadcasts, not in classrooms.

Nonetheless, educators tend to view the recent upsurge in media attention to education as a good thing. In their view, the basic problems have existed for several decades with little media attention being paid to them. When the mass media publicize educational issues, however, political leaders feel compelled to address them. The trouble is that although political leaders are addressing the broad subject of educational reform, they are doing so in terms of the issues formulated by the media. More often than not, these are marginal or even pseudo-issues. Moreover, most of our political and educational leaders need to be perceived as supportive of educational reform and optimistic about its prospects. It is hardly surprising that President Reagan and his first Secretary of Education Bell perceived "a tidal wave" of reform taking place. The Reagan administration is acutely sensitive to the criticism that it is "antieducation" because of its cutbacks in federal aid to education. If educational reforms are being achieved despite reduced federal aid to education, the Reagan administration would benefit politically in a big way. At the same time, governors and state legislators are in no position to state that reform is hopeless, even if they believe this to be the case. Such sentiments would require an explanation; but the explanation would put them on an unwanted collision course with key interest groups. Much the same rationale applies to school board members; recognition of the obstacles to reform calls for basic changes in the way school boards function. Needless to say, it is always easier to reform someone else than yourself.

Educational leaders at all levels also have a major stake in being perceived as supportive of reform. A school superintendent is most unlikely to tell his board or community that the prospects for educational reform are nil. This would be perceived as "negativism" or as opposition to reform. Furthermore, most school administrators are very sensitive about the issue of public confidence in public education, since it is so closely related to public support for it. For this reason, they are usually cheerleaders, not critics, of public schools.

To our nation as a whole, the important question is whether educational improvement is taking place. To key individuals, however, the critical question, that is, the one most important to their own welfare, is whether they are perceived as active participants in the reform movement. The upshot is that there is a large and influential group that is more interested in the appearance of reform than in the reality of it. To this group it would be nice if reform becomes a reality, but their careers depend more upon whether they are seen as apostles of reform than upon whether reform is actually achieved.

Such leaders are not insincere, although there is much more skepticism about educational reform than appears from media treatment of the subject. Perhaps the critical difference between the approach adopted here and the one adopted by the reformers is this: The latter regard previous failures as a failure of will or energy or enthusiasm; in short, they have a hortatory approach. It is my view, however, that educational reform is not primarily a hortatory or an incremental process, to be achieved by more effort, more resources, or more enthusiasm. Instead, it requires a careful diagnosis and a program and strategy designed to overcome specific obstacles to improving education. All of these critical elements are missing from the educational reform movement.

This conclusion has yet to be supported by the analysis; even if the analysis confirms it, a difficult question remains. How or why would so many prestigious educational and noneducational leaders ignore the hard questions about reform? This is a fair question, which deserves (and receives) a responsible answer. Initially, however, it is most important to establish the substantive deficiencies in the reform movement. Once that task has been accomplished, it will make sense to discuss how and why the deficiencies occurred.

The Meaning and Modes of Entrepreneurial Schools

An "entrepreneur" is someone who arranges the factors of production in ways that add economic value to them. Thinking "entrepreneurially" means thinking of ways to generate value. Policies that encourage entrepreneurial schools can be implemented in a variety of ways. Because it is important not to limit the concept to only one possible form they might take, let me suggest some of the forms entrepreneurial schools can and probably will take.

- Individual schools operated as an independent business.
- Franchised schools, perhaps specializing by grade level or program.
- Schools operated by private enterprise under contract with school boards or state educational agencies.
- A mixed mode in which schools may be neither wholly public nor wholly private and entrepreneurial but a mixture of both.

In the last form, the school may offer some services without charge; others may require a fee, either to the school or to private-sector teachers or companies that operate out of public schools or in cooperation with them. For instance, school districts may wish to make certain instructional services available even though the districts cannot provide them. In such cases, the schools may arrange for such instructional services; the school district may or may not serve as the middle man in these arrangements. It may lease space and/or facilities to private entrepreneurs; the financial arrangements between the students and the service providers may be handled directly by the latter or through the school district.

At the same time, schools are likely to become more active in pursuing opportunities to increase school revenues. These opportunities may or may not be related to education. For example, schools may rent space and equipment to private companies for training purposes. A school with declining enrollment will nevertheless maintain certain capabilities that can generate revenues; for example, it may have a cafeteria facility that can be used to feed senior citizens, or classrooms and facilities that can be used to operate day care programs as an entrepreneurial operation.[10]

Once public schools become alert to the opportunities to become "entrepreneurial," we can expect a tremendous variety of new relationships between public schools and the private sector. At the present time, a custodial mentality dominates educational thought and practice; as this changes, we may see incremental changes toward entrepreneurial schools. Over time, such changes would be reflected in every dimension of public education; schools might still be legally "public" but entrepreneurial in spirit and practice.

The point of view adopted here is not to regard any of these alternatives as necessarily superior to the others. Instead, the issue to be faced is which alternative is most appropriate for what set of circumstances. Given the diverse ways the states regulate education, and the disparate circumstances of local school districts, we can expect all of these alternatives to materialize in some school districts. Which, if any, predominates over the long haul can be resolved only by experience.

Preliminary Considerations

Unquestionably, entrepreneurial schools do not command widespread public or professional or political support at this time; to be candid about it, they are not even in the mainstream of the current debate over educational reform. For this reason, and to avoid premature rejection of a position that can be easily misinterpreted, a few preliminary comments may be helpful.

First of all, the argument for entrepreneurial schools is not based upon an ideological commitment to the free enterprise system as the answer to every social problem. Although data from other fields are cited to support the recommendation, such data are only suggestive. The argument itself is based upon the circumstances of public education. In other words, this book is not a general appeal to a free enterprise solution that uses public education as an example. It is an argument for a free enterprise solution or perhaps a free enterprise approach to the basic problems of public education; the book does not take a position on such an approach to other social problems.

One other caveat needs to be emphasized. It might be assumed that policies that would encourage profit-making schools are most likely to be supported by political conservatives and opposed by political liberals. Although this is a possibility, the politics of the issue are likely to be much more complex. The private school forces (such as denominational schools) that currently support political conservatives do so because the latter typically support tuition tax credit/ vouchers. However, such support on both sides is currently limited to private *nonprofit* schools. Any effort to strengthen private *profit-making* schools is likely to be opposed by the private school lobby; entrepreneurial schools pose a threat to them as well as to public schools. For this reason, conservative political leaders may be more embarrassed than pleased by proposals that would encourage profit-making schools. The fact that entrepreneurial schools do not have a political constituency at this time is important but not necessarily fatal to their rapid emergence.

Of course, there would be no point to encouraging entrepreneurial schools apart from a belief that such schools can generate a politically significant constituency. The composition of such a constituency, however, is not likely to follow existing political alignments on educational issues. All of these considerations will be discussed later in more detail; at this point, my objective is simply to avoid unwarranted assumptions about a position that cannot be understood apart from its context and the specifics of its implementation.

NOTES

1. National Commission on Excellence in Education, *A Nation At Risk: The Imperative for Educational Reform* (Washington, D.C.: U.S. Government Printing Office, 1983), p. 39.

2. Ibid., pp. 8-10, 18-23.

3. One exception is Edward B. Fiske, "Beyond the Classroom," New York *Times, Education: Spring Survey*, April 14, 1985, pp. 1, 43.

4. For example, see James T. Bennett and Manuel H. Johnson, *Better Government at Half the Price* (Ossining, N.Y.: Caroline House, 1981); "Public Services and the Private Initiative," Special Edition, *Government Union Review* (Vienna, Va.: Public Service Research Council, 1983).

5. Ernest L. Boyer, *High School: A Report on Secondary Education in America* (New York: Harper & Row, 1983).

6. Some of the books that have made this point since 1949 include: Mortimer B. Smith, *And Madly Teach* (Chicago: Regnery, 1949); Arthur E. Bestor, *The Retreat from Learning in Our Public Schools* (Champaign: University of Illinois Press, 1953); Albert Lynd, *Quackery in Public Schools* (Boston: Little, Brown, 1953); Mortimer B. Smith, *The Diminished Mind* (Chicago: Regnery, 1954); H. G. Rickover, *Education and Freedom* (New York: Dutton, 1959); H. G. Rickover, *American Education: A National Failure* (New York: Dutton, 1963); James B. Conant, *The Education of American Teachers* (New York: McGraw-Hill, 1963); James D. Koerner, *The Miseducation of American Teachers* (Boston: Beacon Press, 1963); and James D. Koerner, *Who Controls American Teachers?* (Boston: Beacon Press, 1968).

7. George H. Gallup, "The 1983 Poll of the Public's Attitudes Toward the Public Schools," *Phi Delta Kappan*, September 1983, p. 38.

8. Samuel H. Preston, "Children and the Elderly in the United States," *Scientific American*, December 1984, pp. 44-49.

9. James B. Conant, *The American High School Today* (New York: McGraw-Hill, 1959).

10. This development is predicted in a futures study sponsored by the American Association of School Administrators. See Marvin Cetron, *Schools of the Future* (Arlington, Va.: AASA, 1984).

2

TEACHER UNIONS AND
EDUCATIONAL REFORM

The previous chapter asserted that the reform movement has ignored several major obstacles to educational reform. This chapter illustrates the point by considering the role of teacher unions in educational reform. I begin with this subject not only because of its importance but also because the neglect of it by the reform movement is beyond dispute.

Let me begin with my own conclusions on the subject. Generally speaking, individuals forced to rely solely upon their own resources are unable to protect themselves against unfair government action. In totalitarian countries, unions, religious bodies, employer associations, and other interest group organizations are dominated by government; they are instruments of oppression, not a means of protecting individual rights and liberties. In my view, therefore, organizations of public employees are essential. In the absence of organizations, teachers, like other public employees, would be much more vulnerable to unfair treatment in one way or another.

Notwithstanding this point of view, the following analysis is devoted largely to criticisms of the role of teacher unions. Such criticism does not imply advocacy of their elimination. Instead, my view is that we have not as yet found the way to retain the defensible and even essential aspects of teacher unionization while eliminating the undesirable aspects of it. The existence or nonexistence of teacher unions is not an issue arising from the analysis. What is an issue is the most appropriate way to structure their functions and obligations, and the way these things are carried out.

Notwithstanding this point of view, teacher unions, and collective bargaining by teachers, are major obstacles to educational reform. In the short run (three-five years), these obstacles will be insurmountable. In the long run, they can be overcome only by the expansion of private schools to the point where teacher unions might accept the reforms that are needed, or by technological changes that render teacher unions unable to block reforms. In the abstract, teacher collective bargaining might be limited legally but adverse judicial decisions are the only realistic possibility of achieving this outcome for decades to come.

To present this argument, this chapter will discuss the following related matters: the process of collective bargaining; the extent of collective bargaining in public education; educational reform and the scope of bargaining (that is, what reforms are subject to collective bargaining between unions and school boards); union ability to block educational reforms; union positions on educational reform issues; and the cognizance issue (that is, the attention paid to teacher unions and collective bargaining in major reform proposals).

THE PROCESS OF COLLECTIVE BARGAINING

Collective bargaining is a process for resolving terms and conditions of employment. Section 8(d) of the National Labor Relations Act, and many of the state laws providing bargaining rights for teachers, defines it as follows:

> For the purposes of this section, to bargain collectively is the performance of the mutual obligation of the employer and the representative of the employees to meet at reasonable times and confer in good faith with respect to wages, hours, and other terms and conditions of employment, or the negotiation of an agreement, or any question arising thereunder, and the execution of a written contract incorporating any agreement reached if requested by either party, but such obligation does not compel either party to agree to a proposal or require the making of a concession . . .

The "representative of the employees" is, of course, the union, if any, which the employees have chosen to be their exclusive representative on matters subject to bargaining. Inasmuch as these matters include actions required for reform, the union's position on them inevitably plays a critical role in the reform process.

COLLECTIVE BARGAINING IN PUBLIC EDUCATION

Obviously, the importance of teacher collective bargaining depends partly upon how widespread it is. Whether or not school boards are required to bargain collectively with teacher (or other) unions is a state decision. As of the spring of 1984, 34 states had enacted some type of bargaining statute governing school district employment relations.[1] These state laws frequently differ from the National Labor Relations Act and from each other in significant ways, such as the scope of bargaining, whether strikes are legalized, the conduct to be regarded as an unfair labor practice (and therefore prohibited), the kinds of employees accorded bargaining rights, and the procedures to be followed in cases of an impasse between the union and the school board. From the standpoint of educational reform, however, the differences between these laws are not as important as their similarities. The following discussion, therefore, is based upon the typical characteristics of teacher bargaining in states that have legalized it. Significantly, of the ten most populous states, only Texas has not legalized teacher bargaining on a statewide basis. It should be noted, moreover, that teacher unions frequently exercise de facto bargaining rights even in states that have not enacted bargaining statutes. For these reasons, it is readily understandable why the vast majority of public school teachers are unionized. According to a recent estimate, 73 percent of the nation's public school teachers are covered by collective bargaining agreements. Thus, if teacher unions are an obstacle to educational reform, it is virtually certain that they are an obstacle on a national basis. Although collective bargaining by bus drivers, cafeteria workers, custodians, and other nonteaching employees often leads to difficult problems, the following discussion is limited to collective bargaining by teacher unions.

EDUCATIONAL REFORM AND TEACHER BARGAINING

In most school districts, 50 to 75 percent of district revenues are spent for teacher salaries and benefits. Collective bargaining is the procedure used to determine how much school boards will spend for this purpose, and how the funds will be distributed among the staff. Equally if not more important, collective bargaining is now the predominant procedure for establishing, revising, and/or abolishing personnel policies affecting teachers. Obviously, changing such policies is essential to educational reform; in fact, it is the reform in many instances. This is evident from merely listing some of the proposals currently receiving the most attention in the reform programs, as well as in the media and professional journals:

- Increase the teacher workyear (from 180 to 220 workdays)
- Increase the teacher workday
- Reward outstanding teachers (merit pay)
- Make it easier to dismiss incompetent teachers (that is, weaken or abolish teacher tenure)
- Require rigorous in-service training for teachers as a condition of employment
- Stop giving teachers salary credit for "Mickey Mouse" courses
- Lay off marginal teachers with greater seniority before laying off outstanding teachers with less seniority
- Require teachers to provide more assistance to pupils outside of regular class hours
- Require teachers to be more accessible to parents
- Require teachers to devote more time to assigning and grading homework
- Permit nonschool personnel, such as recently retired or privately employed mathematicians and scientists, to teach part-time in secondary schools

For present purposes, it hardly matters whether these changes would improve matters. Whether they be "reforms" or merely changes, all would normally be subject to bargaining. This fact is of the utmost practical importance. Suppose, for example, that a school board wishes to pay higher salaries to outstanding teachers. If the board has negotiated a contract with its teacher union, it will not even be in a position to propose "merit pay" until the contract expires. This may be one, two, or even three years in the future. Needless to say, it is difficult to launch reforms when you cannot even raise the issue for two or three years.

Most importantly, many reforms that are legally not subject to bargaining are nevertheless subject to it as a practical matter. This results from the fact that school boards are frequently required to bargain on the "impact" of decisions that are supposedly not themselves subject to bargaining. For instance, suppose a school board decides to replace several personal development courses with courses in science, mathematics, and computer technology. I know of no state, except perhaps Ohio, where such a curriculum decision would be subject to bargaining. On the other hand, what will happen to the teachers in the courses being dropped? Will they have to be fired? The teacher union will be vitally concerned about this "impact" of the curriculum decision. It will propose retraining and continued employment in some capacity of teachers who would otherwise be laid off. It will demand that any staff reductions be accomplished through attrition; failing this, it will bargain hard for severance pay, assistance in finding employment, continuation of insurance benefits, and other concessions designed to avoid any layoffs or cushion them liberally if they are made.

Quite frequently, bargaining on the impact of nonnegotiable management decisions becomes so protracted, so unpleasant and expensive that the decisions are reversed or greatly amended. Requiring, as many states do, that school boards bargain on the effects of supposedly nonnegotiable decisions is really a back-door way of requiring the boards to bargain on the decisions themselves. As a result, the union's ability to block or delay or subvert change applies to many decisions that are legally outside the scope of bargaining.

UNION ABILITY TO BLOCK EDUCATIONAL REFORM

Teacher unions, like unions of state and local public employees generally, have more power than private-sector unions to block changes opposed by the union. To understand why this is the case, we must first understand some critical differences between private- and public-sector bargaining. As we shall see, these differences have major implications for educational reform.

In both the public and private sectors, the employer's legal obligation is to bargain in good faith with the union. Legally speaking, the employer is not required to make concessions or agree to union proposals.

What happens if there is no agreement? In both sectors, if the employer has met its obligations to bargain in good faith, and there is still no agreement, the employer can act unilaterally, that is, without the consent of the union. Thus in both sectors it appears that the employer maintains its basic rights to manage. In theory, therefore, if a school board feels strongly enough about an issue, it is entitled to adhere to its position and eventually implement it, even in the face of union opposition.

Upon closer examination, however, it becomes clear that school boards do not have as much power as private-sector employers to implement policies opposed by unions. In the private sector, disagreements are resolved rather quickly. The union either accepts the employer's best offer or goes on strike. This dilemma forces everyone to face the moment of truth immediately. Employees risk their jobs by striking for economic concessions. Similarly, the employer faced with a shutdown or attempted shutdown of operations is forced to assess its bargaining position realistically. These pressures are usually sufficient to resolve the issues promptly.

In contrast, collective bargaining in public education does not lead to prompt settlement of disputes between teacher unions and school boards. One reason lies in the history of the state bargaining laws that legalized teacher bargaining. When most of these laws were enacted, the legislatures did not want to legalize teacher strikes. On the other hand, they were impressed with the argument that if school boards knew that teacher strikes were illegal, they would simply refuse to make any concessions. According to the union argument, since unions had no effective leverage on the school boards, the latter would not really bargain in good faith.

To remedy this potential problem, the legislatures frequently enacted complex, protracted impasse procedures. In 1983, at least 32 states provided mediation in the event of persistent disagreement; at least 30 states required the parties to submit disputes to fact-finding if mediation failed to bring about agreement or was not utilized. At least 22 states provide that disputes over what should be terms of the contract (as distinguished from grievance arbitration) may or must be submitted to arbitration.[2] In most states, boards had to complete these procedures before they could act unilaterally, that is, without the union's agreement. This was supposed to ensure that the school boards would consider the union's position carefully before acting unilaterally.

Unfortunately, the primary effect of these impasse procedures has been to prevent school boards from acting promptly, even after they have negotiated on the union proposals in good faith. To see why, let us assume that the parties cannot agree on salary, layoffs, insurance benefits, binding arbitration of grievances, and compulsory payment of union dues as a condition of employment. After several negotiating sessions, usually held over a period of several months, one or both requests a mediator.

Depending upon the time of the year, mediators may or may not be very busy. If they are busy, it may be impossible to arrange a session with the mediator for several weeks. Usually more than one mediation session is required, even for relatively simple disputes. Quite often, five to ten or even more mediation sessions, scheduled over two to three months, are required.

What happens if mediation does not culminate in a contract? Mediators do not like to admit failure, so they are apt to drag out the mediation process. There is, however, a more practical reason for mediators to continue mediation. The "success" of the mediation agency is based upon the percentage of disputes settled through mediation. If the mediator concedes inability to bring about a settlement, the agency's "success" rate is lower. Inasmuch as most disputes are eventually settled, there is a tendency for public-sector mediators to drag out mediation, waiting for the settlement that will boost their "success" rate. In the private sector, mediation is not imposed because it is not effective unless both parties desire mediation. This view does not prevail in most state teacher bargaining laws. Mediation is imposed on the parties.

Let us assume that mediation is finally terminated, still without an agreement. Typically, the next step is fact-finding. Each party presents its positions and arguments to a fact finder, who subsequently makes recommendations to the parties and perhaps to the community on what should be the resolution of the dispute. Selection of a fact finder usually requires a few weeks. Once selected, the fact finder must schedule hearings. After the hearings, the fact finder must have time to digest the evidence and draft the recommendations for resolving the dispute. Taking into account work schedules, holiday seasons, illness, and other factors, the process may require more than a year, especially if several issues are in dispute.

Eventually, a fact-finding report is issued. The state bargaining laws typically prescribe what happens or what may happen next. Many, perhaps most, require a period of negotiations over the report, that is, more delay before the school board can take action.

One point about these delays is absolutely critical: Legally, a school board cannot act unilaterally on matters subject to bargaining until the impasse procedures are exhausted. A school board that acted without the union's consent on such matters would be committing an unfair labor practice, that is, an act prohibited by law. In effect, therefore, the state bargaining laws accord a private interest group, say the teacher union, a veto power over most reforms. The duration of this veto power varies from state to state; the most critical factor is the impasse procedure mandated by the bargaining statute. In states where the impasse procedures include both mediation and fact-finding, it can easily take a year or more to complete the impasse procedures.

Impasse Procedures and Educational Reform

Let us now relate the impasse procedures to educational reform. One relationship is this: If a teacher union is strongly opposed to any reform involving terms and conditions of employment, as most reforms do, the teacher union can legally prevent implementation of the reform for a substantial period of time. It can do so merely by refusing to agree to the change in negotiations.

The reader's reaction may be: "Such delays are regrettable, but not necessarily fatal to proposed reforms. After all, the school boards can eventually implement the reforms by maintaining their positions throughout the bargaining and the impasse procedures."

This point of view is understandable but extremely unrealistic. Essentially, it is based upon a failure to understand the critical difference between private- and public-sector bargaining and the dynamics of the latter.

In the private sector, collective bargaining is essentially a test of economic power. The union's ability to inflict economic damage upon the employer is the basis of its bargaining power. This is not the case with teacher bargaining. As with public-sector bargaining generally, bargaining power is not based upon ability to inflict economic damage upon the public employer. As a matter of fact, school boards often "make money" as the result of a teachers' strike. Furthermore, school board members personally are not adversely affected economically by a teachers' strike, as private-sector managers might be.

In public-sector bargaining, bargaining power is based upon the union's ability to inflict *political* damage on the employer. In large part, teacher bargaining is a contest for public opinion. It is hardly possible to overestimate the importance of this fact, especially in conjunction with the legal power of teacher unions to block changes for a considerable period of time.

The teacher union that is resisting a change at the bargaining table is not doing just that. During the bargaining, it will unleash a stream of antiboard propaganda, depicting the board as "antiteacher," "not caring about children," and "not trusting teachers." If the board wants to introduce merit pay, it will be accused of wanting to reward boot-lickers and teachers who don't protest lousy conditions. If it wants to weaken tenure, it will be accused of adopting a "punitive" approach, instead of working with teachers to improve instruction. If it wants more homework, it will be accused of butting in where teachers know best. Tell me what the union is objecting to, and I can tell you what evil lurks in the mind of its board members. The facts of the situation play about the same role, and have about the same influence, as facts generally do in political affairs, that is, they are usually a negligible factor.

Very few school boards are prepared to stay the course in the face of such a campaign. As pointed out previously, the teacher union is frequently the sole, or the major, interest group active in school board elections. The interaction between the bargaining and the political process gives the teacher union an enormous advantage over private-sector unions; in district after district, school board members lose an election because of teacher union opposition or win because of union support.

If the school board election is conducted separately from a general election, as is often the case, an extremely small proportion of the electorate can elect board members. The teacher unions are thus able to wield influence all out of proportion to their numbers. Quite often, it is unnecessary for the union to become active formally. The mere possibility that it might be active often weakens board adherence to positions opposed by teacher unions. In short, the problem is not simply that school boards are limited in their ability to carry out reforms. It is also the fact that a reform platform is likely to be a losing one politically—not necessarily because most citizens oppose it, but because most do not participate in school board elections.

It must also be noted that certain obstacles may interact in such a way that their total effect is much greater than their effects in isolation. The tendency for teacher bargaining to extend over a long period of time illustrates this point. In isolation, one might suppose that it would cause irritating delays but not pose any major problems. When the delay in reaching agreement interacts with the political dimension of teacher bargaining, the situation is drastically different from each factor considered independently. The inability of boards to act promptly would not be such a problem if the interim period was not given over to political attacks upon the board for its support of reform; the attacks upon the boards would not be so harmful if they were confined to a much briefer period of time. In practice, however, they continue as long as the impasse continues. This often means conflict on a year-round basis in the school district. This is especially likely where school boards must bargain with unions of bus drivers, custodians, cafeteria workers, and other nonteacher employees.

Bargaining Rights for Principals

In 32 states, supervisors, often including principals, have bargaining rights.[3] In the states where principals can bargain, the principals have a vested interest in the success of the teacher union; any benefit achieved by the latter is virtually certain to be made available to principals. Furthermore, the principals do not oppose arguments that the principals expect to use when their union bargains with the school board. For instance, if the teacher union proposes that all vacancies be resolved by seniority, the principals are not likely to object vigorously. To do so would be to weaken their own argument that vacancies among principals be resolved strictly by seniority. Thus the emergence of unions of principals tends to give principals a stronger stake in the success of the teacher union than in carrying out the policies of the school board.

As damaging as this is, it is by no means the worst situation. In several states, principals are included in teacher bargaining units. This means that the salaries and terms and conditions of employment for principals are negotiated by the same union that represents teachers. The implications of this fact are serious indeed.

Suppose principals in a district are eager to carry out certain reforms. They resolve to evaluate teachers more rigorously, to weed out the marginal teachers. They insist upon more homework and that teachers grade it conscientiously. They institute a stricter policy intended to prevent teacher tardiness and abuse of sick leave. In short, they do everything that principals could do to improve education in their schools.

What happens when the union, composed predominantly of teachers supervised by such principals, negotiates the salaries and working conditions of the principals? A little reflection suggests that our initial assumption is probably premature. If the teacher union also represents principals, the latter are very unlikely, or much less likely, to do a good job of supervising teachers. In the private sector, providing bargaining rights for supervisors turned out to be disastrous, for precisely the reasons suggested by our example. Notwithstanding the dangers of union representation of supervisors, many states nevertheless enacted bargaining rights for supervisors and even managerial employees. Needless to say, in such states the ability of a local board to implement reform is even more limited than I have previously suggested.

The fact that some states enacted bargaining rights for principals illustrates another important point about the effects of collective bargaining. It is true, as previously noted, that some states do not have teacher bargaining, and that it is present in a relatively weak form in others. On the other hand, in many of our most populous states, the bargaining rights accorded teacher unions greatly exceed those accorded private-sector unions. For instance, in the private sector, the employer can replace striking employees, permanently if necessary. Not so with teachers in California, Ohio, and many states with both bargaining and teacher tenure laws. Striking teachers are still entitled to the benefits of a tenure hearing. No one takes seriously the idea that a large school district in one of these states is going to conduct thousands of individual hearings in order to fire thousands of striking teachers. This is only one of several reasons why teachers and unions alike have little to fear from concerted opposition or even outright insubordination to school board policies.

Let us now summarize the situation. Most educational reforms require changes in personnel policies. These changes will usually be opposed by the teacher unions. These unions have the legal power to block the changes for a considerable period of time. In the meantime, the unions are likely to be campaigning against the changes and/or the board members who support them. Typically, the community as a whole or the parents will have little understanding of the issues, either at the bargaining table or in the school board election.

In any event, the reforms are subject to the continued support of a board whose members have staggered terms, whose options are severely limited by existing contracts, state regulation, and state aid, and who are typically vulnerable to political and bargaining pressure from teacher unions. In addition, the reforms must run a long and difficult gauntlet in the bargaining process. Conflict with the union requires more board meetings, more meetings with board negotiators, more risk of committing an unfair labor practice, more district funds ostensibly diverted from classroom needs, and so on. Additionally, many boards simply lack adequate remedies to counter concerted teacher refusals to carry out board directives. Finally, the benefits of most reforms require several years to become evident, whereas the critical time span for school board members is much briefer. Given the choice of a protracted, politically costly struggle to achieve reforms, which may not be evident until five to ten years in the future, and a noncontroversial adherence to the status quo, most school board members opt for the status quo. In doing so, they are behaving as political leaders normally do when faced with a decision of this kind. One need only review the way Congress avoided reform of the social security system year after year, despite widespread knowledge that reform was essential to avoid insolvency. The problem, therefore, is not to be resolved by electing better board members. There will never be enough martyrs around to meet the need, either in Congress, the state legislatures, or on boards of education.

Comparability in Bargaining and Educational Reform

In the preceding discussion, my main argument might have been summarized this way: "If you consider teacher bargaining simply as a legal process, and limit your analysis to the legal issues, it is a problem but not an insurmountable obstacle to educational reform. We should not, however, limit our analysis this way. If we wish to achieve reform in the real world, our analysis must take into account the dynamics of the process. That is, we must give due regard to what happens and why in collective bargaining. Only when we do that can we fully appreciate why teacher bargaining poses insurmountable obstacles to educational reform."

In this connection, at least one other aspect of teacher bargaining should be pointed out. In bargaining, school boards and unions submit proposals. Good faith bargaining requires that reasons be given why the other party should accept the proposals. Sometimes the reasons have nothing to do with the merits; for example, "If you don't raise our salaries, we'll raise hell until you do." Most of the time, however, at least lip service is paid to the idea that reasons other than coercion should dominate the give and take.

Comparability is one of the most common reasons adduced to support a proposal. For example, if the union proposes that everyone be compelled to pay union dues or be fired, the extent to which other contracts include the requirement is important. If no other teacher contract in the area has such a requirement, it is more difficult for the union to strike over it, or insist upon it to the point of impasse. At the bargaining table, management can raise several questions: Why is the issue more important here than anywhere else? If unions elsewhere can flourish without such a clause, why can't this one? Why should this district be the first to make such a concession? Conversely, if all other contracts in the area include such a clause, it is more difficult for the school board to reject the proposal. The burden of persuasion now falls upon the school board. The issue no longer is why should this district be the first to grant the concession. It is why should this district be the last to do so. In short, what other school boards and unions have or have not done is a very important factor in the bargaining process.

In the context of educational reform, however, the comparability factor will usually have a negative impact. Suppose, for example, a school board wants to pay a salary differential to outstanding teachers. If no other school board in the area does so, it becomes very difficult for the board to maintain its position in the bargaining process; it is holding up an agreement for a concession that no other board has made. Furthermore, if the issue arises in a school board election, candidates who support merit pay are in a weaker position if no other school board does so.

The unions, of course, are aware of the dynamics of bargaining. They understand that if you can keep the camel's nose out of the tent, you can keep the camel out. So they will be adamant in resisting reforms inimical to teacher welfare, knowing that the entire effort will lose momentum as a result.

UNION POSITIONS ON EDUCATIONAL REFORM ISSUES

Thus far, the analysis has emphasized that teacher unions have enormous power to block, delay, and/or weaken reform proposals. Nevertheless, although I have asserted that the unions will be hostile to reform, I have not confronted this issue directly. Let me do so now, and then raise an important issue. To what extent have the major reform proposals taken into account the role of teacher unions in the reform process? As we shall see, the answer is hardly conducive to the prospects for reform.

One important preliminary point: We must always be prepared to distinguish the "union" from the "teacher" point of view. Although the two overlap, they reflect different interests and priorities. Individual teachers tend to be motivated by their interests. On the other hand, union staff will tend to give more weight than teachers to the impact of proposals upon the union as an employer and an institution. For example, beginning teachers might desire to abolish seniority, believing that it stands in the way of rapid advancement. Union leaders, however, are apt to be concerned about the possibility of intraunion conflict if seniority is abolished. If, for example, teachers must be laid off, it is better from a union perspective that seniority be the governing criterion.

Superficially, there is no conflict: What's good for teachers is said to be good for the union, and vice versa. Realistically, this is nonsense, and most union leaders concede it privately if not publicly. In thousands of contracts, concessions to the union's interests are made or requested as trade-offs for concessions to teacher interests—for example, exclusive union rights to use district bulletin boards and mail systems, and the denial of such contractual rights to individual teachers or other organizations. (Such clauses make it more difficult for a rival union or an insurgent group within the union to campaign among teachers. For this reason, they weaken opposition to the union or to union leadership, but it is difficult to see how they could be in the interests of rank-and-file teachers.)

Furthermore, when there is conflict between the union's interests and the interests of teachers, the union's interests are likely to prevail. The conflict usually arises at the bargaining table. The teacher bargaining team usually consists of three to seven teachers from the district, with the full-time union representative serving as their chief negotiator. The latter usually serves in this role for several teacher unions in a given area. Because of the greater knowledge, experience, and prestige of the full-time union representatives, they are usually able to persuade the teacher bargaining team to see things their way. In many cases, the teachers are not even aware of the union's stake in a particular issue.

Another reason why the union's interests prevail is that the conflict between union and teacher interests is inherently stacked in favor of the union. The teachers challenging the union position must devote their own time and resources to the challenge. In contrast, union leaders control union publications and channels of communication. In other words, they are using union resources, not their own personal resources, to overcome any intraunion opposition. Regardless of whether teachers want to get rid of the union, change its leadership, or change the union's position on an issue, incumbent union leadership has the advantages of incumbency. In theory as well as in practice, these advantages are similar to those of incumbents holding political office.

Paradoxically, the larger the union, the easier it is for its leadership to promote policies to which many members are indifferent or even opposed. How is the individual teacher going to launch and support a campaign to change the policies of the National Education Association (NEA)? Individual teachers who can change the policies of a small local union may be helpless to change the policies of a state or national union, even when a majority supports or would support the change.

These considerations underlie the need to assess reform proposals from a union as well as a teacher point of view. I am not contending that the divergence is significant on every issue, or even on most issues, but it does play a role that should not be ignored in some basic issues.

Except in small school districts, most union contracts include clauses on the salary schedule, the workday and workyear, assignments, transfers, adjunct duties, leaves, evaluation procedures, and many other such personnel matters. In negotiations on such issues, what is the role of the teacher union? It is to maximize the benefits to teachers while minimizing their work load. The union does not exist to achieve less pay, longer hours, reduced benefits, weakened job security, an emphasis upon performance and productivity, higher standards for continued employment, and other changes it deems inimical to the interests of teachers. Nor is the union's role the protection of the public interest in education, the elevation of standards of student achievement, or the moral and/or sexual development of pupils.

A union is an organization chosen by teachers to advance the interests of teachers. In doing so, it will try to equate teacher interests with the public interest, or with the interests of students. But just as what is good for General Motors (GM) is not necessarily good for the nation, what is good for teachers and teacher unions is not necessarily in the public interest or in the interest of students. On the contrary, the demands of a teacher union are usually more directly in conflict with the public interest than the bargaining proposals made by GM; after all, except when government is the purchaser, it is not involved in a direct conflict of interest with GM. When government is the purchaser, it stands to benefit from GM efforts to minimize wages and benefits; such efforts reduce the costs of government purchases from GM and inflationary pressures. In contrast, a conflict with the public interest is inherent in a situation wherein a teacher union negotiates with a school board.

As a general rule, teacher unions are opposed to any reform that does not provide more pay, easier working conditions, and/or less work. They are also opposed to any concessions that weaken union prerogatives, such as paid leave for union officers, union rights to use school equipment and facilities at no cost, released time with pay for bargaining and processing grievances, and termination of teachers who do not pay dues or a "service fee" to the union. Less obviously but equally important, teacher unions are also opposed to changes that create or maximize intraunion conflict or problems of union representation. Thus they are opposed to replacing seniority with managerial discretion in layoffs, transfers, assignment to extracurricular duties, and promotions; to having teachers accountable for their evaluations of other teachers; to permitting individual teachers to reach agreement on matters subject to bargaining without union representation, and to merit pay. We can also expect the unions to oppose any diminution of unit work, inasmuch as such action would reduce the job opportunities for teachers and the number of dues-paying teachers. We can expect such union opposition regardless of whether the reduction of unit work is due to technological change, use of non-teachers to perform "instructional" tasks, changes in the educational program, or any other reason.

Teacher unions are also opposed to policies that would increase teacher accountability. For example, the unions oppose more frequent and more rigorous observations and evaluations of teachers as "harassment." As will be discussed in Chapter 4, they oppose policies and/or legislation designed to make it easier to fire incompetent teachers. They negotiate for teacher rights to be absent for unexplained personal reasons, and for severe restrictions on management rights to ascertain whether teacher absences were justified. They oppose any increase in teacher work time, unless the additional time is paid for. This opposition applies to in-service training requirements, more frequent meetings after school with parents, more homework to be graded after school, more faculty meetings after school, and any other increase in teacher work time, regardless of purpose or need.

None of this is speculation. These have been the negotiating objectives of teacher unions since collective bargaining emerged in education in the early 1960s. I base this conclusion not only on my own experience in negotiating teacher contracts in six different states, or frequent discussions with scores of experienced negotiators at conferences, or an analysis of the literature on the subject. In some large states, the state NEA affiliate prepares a proposed master contract of several hundred items that is disseminated to its local unions. The latter simply submit the proposal as their own to their local school boards, which are legally obligated to bargain on each proposal.

Without fail, these union proposals emphasize higher pay and benefits, less work, less teacher accountability, severe restrictions on teacher evaluation and disciplinary action against teachers, compulsory payment of union dues by all teachers, released time with pay for teachers to perform union business, and a host of other benefits for teachers and unions. As for parents, the union boilerplate contract typically proposes that parental complaints must be in writing and that teachers be entitled to union representation during a complaint in person by a parent. These proposals would inhibit complaints and grievances by most parents, especially low-income and non-English-speaking parents who are the most likely to be deterred by formal, legalistic procedures for expressing their concerns.

A recent study of the effect of collective bargaining upon teacher time is undoubtedly consistent with developments on other issues. The study, based on a national survey of 3,000 elementary teachers, concluded that

> teachers covered by collective bargaining spend approximately 3 percent less time in instruction per day (or one less week a year) than teachers not covered by collective bargaining . . . the best we can say is that collective bargaining has a *tendency* to reduce student achievement by reducing time spent in instruction.[4]

Educational Reform and Union Dynamics

As we have seen, interest groups threatened by reform become very active to prevent the reform from taking place. Inasmuch as others do not benefit very much individually from any specific reform, most people are not reform activists. For example, proposals to increase the teacher workday would immediately affect teachers adversely if implemented. In contrast, the benefit to any particular student (or parent) is highly speculative. It is therefore understandable why teachers would actively oppose the reform while parents are unlikely to devote much time and energy to achieving it.

Of course, some reforms would not adversely affect most teachers. Therefore, it might seem unrealistic to anticipate strong union opposition to them. For example, why would a teacher union object adamantly if a school board wanted to replace two teachers out of 300, in order to offer courses in mathematics and physics instead of driver education and personal development? Inasmuch as most teachers would not be affected by the change, why would the union be adamantly opposed to it?

The reason is that the dynamics of the process apply within the union. To follow our example, the two teachers in danger of being laid off are going to be much more active than the vast majority unaffected by the impending layoff. They are more likely to attend union meetings and try to influence union strategy to protect their interests. They may even try to be on the bargaining team to be assured of timely information and of protection against the anticipated layoff.

Every experienced negotiator has to deal with this problem. A highly motivated minority in the bargaining unit frequently achieves undue influence or even outright control over the union's bargaining team. This minority is quite willing to sacrifice the interests of the majority, if need be, to achieve its own objectives in the bargaining. To put it mildly, there is nothing like the fear of losing a job or some important benefit to motivate a minority this way. Teachers about to lose their jobs will gladly give up a raise for all teachers for their own job security. I am not asserting that the minority prevails in every situation; it does not. But the situation arises frequently and often has a profound effect upon bargaining.

Essentially, unions are political organizations. They are political organizations devoted to economic ends, but the basis of control over the union is political (one employee, one vote). In this respect, unions can be contrasted with corporations, where control is formally vested in the persons representing the largest number of shares.

For present purposes, this point must be seen as a factor affecting the conduct of bargaining. A union representative will normally try very hard to avoid having a highly disaffected minority within the union. Such minorities are the basis for campaigns to replace union leadership. Teachers who receive a 7 instead of an 8 percent salary increase may not be pleased, but that is not the kind of issue or disappointment that ordinarily leads to a challenge to union leadership. In contrast, failure to prevent dismissals or acceptance of more onerous conditions for most unit members poses some real dangers to the union leader who agrees to them. This is why these things do not happen very often.

To summarize, the dynamics of bargaining have an important bearing upon the fate of educational reform. We can expect adamant union opposition to any reform that threatens the basic interests of even a small number of teachers. Although such proposed reform may affect only a small minority in the union, its effects are to activate those who would be directly affected by it. Their activity changes every dimension of the bargaining, primarily by making it much more difficult to achieve an agreement that does not meet their needs. Educational dilettantes may ignore this important point; anyone interested in actual reform cannot afford to do so.

Of course, union success in negotiations varies a great deal. As a practical matter, the unions are often required to accept contractual provisions that serve managerial instead of union objectives. In fact, the American Federation of Teachers (AFT) concedes that local unions will sometimes have to accept reforms they regard as unwise, merely because the public thinks they have merit.[5]

The AFT position paper explicitly recognizes that union concerns and teacher concerns are not identical. Nevertheless, it provides no basis for optimism that AFT locals would accept educational reform contrary to AFT policies; for instance, the paper expresses concern that certification requirements might make it easier to license teachers and thereby break a teacher strike. In any event, there is a big difference between accepting a change under duress, only in order to forestall even greater "take-aways," and affirmatively supporting the change.

Are there any "reforms" that teacher unions are likely to support? Yes, there are several, such as higher salaries for teachers, smaller classes, stronger measures to exclude unruly pupils, and paid in-service training programs and sabbatical leaves.

In short, teacher unions support changes that pay teachers more, require them to do less work, reduce their accountability, and/or otherwise make life easier for teachers. Although such reforms may be justified in some situations, they could hardly have much effect outside of a few districts with special problems.

NEA/AFT Approaches to Reform

Although teacher union responses to reform are limited by union realities, the NEA and the AFT differ somewhat in their approach to reform. The differences are partly cosmetic and may disappear in the future, but they should be noted briefly. Prior to 1985, the NEA's response was to accept everything that enhanced teacher welfare, to reject everything perceived as contrary to teacher welfare, and to straddle the other issues. As a result, the NEA was widely perceived as "antireform." At its 1985 convention, however, the NEA endorsed tests for new teachers and the dismissal of incompetent experienced teachers. These are hardly revolutionary positions, but they were widely perceived as reflecting a more flexible posture by the NEA.[6] The AFT's response has been much more sophisticated. It has carefully avoided a militant posture, even on issues where locals will be militant if and when certain issues are pressed to the utmost. Instead, the AFT position papers on reform issues are moderate in tone, objective in defining the issues, and rather candid in identifying the union interest in an issue. Furthermore, the position papers recognize that locals may accept proposals to which they are strongly opposed on the merits.

The differences between the NEA and the AFT on reform issues are largely differences at the national level. Because of its internal structure, the NEA lacks strong elected leadership. As a result, the NEA policies are almost always reduced to the lowest common denominator of union ideology. In contrast, the AFT is headed by Albert Shanker, an elected president whose prestige and security as national president provide considerable latitude for leadership. As Shanker himself has said, his unchallenged position as AFT president enables him to be an "educational statesman" on occasion.

Shanker's assessment of the reform movement goes a long way toward explaining the AFT's reactions to it. For several years he has contended that public education is seriously jeopardized by tuition tax credits and/or vouchers. Speaking on the reform reports at the 1983 AFT convention, Shanker stated:

> We must show a willingness to move far in the direction of these reports, cooperatively and eagerly, because we stand a great chance that these powerful report sponsors will say yes, the nation is at risk, we were willing to spend a lot of money and we wanted to make a lot of changes, but you know, it is hopeless because we came up against inflexible unions, school boards and administrators. If these leaders of government and industry after having invested time, effort and prestige on a program to rebuild American education find their efforts frustrated, there is no question as to where the tilt of public policy will go. We will lose the support that we now have. There will be a massive move to try something else, and it will all be over.[7]

Shanker's membership on the AFL-CIO Committee on the Evolution of Work has also affected his attitude toward the reform movement. This committee was established by the AFL-CIO Executive Council in August 1982. Ostensibly intended to review and evaluate changes in the labor force, the committee has devoted considerable attention to the future of unions in the United States. The committee reports may be viewed as an effort by the AFL-CIO to reassess its goals and its strategy and tactics for achieving them.

The first two reports published by the committee suggest several interesting changes in the role and programs of unions.[8] For example, the 1985 report points out that many workers who support the concept of organization nevertheless are opposed to traditional adversarial bargaining relationships between employers and employees. The report also mentions the fact that these employees feel that unions have neglected issues of concern to them. Such data led the committee to recommend a variety of approaches to collective bargaining. Instead of the traditional comprehensive contract spelling out terms and conditions of employment in detail, unions were urged to consider such nontraditional approaches as minimum guarantees as a floor for individual bargaining.

Although insisting that unions need the capacity to respond to employer confrontations, the report avoids the error of treating such confrontations as primarily the fault of employers. Needless to say, if the spirit and substance of the report were actually implemented by teacher unions, at least some of the negative conclusions concerning their role in educational reform would have to be modified. In any case, the AFT's more open-minded approach to reform seems to be based upon a more realistic understanding, or at least a different perception, of worker attitudes than prevails in the NEA. The long-range effects of these differences are nevertheless difficult to predict. After all, teacher union responses to reform proposals are determined by local, not by national, union officers. We should be skeptical as well as hopeful concerning the reorientation of the local union officers and representatives.

Notwithstanding the foregoing, it may appear that I have still exaggerated the effectiveness of union opposition to educational reform. Although "reform" is not synonymous with less pay for more work, the union posture toward such employer demands in other fields seems inconsistent with my analysis. In recent years, a number of large and powerful unions have accepted "takeaways" and agreed to forego wage increases and restrictive work rules for varying periods of time. There are at least two reasons, however, why teacher unions, like public-sector unions generally, will be more effective in opposing changes required to increase teacher productivity.

First of all, the private-sector unions that have accepted takeaways did so because of competitive factors that neither the union nor its employer could control. For example, unionized airlines with inefficient work rules could not compete with nonunionized airlines. In this situation, the union had to accept takeaways or face the fact that its employer would be out of business in the near future—literally within a matter of days on some occasions. Teacher unions, however, are not faced with this problem. There is no educational equivalent of People Express or Nissan, ready immediately to service the customers of employers at the verge of bankruptcy. For this reason, teacher unions are in a much stronger position than the private-sector unions, which have accepted drastic measures to increase the productivity of the employees they represent.

Unlike private-sector unions, teacher unions are not restrained by the possibility that inefficiencies will result in lower revenues for the employer. Employers in the private sector have to pass on increased costs to the buyers of their goods and services. With or without competition, the increased costs may lead to higher prices and, consequently, to a decrease in sales and revenues. In contrast, school districts' revenues are rarely affected adversely by inefficiencies; for instance, federal and state aid to school districts is based on the number of pupils, not on the efficiency of the districts. This weakens union incentive to maximize teacher productivity. It is also one of the reasons why both the NEA and the AFT are likely to oppose the changes needed to restore public confidence in public education. Unions are most successful in their aggressive mode; they are not as successful as defensive institutions.

In assessing the ability of teacher unions to block reforms, we should not overlook the enormous resources available to them. For example, the dues income of local, state, and national teacher unions in the United States probably exceeds $500 million annually. In addition to other revenues, the teacher unions have enormous personnel resources to use in a struggle for public opinion. These resources include the time of thousands of union staff members as well as the substantial time available to teachers after school, during holiday seasons, and in summer vacations.

THE COGNIZANCE ISSUE

The analysis has shown how and why collective bargaining poses major obstacles to educational reform. To what extent do recommendations for reform take cognizance of these obstacles? What strategy or program do they propose to overcome these obstacles?

The answer is clear: No recognition, no strategy, and no program. Difficult as it may be to comprehend, the subject is ignored by the reform leaders and in the reform proposals currently receiving most of the attention. For instance, *A Nation At Risk*, the report of the National Commission on Excellence in Education, is unquestionably the leading reform proposal of our time.[9]

In preparing its report, the commission funded 40 studies on various topics and issues. Not a single one dealt with teacher unions, or the relationships between collective bargaining and educational reform. Furthermore, nothing in the commission's report itself suggests that the role of teacher unions must be considered in a reform strategy. It is as if a commission were to study what must be done to restore our automobile manufacturing industry to world leadership, and then come up with a series of recommendations on labor policy that totally ignored the existence of the United Auto Workers. As naive as this would be, it is the intellectual level of *A Nation At Risk*. The complete failure to consider the role of teacher unions is not the only major oversight in the commission report or the only reason the report is an exercise in futility. It is, however, a sufficient reason. It is all the more deplorable because it substantially decreased instead of increased public understanding of the difficulties in achieving educational reform.

The same conclusions apply to *High School*, the highly publicized reform proposal sponsored by the Carnegie Foundation.[10] The index to *High School* does not mention "union," "collective bargaining," or "American Federation of Teachers." The *only* reference to the National Education Association is to a study it sponsored in 1913.

Similarly, from reading the other reform proposals, one would not be aware that teacher unions exist, let alone that they constitute any kind of obstacle to educational reform. With one negligible exception, not one of the reform proposals takes any cognizance whatsoever of teacher unions. None discusses their actual or potential role. None suggests that teacher unions may be strongly opposed to most measures necessary to achieve reform. These omissions would not be so disturbing if the reformers had explicitly considered the issues and, for whatever reason, concluded that teacher bargaining was not an important obstacle to educational reform. As it is, however, the omissions greatly undermine the value of the reform reports as a guide to action.

As with collective bargaining in other fields, its impact on education is a matter of dispute. Most of the published research, whether "pro" or "anti" union in its conclusions, is intellectually pathetic. One such study, based upon interviews with principals, teachers, and union representatives in six "representative" school districts, concluded that "there was virtually unanimous agreement among both teachers and administrators that collective bargaining continue to be necessary in today's schools—necessary to protect teachers from abuse, to ensure fair wages, to represent collective interests, and to defend educational budgets during a time of declining resources. . . ."[11] This sounds great. Unfortunately, the total school district budget is not subject to bargaining anywhere.

In bargaining, union and district representatives talk to each other, not to third parties. Against whom would they "defend educational budgets" in bargaining? Whether against each other or third parties, the conclusion makes no sense, whether reached by the persons interviewed or derivatively by the author of this piece of unwitting union propaganda.

The other major conclusion reached in this study is that unionized teachers are more dissatisfied with their working conditions than nonunionized teachers. The authors suggest that unions emerge from highly unsatisfactory working conditions. Thus although unions may improve these conditions, they are unable to bring the teacher level of satisfaction to the level of the nonunion districts. In fact, the explanation is fallacious. Teacher unions have emerged as much or more where conditions were superior as where they were poor. Furthermore, at least some of the time, the greater dissatisfaction among unionized teachers is not the cause but the direct result of unionization. Unions typically seek to arouse dissatisfaction in order to develop teacher militancy or demonstrate the need for the union. For this reason, teacher dissatisfaction is frequently greater in unionized than in non-unionized districts with inferior terms and conditions of employment.

To put the point in a different way, the same working conditions that are perceived very favorably by teachers in one district may be perceived very unfavorably by teachers in a different district. The difference in perception is not due to the conditions of employment, which are the same in both districts. It is due to differences in the levels of expectation. Teachers who have been treated better expect more, and are therefore more likely to be dissatisfied with modest improvements. Because their expectations are lower, teachers with relatively poor conditions of employment are more likely to be satisfied with modest improvements.

TEACHER UNIONS AND ENTREPRENEURIAL SCHOOLS

Entrepreneurial schools could develop in several different ways. It can be safely stated, however, that regardless of their pattern of development, they would avoid most if not all of the problems associated with teacher unions.

Preliminarily, we should note that union membership generally is much lower in the private than in the public sector. Nationally, union membership as a percentage dropped from 23.0 in 1980 to 18.8 in 1984. Almost every category showed a decline; for example, in manufacturing (which includes the automobile industry) the percentage of unionized workers dropped from 27.8 in 1980 to 26.0 in 1984.[12] Although we lack reliable data on the status of union membership in private schools, it is clearly minuscule, especially in comparison to its prevalence in public education. This situation is not likely to be greatly affected by changes from nonprofit to profit-making private schools.

In the first place, union success in organizing both public- and private-sector employees has always been closely related to the legislative environment governing the subject. This has been true under both state and federal law. Indisputably, the growth of teacher unions has been made possible by state collective bargaining laws. Some apply to state and local public employees generally; some apply only to school district employees. No one, however, seriously disputes the fact that these state laws have encouraged teacher unionization.

In contrast, entrepreneurial schools would not be subject to such laws. For this reason alone, teacher unions would be at a severe disadvantage in organizing such schools. The latter could take all sorts of actions to avoid unionization that would be illegal under the state bargaining laws.

In public schools, teachers were often members of the NEA or the AFT before these organizations became fully unionized. Even in the precollective bargaining days (prior to 1965), teacher organizations exhibited some of the characteristics of unions. Teacher unionization was a matter of changing the functions of existing organizations much more than it was the establishment of new organizations. It is very unlikely, however, that teacher unions would have a similar presence in entrepreneurial schools. For the most part, their organizing efforts would be unsupported by any existing organization in the entrepreneurial schools. This would be an immense obstacle to union organization. Instead of having teachers on the site who could encourage organization, the unions would have to depend on union representatives, that is, "outsiders," who would normally be more costly to support and less effective than "fellow teachers" in organizing.

A third major factor would be the strategic vulnerability of unions in entrepreneurial schools. Currently, teacher unions can demand all sorts of benefits that would normally be opposed by parents. For example, the unions may seek to limit the teacher workday to 15 minutes before and after the pupil day. Or they may limit the number of evening (PTA) meetings teachers must attend, and so on.

On the other hand, the popularity of entrepreneurial schools is likely to depend in part upon their avoidance of such limitations upon school responsiveness to student and parent needs. The teachers in entrepreneurial schools will be aware of the fact that typical union demands will threaten the popularity, perhaps even the existence, of entrepreneurial schools. Unlike public schools, which depend largely upon state and federal aid that is independent of client satisfaction, entrepreneurial schools will be directly dependent upon their ability to satisfy clients. Consequently, union appeals that may be successful in public schools will be correctly perceived as a threat to teacher well-being in entrepreneurial schools.

These reasons alone would probably be sufficient to minimize the union role, even its existence, in entrepreneurial schools. To be sure, there are a few reasons why teachers might be more rather than less likely to unionize in entrepreneurial schools. For instance, they will not have the protection of the state tenure laws, hence they may be more receptive to the need for union protection of job security. Nor can we ignore the possibility that entrepreneurial school management may ineptly generate employee dissatisfaction and receptivity to union organization. Nevertheless, the number and influence of teacher unions would be much less in entrepreneurial than in public schools; it is doubtful whether union leaders themselves would question this conclusion.

NOTES

1. Educational Finance Center, Education Commission of the States, *Cuebook II, State Education Collective Bargaining Laws* (Denver: Education Commission of the States, 1980); and update dated July 1984.

2. Ibid.

3. Ibid.

4. Randall W. Eberts and Lawrence C. Pierce, *Time in the Classroom: The Effect of Collective Bargaining on the Allocation of Teacher Time* (Eugene: Center for Educational Policy and Management, University of Oregon, 1982), p. 17.

5. See *AFT Issues Papers* (Washington, D.C.: American Federation of Teachers, n.d.)

6. New York *Times*, July 7, 1985, p. E7.

7. President Albert Shanker, *Address to the 1983 Convention of the American Federation of Teachers* (Washington, D.C.: American Federation of Teachers, n.d.), p. 9.

8. AFL-CIO Committee on the Future of Work, *The Future of Work* (Washington, D.C.: AFL-CIO, 1983); and *The Changing Situation of Workers and Their Unions* (Washington, D.C.: AFL-CIO, 1985).

9. National Commission on Excellence in Education, *A Nation At Risk: The Imperative for Educational Reform* (Washington, D.C.: U.S. Government Printing Office, 1983).

10. Ernest L. Boyer, *High School: A Report on Secondary Education in America* (New York: Harper & Row, 1983).

11. Susan Moore Johnson, *Teacher Unions in Schools* (Philadelphia: Temple University Press, 1984).

12. News Release, Bureau of Labor Statistics, U.S. Department of Labor, as reported in the New York *Times*, February 8, 1985, p. B5.

3

FACT AND FICTION IN
TEACHER SALARIES

As we have seen, many proposed reforms would adversely affect terms and conditions of teacher employment. Naturally, teachers do not regard such proposals as "reforms." In their eyes, such proposals are merely an excuse to further exploit teachers.

On the other hand, the reform reports unanimously agree on the urgent need to increase teacher salaries substantially. Teachers understandably view such proposals as "real" or "genuine" reforms, not "fads" or "quick fixes." Therefore, let us consider the reform most strongly supported by teachers. After all, if their opposition is a major roadblock to reform, perhaps reforms they enthusiastically support have a better chance to succeed.

THE CASE FOR HIGHER TEACHER SALARIES

What is the case for a material improvement in the relative economic status of teachers? Let us first consider this question in terms of the entire teaching profession.

Preliminarily, it is essential to see how and how much teachers are paid.[1] As illustrated by Table 3.1, the vast majority of teachers are paid solely according to their training and years of experience. Salary schedules differ primarily in (1) the number of steps (that is, the number of years that receive salary credit), (2) the number of columns and the amount of credit required to move horizontally (that is, from one column to another), and (3) the amount of salary credit, if any, for advanced degrees, longevity above the regular schedule, and credit

46

Table 3.1 Teachers' Salary Schedule, Berea, Ohio, City School District (Salary grid: 1.96, $16,650 base; effective January 1, 1985)

Years of Service	B.A. Degree	B.A. Plus 10 S.H.*	B.A. Plus 20 S.H.	B.A. Plus 30 S.H.	M.A. Degree	M.A. Plus 12 S.H.	M.A. Plus 24 S.H.	M.A. Plus 36 S.H.	M.A. Plus 48 S.H.
					College Training				
0	16,650	17,066	17,483	17,899	18,115	18,731	19,148	19,564	19,980
1	17,443	17,880	18,315	18,750	19,337	19,760	20,181	20,604	21,014
2	18,235	18,695	19,148	19,600	20,360	20,789	21,215	21,645	22,048
3	19,028	19,509	19,980	20,451	21,382	21,818	22,249	22,686	23,082
4	19,820	20,323	20,813	21,302	22,404	22,847	23,283	23,726	24,116
5	20,613	21,137	21,645	22,113	23,427	23,876	24,317	24,767	25,150
6	21,405	21,951	22,478	23,004	24,449	24,905	25,351	25,808	26,184
7	22,198	22,766	23,310	23,854	25,471	25,934	26,385	26,848	27,218
8	22,990	23,580	24,143	24,705	26,493	26,963	27,419	27,889	28,252
9	23,783	24,394	24,975	25,556	27,516	27,992	28,453	28,929	29,286
10	24,575	25,208	25,808	26,407	28,538	29,021	29,487	29,970	30,320
11	25,368	26,022	26,640	27,258	29,560	30,050	30,521	31,011	31,354
12	26,160	26,836	27,473	28,109	30,583	31,079	31,555	32,051	32,388
13	26,953	27,651	28,305	28,959	31,605	32,108	32,589	33,092	33,422
14	27,739	28,472	29,138	29,804	32,634	33,134	33,633	34,133	34,466
38	30,889	31,622	32,288	32,594	35,784	36,284	36,783	37,283	37,616

*S.H. = semester hours.

Teachers who work beyond the 186 days shall be paid at their daily rate. This raise is contingent upon the passage of additional millage in 1984. If additional millage is not approved by November 7, 1984, the Association and Board will reopen negotiations for salary with five (5) days of the above date.

In addition, the contract includes 13 pages setting forth additional pay for board "pick-up" of teacher contributions to the state teachers retirement system, longevity, curriculum writing during summer, summer school and adult education courses, home tutoring, camp supervision, service as department chairman or teacher team leader, athletic coaching and supervision, and supervision of extracurricular activities.

Source: Agreement Between the Berea Education Association and the Berea Board of Education, Revised, January 1984. The additional millage was approved in November 1984.

for prior teaching service. There may be some variation also in the extra-duty schedule, that is, coaching, class adviser, band leader, and so on, and whether additional amounts are paid for degrees as distinguished from mere accumulation of credit.

As in Table 3.1, most teacher salary schedules do not provide salary differentials according to the subject or grade level. It is not unusual, however, to pay school psychologists, counselors, special education teachers, and a few other categories a stipend above the schedule. Even in these cases, however, the additional stipend often reflects either a longer school year or additional training required or both.

It was not always thus. In the early 1900s, common practice was to pay secondary more than elementary teachers. The differentials were both cause and result of the fact that elementary teachers were overwhelmingly female, whereas high school teachers were more evenly divided between the sexes. The movement toward a single schedule covering grades K-12 resulted from the fact that there are twice as many elementary as secondary teachers. It became impossible to achieve a leadership position in the NEA or the AFT without supporting a single schedule covering all grades.

Actually, there was a time in the early 1960s when many school districts might have adopted different salary schedules for different grade levels. Today, it is widely agreed that the 1961 collective bargaining election among New York City's teachers was the single most important stimulus to teacher bargaining and teacher unions in the 1960s. One of the critical issues in this election was whether all teachers should be in the same bargaining unit. For tactical reasons, the NEA supported the idea that elementary, junior high, and senior high school teachers should separately choose a union to represent their own grade level. If the NEA position had prevailed, it is virtually certain that many school districts would have reverted to the practice of paying secondary more than elementary teachers. The NEA position did not prevail, and today the issue is moot.

Needless to say, the elimination of salary differentials for higher grade levels could not be ascribed to the political ramifications of the fact that elementary outnumbered secondary teachers in teacher unions by a 2 to 1 margin. Instead, it was justified by the alleged importance of the first few years of schooling and by the fact that elementary usually worked as many days as secondary teachers. Neither reason is very impressive. We do not pay high school mathematics teachers as much as university professors of this subject, even though we could make the same argument about the importance of the early years. The fact is that salaries are influenced less by the importance of the work than by the availability of the skills needed. In general, we pay enough to get the job done adequately, no more. Nor is the fact that elementary teachers work as many school days particularly important. So do school custodians and secretaries, but no one contends they should be paid as much as teachers for this reason.

How Much Are Teachers Paid?

How much are teachers paid? Perhaps the most accurate as well as the most surprising answer is that nobody knows. There is a wealth of data on the subject, but it is incomplete on certain critical points. This is an extremely important point because the teacher unions, especially the NEA, are our primary source of data on teacher salaries; even federal agencies, such as the National Institute of Education, rely upon the NEA for information on teacher salaries and salary trends. As we shall see, the missing data would show significantly higher levels of compensation than those accepted by the reformers or the public generally. In my opinion, the relevant data are missing precisely because they would weaken union claims that teachers are underpaid.

Another important question is this: Who is included in determining average salaries? In conducting its salary surveys, which are widely used by government agencies and the media, the NEA uses two categories: "classroom teachers" and "instructional staff." The latter includes supervisors of instruction, librarians, guidance counselors, psychologists, and principals and is significantly higher than the average for classroom teachers. For example, the NEA estimated that in 1981-82 the average was $19,270 for classroom teachers and $20,114 for instructional staff.[2]

The Excellence Commission report illustrates the inaccurate, not to say haphazard, treatment of teacher salaries. The report states: "The average salary after 12 years of teaching is only $17,000 per year, and many teachers are required to supplement their income with part-time and summer employment."[3] Although not stated in the report, the $17,000 figure was meant to apply to the 1981-82 school year. Actually, as we have seen, the NEA estimated the average teacher salary in 1981-82 to be $19,142, that is, 12.6 percent higher than the commission figure.

As do most discussions of teacher salaries, *A Nation At Risk* says nothing about the fringe benefits paid to teachers. I am not now referring to their shorter workyear and workday, which will be discussed later. Instead, I am referring to payments made for the following benefits: teacher retirement, health and welfare benefits, leave benefits, extra-duty pay (coaching, for example), unemployment insurance, and worker compensation.

As in the private sector, health and welfare benefits, primarily medical and hospital insurance, have become a major component of teacher compensation. Additionally, the data on teacher salaries do not ordinarily include the amounts paid by school boards and state governments for teacher retirement. Nevertheless, these important elements of total compensation were ignored by the national commission as they are generally in discussions of teacher salaries. These omissions alone result in significant understatements of teacher compensation.

Like public employee pension systems generally, teacher retirement systems tend to be much more generous than the retirement benefits available to most private-sector employees. Nationally, contributions for teacher fringe benefits averaged about 22 percent of salary in 1983-84; the comparable figure for all workers outside of teaching is 19 percent. It appears also that in some states (California, Michigan, New York) school district contributions for fringe benefits are 35 percent of salary.[4] Note also that teacher fringe benefits are likely to increase even more rapidly in the near future. Some states emphasized higher pension benefits instead of direct salary increases in the 1970s. In these states, substantially greater school district/state contributions will be required as teacher retirements increase.

Minimally, omission of any reference to teacher fringe benefits reflects a lack of candor if not of competence. These deficiencies typically characterize teacher salary discussions at the local level. Teacher unions frequently opt for increases in fringe benefits instead of teacher salaries. This often occurs because the fringe benefits are not taxable to the teachers; on the other hand, the additional income to teachers would be taxed if the money used to pay for health and welfare benefits were instead added to the salary schedule. What typically happens, however, is that the teacher unions ignore the fringe benefits in their efforts to persuade communities that teachers should be paid more. The unions frequently cite data to show that teacher salaries have lagged behind the cost of living—while simultaneously ignoring the fact that the school board is paying for medical and dental costs, which have escalated more than any other component of the cost of living. Such tactics would be futile except for media incompetence in reporting upon public-sector labor disputes.

As this is written (Fall 1985) the Reagan administration has introduced legislation that would eliminate the tax-sheltered status of health insurance benefits. Such proposed legislation has already aroused intense union opposition, and its fate is uncertain. Nevertheless, in addition to providing a much-needed brake on the costs of health care, the change would clearly be consistent with economic realities.

The Teacher Workyear and Workday

In discussing teacher salaries, some but not all of the reform proposals pay much attention to the teacher workyear and workday. One reason may be that the amount of time teachers work is even more unsettled than their total compensation. The number of workdays is seldom in issue; we can use 180 days as a reasonably accurate national average. Serious controversy exists, however, with respect to the average amount of time teachers work each day. In the typical situation, teachers work a defined school day, usually 6-7.5 hours including lunch and preparation periods. The lunch period is usually at least 30 minutes but it is not always duty-free, even when this is mandated by state law. On the other hand, preparation periods are usually not used for preparation. Instead, for all practical purposes, they are used as the teachers see fit, for personal as well as professional tasks or simply for rest during the day.

The major issue, however, is over how much time teachers devote to their work outside the regular school day. The NEA asserts categorically that "teachers average 46 hours of work a week."[5]

This conclusion was based upon teachers' subjective judgments and recollections of how much time they devoted to school tasks. Given the self-serving nature of the NEA studies, and the procedures used, a healthy skepticism seems warranted. Of course, there are teachers who average 46 hours, or even more than this (despite, it must be said, some union efforts to discourage voluntary work because it weakens union efforts to have it compensated). But until there is better evidence than the NEA's self-serving studies, we cannot accept the conclusion that most teachers average 46 hours of work per week without additional compensation.

To summarize, both the rate and the amount of teacher compensation are typically understated while their hours of work are overstated. Let us ignore these considerations, however, and turn to the contention that it is imperative to raise the relative economic status of teachers. Why precisely is it imperative, or even desirable?

The reasons most often cited are that (1) teaching is not as good as it should be because teachers are recruited largely from the lower ranks of high school and college graduates, and (2) it is impossible to attract teachers to certain fields because the salaries in those fields are too low. As *A Nation At Risk* observed, "too many teachers are being drawn from the bottom quarter of graduating high school and college students." The National Commission report went on to point out that "the shortage of teachers in mathematics and science is particularly severe. A 1981 survey of 45 states revealed shortages of mathematics teachers in 43 states, critical shortages of earth science teachers in 33 states, and of physics teachers everywhere."[6]

To remedy these problems, the National Commission recommended that

> salaries for the teaching profession should be increased and should be professionally competitive, market-sensitive, and performance-based. Salary, promotion, tenure, and retention decisions should be tied to an effective evaluation system that includes peer review so that superior teachers can be rewarded, average ones encouraged, and poor ones either improved or terminated.[7]

The commission did not provide any specifics on how large an increase would be required to achieve these objectives. In this respect at least, its recommendations contrast markedly with those made by Boyer, who recommended that "the average salary for teachers should be increased by at least 25 percent beyond the rate of inflation over the next three years, with immediate entry-level increases."[8]

Like the National Commission and the other leading reformers who have considered the matter, Boyer emphasizes the fact that teaching is not economically competitive with other professions. He also contends that low salaries force teachers to moonlight extensively, thus reducing the time that should be devoted to their teaching positions or to professional improvement. Despite differences in language and emphasis, these are the major arguments for increasing teacher salaries.

These arguments are expressed as if their validity were self-evident. To this observer at least, they are neither valid nor persuasive. In the first place, none of the arguments demonstrates a causal relationship between the decline in scholastic aptitude among beginning teachers and the actual decline in student achievement. The causal relationship is assumed without question. Nevertheless, if one assumes (as I do) that the decline in student achievement has multiple causes, then we should have at least a rough idea of how it is affected by the talent level of teachers. Yet to my knowledge, no one seems to have any idea of either how much additional teacher talent would be attracted by increases in teacher compensation, or how much students would learn if teachers were paid more.

The more one considers the matter, the less impressive is the argument for a significant general increase in the level of teacher compensation. Consider the National Commission's recommendation that teaching salaries be "professionally competitive." The American Association of School Administrators (AASA) conducted a survey in 1983 to determine the costs of the commission's recommendations.

It did so by means of a survey of 28 school districts: urban, rural, and suburban, large and small, and from every region in the country. Using a survey conducted by the Bureau of Labor Statistics, U.S. Department of Labor, AASA estimated that the *lowest* average entry-level salary for professionals with a bachelor's degree was $18,820 per year. It then asked the survey school districts the following question: "What would be the cost to raise starting teachers' salaries to $18,720 per year?"

The responses highlight the unrealistic nature of the National Commission's recommendation. The average current starting salary in these 28 districts was $13,853. The cost of raising beginning salaries to $18,720, just in these 28 districts, was $273,907,291! Such a raise would have increased average salaries in the 28 districts from 14.2 to 58.5 percent and would have increased the *total* budgets of all 28 districts by 12.9 percent.[9]

Again, let me emphasize that this increase would result from just one commission recommendation, and not the most expensive one at that. Even so, the AASA study grossly understated the cost of implementing this one recommendation. In the first place, it was based upon increasing only the beginning teacher salary and any others currently below $18,720. It would be extremely unlikely that a district could or would do this without raising at least some other salaries; it would be absurd to assume that administrators, teachers already earning over $18,720, and nonteacher employees and their unions would accept a situation in which beginning teachers received raises of 16.5 to 58.3 percent, and they received the short end of the stick. Even apart from this, the AASA estimate of the costs is much too low. If school districts did indeed raise their beginning salaries to $18,720, many firms that pay this salary to beginning professionals would increase it to meet the competition from the schools. Just how high the bidding would go is anybody's guess, but $18,720 would merely be the start of the auction, not the end of it. Significantly, none of the reform proposals pays any attention to the impact of higher teacher salaries on the other fields that would lose some of their talented college graduates. Without this information, we are hardly in a position to conclude that our society would be better off if a much larger proportion of our ablest college graduates were teachers.

My point here, however, is not the cost of the salary recommendations in *A Nation At Risk*. It is the absence of any concrete idea of what benefits would accrue from them, or when or how. To be candid, there are only general appeals to raise teacher salaries, without the slightest indication of what levels of improvement would result from increases in teacher compensation. Long before any such calculations are made, however, the futilitarian nature of the reform proposals should be clear to everyone. Take, for example, Boyer's recommendation that teacher salaries be increased by 25 percent above the rate of inflation over the next three years. The estimated average salary of 2,150,000 public school teachers in 1982-83 was $22,000, not including any fringe benefits. Boyer's recommendation would cost over $11.8 billion, not including increases in mandated costs based upon teacher salaries or increases for other employees certain to take militant action to get their share. Little wonder that Boyer is being praised as an educational statesman in paid union advertisements![10]

One additional challenge to the conventional wisdom should be noted. There is widespread belief that private schools educate at least as well as public schools. Be that as it may, teachers in private schools are paid less, and receive less in fringe benefits, than teachers in public schools. Of course, the differences vary from area to area and school to school, but most private school teachers probably earn only two-thirds to three-fourths as much as public school teachers.

How can this be? That is, how can it be argued that higher salaries for public school teachers are essential, while teachers in private schools are paid less but presumably perform as well or better? Clearly, the lower average salaries in private schools cannot be explained by the presence of a small number of teachers who are members of religious orders; the differentials apply to lay teachers, who comprise the vast majority anyway. It is often asserted that private schools can recruit good teachers in spite of their lower salaries because other conditions of employment in private schools are superior. Allegedly, private school teachers have more autonomy, more freedom from bureaucratic demands, and more input into professional decisions, such as textbook selection. To my knowledge, however, these claims have not been substantiated on a systematic basis.

Understandably, some teachers may prefer to teach at a lower salary, if the school has higher morale and fewer unruly pupils and security problems. Nevertheless, it is not clear that superior nonsalary conditions of employment prevail in private schools, let alone explain their alleged ability to attract competent teachers at lower salaries than are paid to public school teachers. For instance, class size, which is an important condition of employment, is usually higher in private than in public schools. At any rate, the situation poses some difficult questions for the argument that a higher salary level is essential to improve education.

HIGHER SALARIES FOR SUBGROUPS: AN OVERVIEW

Let us put aside rhetoric about raising the economic status of teachers generally and turn to some less grandiose salary proposals. Such proposals call for substantial salary increases for one or more subgroups of teachers. Those subgroups would be differentiated from other teachers by their function, their subject matter specialization, or their superior teaching performance.

Because these three approaches are often confused, let me begin by illustrating the differences.

A is a "Master Teacher" who helps to train new teachers. B is an excellent teacher who doesn't want to be bothered by training duties and isn't concerned about the salary differential for doing so. If the district pays A more than B because of A's role in training teachers, we have a salary differential based upon different functions. Such proposals are often referred to as "differentiated staffing."

C is a mathematics teacher; D is a history teacher. Both are excellent teachers. Both do everything expected of teachers, in and out of the classroom. Nevertheless, because of the tremendous shortage of mathematics teachers, C is paid $5,000 annually more than D. In this case, we have a salary differential based upon subject matter specialization.

E is an outstanding mathematics teacher; F is an average mathematics teacher. They are the same age, have the same training and experience, and perform the same tasks throughout the day. Nevertheless, the district pays E more than F because it wishes to pay outstanding teachers more than average ones. In this case, the salary differential is based upon differences in the quality of performance.

I shall refer to such salary proposals as "merit pay"; proposals to pay teachers more based upon functional differentiation, or subject matter specialization, are not "merit pay," as the phrase is used here. The AFT's position paper on salaries makes the same distinction and emphasizes that the union's opposition to merit pay does not necessarily apply to other proposals to pay salary differentials to a limited number of teachers.[11]

Although all three kinds of salary proposals are often labeled "merit pay," there are important differences between them—for example, in incentives, costs, ease of administration, and union opposition. Valid objections to one type of proposal do not necessarily apply to the others. Differentials based upon subject matter taught require minimal administrative judgment, are relatively easy to administer, encounter less union opposition, and would probably have more immediate effects than merit pay. A college senior majoring in mathematics is more likely to become a teacher because of subject matter than a merit pay differential. The student would realize that the subject matter differential would be available immediately, whereas the merit pay differential would be uncertain, involve a great deal of judgment, require a multiyear evaluation period, and would likely be resented by more experienced teachers. These comments are not intended to bless one category or criticize another but they underscore the need to examine each proposal on its own merits. Of course, it is possible to have salary differentials that combine elements of all three approaches, but for analytic purposes, I shall consider each type separately.

Higher Salaries in Specific Fields: Mathematics and Science

The reformers have repeatedly noted the severe teacher shortages in certain fields, such as mathematics and science. The cause of the shortages is simple enough: The persons who have the abilities and aptitudes to be competent teachers of these subjects can earn substantially more in private-sector positions.

The explanation for the shortages is valid, but few persons understand the full implications of it. The mathematics teacher has more in common with other persons having mathematical skills and aptitudes than with other teachers. There is a strong nonschool demand for mathematics teachers, or for students who could be mathematics teachers. There is no such strong out-of-school demand for persons who would make good history or physical education teachers.

According to the folklore of education, concern for young people is the primary and common characteristic of teachers. This is utter nonsense. Suppose a university decided that professors of surgery and professors of English literature were really members of the same profession because they both enjoyed teaching, and should therefore be paid the same. The upshot would be either it would overpay professors of English literature, perhaps by as much as $50,000 a year; or it would be unable to hire professors of surgery; even surgeons not qualified to teach surgery would not teach for the salaries paid to professors of English literature.

As absurd as this self-imposed dilemma would be, it is precisely the dilemma facing school districts who pay physics teachers the same as history teachers. They end up without physics teachers, just as a university would end up without surgery professors if it followed such an idiotic policy.

One might expect the teacher unions to experience internal conflict by opposing differentials for mathematics/science teachers. Possibly, but not as much conflict as they would experience—or expect to experience—by accepting salary differentials for fields experiencing teacher shortages. Although single salary schedules do not necessarily eliminate intraunion conflict over salaries, they do tend to minimize it (although that is seldom given as the reason why unions negotiate them). The reasons usually given are that all teachers love children, all are members of the same profession, and all have the same amount of training. Second, the unions view the shortages in specific fields as leverage to achieve salary increases for all teachers. Additionally, salary differentials for mathematics/science teachers could be a disastrous precedent. As John Dewey once observed, once people start thinking, you never know where they will end up. Once it is conceded that market factors are a legitimate concern in salaries for mathematics/physics teachers, why stop there? Why not go on to say that if the school district has 50 outstanding applications for teaching history, and none for mathematics, it should *lower* the salary for history teachers as well as increase the salary offered for mathematics teachers?

At the local level, salary differentials for mathematics/science teachers will usually be casualties of collective bargaining. Teacher unions are not going to propose such differentials, or struggle to achieve them. Mathematics/science teachers will constitute only a very small proportion of the teaching staff, hence of the union's membership. Do not forget that unions are essentially political organizations —they are devoted to economic objectives, but they are governed by a political process in which each member has one vote. For this reason, it is unrealistic to expect teacher unions to negotiate salary differentials for a few teachers. The unions will make an all-out effort to prevent dismissals of a few teachers, but not to achieve salary differentials for a small number of them.

In a few districts, such as Dade County, Florida, the unions have negotiated plans that provide additional compensation for mathematics/science teachers but technically do not violate the single salary schedule. Such teachers are paid additional amounts for teaching during their preparation periods, provided opportunities to work additional days, and otherwise accorded more opportunities to earn additional amounts in accordance with the salary schedule. In the long run, however, such arrangements will not have more than a marginal effect at best upon the underlying problem. After all, if you don't have mathematics/science teachers to begin with, you can't ask them to teach during their preparation period.

The teacher unions try to avoid wage differentials; such differentials lead to internal strife, something the unions don't want. Furthermore, the lower the differential, the less likely it will achieve its purpose; the higher the differential, the less support for it there will be among teachers. The differential is offered because the number of teachers in the subject is very limited. On the other hand, unions seldom negotiate hard for large gains for a few constituents. The union negotiator responds to what most members want—and what they want is more money for themselves, not concessions that indicate their services aren't as valuable as anyone else's.

What is the likelihood that school management will propose and bargain hard for salary differentials for mathematics/science teachers? On a scale of 0 to 10, with 10 representing management determined at all costs to have the differentials, I would rate the likelihood about 1. First of all, we cannot ignore the record and the reasons for it. Shortages of mathematics/science teachers have been with us for several decades. Nevertheless, there has never been much support for locally funded differentials, even in nonbargaining states. Differentials pose problems that management as well as unions would like to avoid.

The fate of management proposals to pay differentials to teachers in scarce fields would depend upon several factors: the extent of the shortage, the amount of the proposed differentials, the duration of the contract, the leadership of the union, and so on. All things considered, however, there is no trend toward such management initiatives.

Let us assume, however, that a local school board decided to require mathematics and physics for a high school diploma. Let us pass over the problems of persuading thousands of local school boards to do so, and begin at the point where the policy is being implemented.

Inasmuch as the courses are required for graduation, there must be teachers to teach them. As we have seen, however, there is an extreme shortage of qualified teachers available in these subjects. Suppose the board wishes to attract the needed mathematics and science teachers by paying them a salary differential. This commonsense solution nevertheless faces several problems in addition to those related to collective bargaining. Students now in college close to graduation have probably made their career choices already. Very few mathematics/science majors have chosen to become high school teachers. How large would the differential have to be in order to stimulate these students to switch to teaching?

As we have seen, a college graduate with a bachelor's degree in mathematics earns only 75 percent as much as a teacher would earn in private industry. This difference, however, applies only to initial employment. Undoubtedly, the differentials after initial employment are much greater, especially for graduates with advanced degrees. A high school teacher with a Ph.D. in mathematics might be paid $500-$1,000 annually more than a teacher with only a bachelor's degree. The differentials outside of education are likely to be 10 to 20 times as much. To influence an adequate number of mathematics/science majors to become teachers (and remain teachers), the salary differentials would have to be substantial. Otherwise, school districts would only end up paying more to persons who were going to teach anyway.

It will not be helpful to have only a few districts pay a meaningful differential. College students who could be competent mathematics/physics teachers are not likely to teach because a few districts announce such differentials—or even implement them. There would have to be a sizable number of school districts committed to the differentials. Otherwise, few if any students in the scarce fields will decide to become teachers. On the other hand, colleges cannot establish programs to train mathematics/science teachers without enough students to make the programs economically feasible.

Personally, I do not see even a remote possibility that districts will offer mathematics/physics teachers a 25 percent differential above other teacher salaries. Even differentials this large, however, might have only a marginal impact upon the recruitment of mathematics/physics teachers. We cannot expect the private sector to ignore the competition for employees with a strong mathematics/physics background. For this reason, as school districts become competitive, the differentials for mathematics/physics teachers would have to be raised again and again. While this is going on, private-sector employers are not going to be pleased by school board policies that exacerbate their own personnel problems.

The colleges have an interest and a stake of their own in this matter. For many, especially the smaller institutions that do not produce many teachers, the economics of the matter would be prohibitive. These colleges might not be able to afford the required courses in mathematics and science. They frequently will be unable to sustain classes having five-ten students as economically feasible. Moreover, if mathematics/science majors begin to enter teaching instead of other fields, the latter are going to become active to avoid losing their clientele.

The school district that has overcome these obstacles must also provide suitable classroom laboratories and facilities. It will be expensive to provide them for a small number of students, especially when there are other needs that affect the student body as a whole. Additionally, adequate supervision of mathematics/science teachers is likely to be difficult. For some purposes, a supervisor does not have to be proficient in the same field as the teacher being supervised. You do not need a physics major to know whether a class in physics is or is not free from disruption. On the other hand, a knowledge of the subject matter is essential for supervision of the subject matter dimension. Needless to say, it will not be easy to recruit competent supervisors in mathematics and science.

State/Federal Funding for Subject Matter Differentials

At the present time, one reason why there is so little local initiative on the differential issue is the expectation, or the possibility, that state and/or federal legislation might fund subject matter differentials. Teacher unions would not be thrilled, but they could live with this solution. Of course, they will try to have the legislation require or permit bargaining on who is eligible for the differential, how many minutes of mathematics/science instruction are required to receive it, which teachers receive priority for assignments receiving differentials, and other details of implementation. If the unions are successful in this effort, the statutory differentials might not be as effective as anticipated by their sponsors. It is unlikely, however, that a significant number of state legislatures will enact subject matter differentials. The shortages in mathematics and science have been around for decades without state action to resolve them. Furthermore, as long as there is a possibility of federal support on this issue, the state legislatures will be correspondingly reluctant to act. (One exception is Iowa, which provides additional state aid for each student enrolled in mathematics/science courses. The approach is interesting but it might be preferable to provide the differential only for students who achieve at specified levels. This would minimize the danger that districts would dragoon unqualified students into the courses leading to the additional state aid.) Even if overall federal aid to education is reduced, some form of federal support for mathematics/science instruction is a distinct possibility since it is seen as closely related to national defense. Whether such federal support will include salary differentials for mathematics/science teachers is, however, rather doubtful. Significantly, the report by a National Science Foundation (NSF) commission, which deals most completely and directly with mathematics/science instruction in public schools, does not formally propose federal aid for this purpose.[12] Instead the NSF commission submitted 14 recommendations for federal action, with a total cost of $1.51 billion annually above current federal spending for education. Of this $1.51 billion, the commission recommended that $829 million be spent for 1,000 elementary and 1,000 secondary schools with exemplary programs in mathematics, science, and technology. The commission calculated the federal share at 65 percent of the total cost, with federal contributions of $276 million a year over a three-year period. Even if this is construed as a back-door way of providing federal support for salary differentials in mathematics/science, the fact that such differentials were not recommended directly is significant.

Reliance upon a new federal initiative at a time when the federal government is reducing federal aid is not very promising, but it may be the only doable way to achieve the reform. Even so, the concept of federally supported differentials raises some troublesome issues. Why should the federal government provide the differentials if local school boards could pay it if they did not adhere to single salary schedules? In effect, the federal government would be subsidizing, and hence perpetuating, highly inefficient local policies on teacher compensation. Should we adopt nationally a policy that says the federal government but not local school boards should be responsive to market conditions? How are we going to get local school boards and our society as a whole to understand that overpayment of some teachers is as much of a problem as underpayment of others—that, indeed, they are inseparable elements of the same problem?

One additional comment seems appropriate. All of the major reform proposals urge more money for education. Indeed, this recommendation is pro forma, as if not to express it implied that the reformer was more interested in reducing taxes than improving education.

This attitude is also supposed to demonstrate realism. In fact, it demonstrates the absence of realism. Before we can decide intelligently whether more money is needed, and if so, how much, we need to examine current educational spending for nonessential, even counterproductive, activities. Educational reform cannot be achieved simply by adding to what currently exists. For one thing, the resources needed for reform, including higher teacher salaries in some fields and more student time, will have to come from savings in nonessential courses, programs, and activities. As long as we take current expenditures, regardless of purpose or consequences, as the base, to which we add but never subtract, educational reform will be a basket case.

Higher Salaries Based upon Functional Differences (Differential Staffing)

Salary differentials based upon the performance of different functions are not new in education. In fact, they have always characterized public education. Superintendents are paid more than principals because of the differences in function. Teachers are paid more than teachers' aides for the same reason.

In the past few years, the idea of paying some teachers higher salaries for carrying out certain functions not shared by most teachers has been the subject of widespread discussion and some legislation. Several governors and legislative leaders have indicated their willingness to increase the salaries of some but not all teachers. State-mandated merit rating was neither politically nor administratively feasible. Thus it became necessary to rely upon functional differentiation as a basis for additional compensation.

What functions are performed by the teachers who receive the higher salaries? The most common one appears to be assisting new and inexperienced teachers. Inasmuch as most of these state plans are just getting under way, we cannot use their actual experience for evaluating them. On the other hand, our past experience with differentialed staffing among teachers demonstrates the problems that any such plan must overcome to be effective. Let us review this experience briefly to assess the prospects for current plans.

Team teaching, one of the most celebrated flops promoted by the Ford Foundation, was essentially an effort to pay teachers more by differentiating their roles. The advocates of team teaching took their cue from the medical profession. The latter includes physicians, nurses, laboratory technicians, nutritionists, physical therapists, and other occupational specialties. Physicians are at the apex of an occupational pyramid. They perform the most highly specialized functions, demanding the most training. The other occupations are subordinate to the physicians and are paid less. It was noted that physicians did not spend their time doing the work of these professionally subordinate groups. To have done so would have escalated the costs of their services; at the same time, it would have reduced the time physicians could use their professional skills (and their income). The principle would be the same if physicians performed the work of janitors or dishwashers. The more professionals perform work that can be performed by less-qualified workers, the less the professionals can concentrate on the work only they are qualified to do.

In principle, the concept makes good sense. One question is: How should the functions be allocated among the educational subgroups? The initial "experiments" started out with teachers and teachers' aides. In elementary grades, aides carried out such nonprofessional tasks as meeting buses, helping children take off or put on overcoats, and collecting or passing out assignments. In the secondary schools, the concept of differentiated staffing was tied to large-group instruction. It is just as easy to lecture to 250 students as 25. Instead of ten classes, each with 25 students, why not have one teacher lecture to 250? This teacher could be the most qualified to teach the particular assignment; furthermore, the teacher would have more time to prepare the lecture, because of the overall savings in time involved. Instead of requiring ten teachers to prepare the same lesson, one teacher could do so. The other teachers could use the time saved to work with individual students or in small-group instruction. Later, the teachers could reverse their roles on some other topic. Thus "teams" could be of varying size and composition.

For a few years, efforts to introduce team teaching emerged all over the country. Most "lighthouse" districts—that is, affluent suburban districts that confused wealth with leadership—jumped on the team teaching bandwagon. Like most educational reforms, team teaching started with enormous fanfare as the "innovation" that could save secondary education; not long afterward, however, it was buried in a shallow unmarked grave, somewhere in Scarsdale or Beverly Hills.

In retrospect, the reasons for its demise are easily understood. Inasmuch as the medical profession was the model, let us see how physicians would have acted if they had followed the education model: Two or more surgeons would have met after graduation from medical school. One would have said, "You can be the doctor, I'll be the nurse this week. Next week, you'll be the nurse and I'll be the doctor."

That is, instead of having clearly defined occupational roles, which relate back to their training, role differentiation in team teaching was based on the ad hoc judgments of teachers about what they would like to do.

In the medical profession, equipment and facilities are based upon the functions performed by the various medical specialties. Nurses, therapists, nutritionists, X-ray technicians, and so on have their specialized equipment and facilities and work stations. These go with the specialization; they are not established subjectively by individuals who divide up the work one way this week and a different way next week.

In medicine, as in other fields in which occupational roles are well defined, personality plays little or no role in who does what. The doctor may be a shy retiring fellow, but he still is in charge, medically speaking. In education, however, things took a different turn. Frequently, teachers' aides were assigned to classrooms with no clearly assigned tasks; they were there to help the teacher. The latter was supposed to figure out what to do with the aides after they arrived. In this occupational structure, personality factors soon began to play a dominant role; aggressive aides or paraprofessionals, often the mothers of the pupils, began to dominate the teachers.

The foregoing are only some of the problems that frustrated differential staffing in the past. Current schemes to pay higher salaries based upon functional specialization do not address these problems. If anything, their rationale and implementation appear to be even more capricious than the earlier efforts.

Most current efforts are "master teacher" plans. Districts are allowed to designate a certain proportion of teachers as "master teachers." The state then puts up a certain amount of money each year for these "master teachers." In this way, districts are able to pay more to their outstanding teachers.

These plans, actual and proposed, vary considerably, but the following requirements appear frequently.

1. Master teachers will be released from teaching for part of the day to help new teachers, work on curriculum, and/or such other duties as may be negotiated or agreed upon. In other words, to avoid having state-mandated "merit pay," the legislation provided for some functional differentiation between master teachers and others. The most common fiction is that the master teacher will work with new teachers or teachers who have having difficulties.

2. The master teachers must teach a specified proportion of a full teaching load (usually 50 to 80 percent).
3. Master teachers cannot supervise or evaluate other teachers. The reason for this is that teachers who supervise or evaluate other teachers are usually excluded from teacher bargaining units by the state bargaining laws. Consequently, if master teachers supervised or evaluated other teachers, the unions would frequently lose them as dues-paying members. Of course, this reason is not articulated publicly.

In practice, master teacher plans are usually counterproductive. Clearly, the additional stipend is irrelevant to keeping talented teachers in the profession. The teachers receiving it are usually at the top of the salary schedule. They have no plans to stop teaching and retire or transfer to a nonteaching job. Frequently, their spouses have settled occupations in the area. As a matter of fact, many master teachers would often continue to teach in the district even if their salaries were reduced instead of increased.

Although enacted to keep good teachers in the classroom, the master teacher programs have precisely the opposite effect. To maintain the fiction of functional specialization, the master teachers are assigned to nonteaching tasks outside of the classroom. Neither the school district nor the teachers really care what these tasks are, since they are only a fig leaf to avoid the implication that the master teachers are receiving "merit pay." In practice, master teacher legislation typically encourages good teachers to get out of the classroom to perform duties that the districts are unwilling to pay for themselves.

MERIT PAY

As I have defined it, "merit pay" exists only if and when teacher A is paid more than teacher B *for performing the same kind of work*, that is, teaching the same grade or subject. Interestingly enough, merit pay has been widely discussed and debated in education for over 75 years. In the early 1900s, merit pay was common, perhaps even a typical characteristic of teacher salary schedules. Salary differentials for male and/or secondary teachers were also common at this time. In the 1930s, however, school districts began to eliminate the differentials for male and/or secondary teachers. Ironically, the differentials based upon merit went down the drain with the differentials based upon sex and grade level. There was a revival of interest in merit pay in the 1950s, but such plans stabilized in the 1960s and declined in the 1970s. It seems likely that the number of districts implementing merit pay has not increased since 1978, when only 115 of all 11,502 districts enrolling 300 or more pupils had merit pay, even as defined much more inclusively than it is here.[13]

The 1979 Educational Research Service (ERS) study cited above deliberately avoided using a specific definition of "merit pay." As a result, the number of districts with merit pay, as I have defined the term, was much smaller than the number reported in the ERS study. In any event, a 1983 study by ERS found only 54 districts (out of approximately 15,500 in the United States) that either had a merit plan in operation or had scheduled such a plan. Although the 1983 study was not conducted as comprehensively as the 1978 one, this fact probably did not affect the conclusion that merit pay was not being adopted very rapidly, if indeed it was increasing at all.[14] In this connection, although the 1978 ERS study found only 115 districts using merit pay, it found another 239 districts that had tried and abandoned merit pay.

Notwithstanding these data, merit pay has a great deal of public and political support. President Reagan endorsed the concept and stimulated national interest in it in a commencement address at Seton Hall University on May 21, 1983. Significantly, the public supports merit pay by a 2 to 1 margin and has done so since 1970—a cautionary note for those who believe that public support is the key to reform.[15]

Merit Pay and Teacher Evaluation

At the present time, merit pay is largely a state instead of a local initiative. Whatever its merits, local school boards are not jumping on the bandwagon. Why is this the case despite public opinion in favor of merit pay?

A brief look at teacher evaluation procedures will help to answer this question. Typically, the building principal has the responsibility for evaluating teachers. Common practice is for the principal to observe teachers in the classroom two or three times a year. If a teacher is on the borderline regarding reemployment, the principal may conduct more observations. Quite often, tenured teachers are formally observed only once every two years or not at all. In any event, the evaluation criteria and procedures are often spelled out in detail in the collective bargaining agreement.

Typically, the principal has a form of checksheet that is used in the process. Figure 3.1 illustrates this. The principal fills out the form on the basis of the observations, then meets with the teacher to discuss the report. The teacher is usually required to sign the report, not to show agreement but to show awareness of it. This is intended to preclude the teacher from challenging dismissal on the grounds that the teacher was not informed of his or her deficiencies and accorded a reasonable opportunity to correct them.

As we would expect, the forms vary from district to district. Often a district can change the form only through collective bargaining. For present purposes, however, the important point is that the quality-of-performance categories have little or no practical significance. The teacher rated "outstanding" is not paid more than the teacher rated "superior," "good," "average," "satisfactory," or even "below average."

As a result, teachers and administrators are not deeply concerned about the distinctions involved. For instance, a teacher would not challenge a rating of "very good" on the grounds that it should be "superior"; at least, in 35 years in education, I have never encountered one such case. In the vast majority of cases, the only rating that matters is whether the teacher is recommended for retention. Teachers concerned about tenure sometimes challenge marginal or weak recommendations, but challenges to a clearly favorable rating, on the grounds that it should have been even more favorable, are rare.

With merit pay, however, distinctions such as those between "outstanding" and "superior" could have important practical consequences. They could now become the basis for paying some teachers more than others. What was formerly merely an academic mark on a piece of paper now becomes, or has the potential of becoming, a highly controversial, even a litigated issue.

Understandably, many administrators do not really want to face this problem. For every teacher recommended for merit pay, several others may be disgruntled over not being chosen. Some are likely to take out their resentment on the principals, or on whatever administrator is perceived as responsible for the injustice. The typical principal is apt to feel this additional headache is not needed.

There is also another problem: Which students are going to be assigned to the merit teacher? The answers to this question could lead to a great deal of friction between parents and teachers, and among the teachers themselves. Parents will naturally want their children to be assigned to the merit teachers. Again, the principal or the school

Figure 3.1 Teacher Evaluation Form

FORMAL OBSERVATION/EVALUATION REPORT

Teacher _____ Activity Observed _____

Center _____

Date/Observation _____ Length/Observation _____
(Minimum 30 minutes)

RATING   COMMENTS

1. *Instruction*

    ____ Outstanding
    ____ Good
    ____ Average
    ____ Below average
    ____ Unsatisfactory

2. *Classroom Environment*

    ____ Outstanding
    ____ Good
    ____ Average
    ____ Below average
    ____ Unsatisfactory

3. *Management/Logistics*

    ____ Outstanding
    ____ Good
    ____ Average
    ____ Below average
    ____ Unsatisfactory

4. *Personal and Professional Qualities*

    ____ Outstanding
    ____ Good
    ____ Average
    ____ Below average
    ____ Unsatisfactory

Attach any informal observation statement forms related to this formal observation/evaluation report. ____ Number of informal observation forms attached.

Comments:

Observer _____ Position _____

Formal Observation/Evaluation # _____

Does a teacher's reply accompany this form?*   YES ____   NO ____

If a decision is to be made at this time would you recommend this person for: (check appropriate block):

	Without Reservation	With Reservation**	Would not Recommend**
Re-employment	_____	_____	_____

* Must be submitted within ten (10) school days of the date of his/her signature indicated above.
** With written statement to justify decision.

Teacher's Signature _____   _____
                                                                                     Date

The teacher's signature indicates that he/she has seen the Evaluation and does not necessarily indicate that he/she agrees in every instance with the Evaluation. He/She may submit a letter to accompany this Evaluation with a copy to the Principal. Teacher must sign and return the evaluation form within five (5) days.

Principal's Signature _____   _____
                                                                                     Date

To be made out in triplicate: One copy for Personnel File in the
                                                   Superintendent's Office,
                                          One copy for the Principal, and
                                          One copy to be retained by the Teacher.

Color Coding:

White   — 1st Evaluation
Blue   — 2nd Evaluation
Yellow — 3rd Evaluation
Green   — 4th or any preceding Evaluation

district is likely to generate more dissatisfaction than goodwill by its actions. Indeed, this is inevitable inasmuch as the students of nonmerit teachers will outnumber those in classes taught by merit teachers.

In addition, the negative consequences of merit rating to the administration are apt to be immediate and personal, whereas its beneficial consequences are remote in time and may be impossible to identify. How much money should be paid to how many teachers? How do you "prove" the time and effort to identify merit teachers was worthwhile? If and when merit rating is adopted, there are bound to be some mistakes or questionable decisions. Such mistakes will increase the vulnerability of the school board, especially if it cannot exercise strong control over its middle management. It must implement merit pay with its existing staff, and its existing staff may be unprepared to implement merit pay effectively.

School administrators do not usually articulate these objections to merit pay. Inasmuch as the concept is popular, they prefer to attribute the absence of merit pay to the opposition of teacher unions. Frequently, school administrators who lament the absence of merit pay have never really tried to implement it.

As a practical matter, the advent of unionization has eliminated merit pay as a viable option in most school districts. In the 1978 ERS study, 18 percent of the 239 districts that abandoned merit pay gave collective bargaining as one of the reasons. Nevertheless, I am not asserting that we would have merit pay in the absence of unionization. The fact is that merit pay does not exist on a significant scale even in states that have not legalized collective bargaining by teachers. My point is this: In addition to all the other obstacles to merit pay, teacher unions constitute still another that would be more than sufficient to block it in most districts. Let us see why this is so.

In the bargaining states, merit pay cannot be implemented without first bargaining on it with the teacher union. From a union point of view, merit pay is extremely dangerous. The reason, however, is not because merit pay would be too subjective and would lead to favoritism. Needless to say, merit pay would not always be implemented properly. However, the policy option is not between a perfect system (no merit pay) and an imperfect system (merit pay). It is between alternative compensation policies, each of which has advantages and disadvantages. Each can be implemented in ways that render the alternative approach much more attractive as a public policy option.

The union opposition to merit pay, however, does not rest upon a calculus of its advantages and disadvantages to teachers. Instead, it is based upon its advantages and disadvantages to unions. Here, the disadvantages clearly outweigh the advantages. Merit pay is a threat, or is at least perceived as a threat, to the unions themselves. The stability of unions depends upon their ability to eliminate or to minimize conflict among members of the bargaining unit. The ideal union contract has just enough in it to satisfy everyone. It avoids giving any subgroup benefits deemed disproportionate to what others are getting. On the other hand, merit pay, to be meaningful—or at least consistent with its avowed rationale—must provide substantial rewards to a minority of teachers. Most teachers who do not receive it will tend to feel or to claim that the district is overpaying the "merit" teachers. Yet if the amount is not substantial, the rationale for merit pay loses force and it is not worth the time and trouble of implementation.

Let us assume a union agrees to merit pay. How would the union respond to a grievance alleging that the grievant was erroneously passed over for merit pay? The claim will be that the grievant is more deserving than another teacher who is to receive merit pay. Such a claim places the union in a no-win situation. For the union to support the grievance would mean assisting a union member, but only at the expense of another union member. To refuse to support the grievance will antagonize the grievant. Either way, the union may be confronted by charges that it has violated its duty to represent all union members fairly. These problems would exist even if the union itself completely controlled the designation of merit teachers. Indeed, such control would exacerbate some of the union problems associated with merit pay.

Understandably, unions want no such dilemmas. They cannot give management a free hand in designating the teachers to receive merit pay. And yet, the deeper the union gets involved in the process, the greater the danger that it will antagonize a portion of its constituency. The only way to avoid such dilemmas is to oppose merit pay.

Of course, outright opposition to merit pay may not be politically expedient. After noting its objections to merit pay, an AFT position paper states:

> Despite these problems, there is one very good reason to remain open-minded to plans like these. There is a popular logic to the idea that better performance deserves higher pay. Numerous polls show that the public is willing to tax itself more if ideas like these are part of what the money will be spent for. This means that shaping these plans into something teachers can support holds out the promise of pay increases that really may solve the problem. And while it is the pay increases—not the

merit differentiations—that will offer real help, the discussion must begin with where public sentiment lies.

II. *AFT Positions*

The most important thing about the AFT's position on these ideas is that *we think they are not the answer to the problem*. Our willingness to talk about them, modify them, maybe even support them in the end, is because *other people think they are*. Confronted with a set of circumstances which include tuition tax credits, no adequate initiatives in federal funding, and a continuing lag in state funding sufficient to create adequate teacher pay standards, popular ideas on how to spend additional dollars on teacher pay must be taken seriously, no matter how flawed. This is where NEA stubbornness resulted in a grave mistake, the defeat of a Tennessee $210 million Better Schools Program which included $110 million for teacher salaries.[16]

As noted in the AFT position paper, the Tennessee Education Association, the state affiliate of the NEA, killed a general pay raise for all teachers in the 1983 session of the Tennessee legislature because the pay hike was tied to a merit pay plan. Subsequently, the 1983 NEA Convention passed the following resolution: "The NEA commends the Tennessee Education Association (TEA) for its strong, courageous stand for teachers and against Governor Lamar Alexander's self-serving, ill-conceived merit pay (master teacher) plan. The NEA urges TEA to continue to advocate for Tennessee teachers."

At the same convention, the NEA passed resolutions denouncing the Reagan administration's support for merit pay as "politically motivated" and stated that "NEA is categorically opposed to any plan, whether designated a merit pay plan or a master teacher plan, or by some other name that bases the compensation of teachers on favoritism, subjective evaluation in the absence of clearly defined performance criteria, student achievement, or other arbitrary standards."[17] It remains to be seen whether any merit pay plans can meet the criteria in Resolution 1983-D.

Teacher Evaluation and "Peer Judgment"

Both NEA and AFT assert that conventional merit pay plans lead to favoritism, bootlicking, awards to administrative lackeys, and other evils too numerous to mention. Consequently, both unions have demanded that "peer judgment" and union participation, both at the local level, be an integral part of any merit pay plan. Presumably, such participation would minimize the likelihood that merit teachers would be chosen on the basis of nonprofessional criteria.

Whatever the evils of merit pay, however, it is unlikely that they would be remedied by involving local teachers or the local union in the process of identifying teachers to receive merit pay. A 1984 incident in the San Ramon Valley Unified School District (California) illustrates the reason. Most of the district's approximately 500 teachers went on strike in 1984; about 115 teachers continued teaching during the strike. Subsequently, a committee elected by teachers was established to recommend teachers to serve as "mentor teachers"; such teachers receive an additional $4,000 annually from state funds. The teacher-elected committee recommended 15 teachers to receive the $4,000 stipend. Not one of the teachers who had continued to teach during the strike was so designated, even though one of them had just been designated "Teacher of the Year" and "Schoolmaster of the Year" by community organizations. The omission of non-strikers was clearly deliberate.[18]

In other words, "peer judgment" and local union participation do not eliminate bias in merit pay. At best, they simply replace one bias with a different bias. In any event, there is no prima facie reason to assume that local union participation in merit pay will not favor teachers who support union positions, and disfavor teachers who are opposed to these positions. Similarly, if teachers can avoid their biases in evaluating fellow teachers for merit pay, school administrators should be able to do so also.

Paradoxically, teacher opposition to merit pay is largely due to union campaigns to discredit it. Polls of teacher opinion show considerable teacher support for merit pay.[19] Granted, there are difficult problems associated with merit pay, and its potential benefits may be exaggerated by its supporters (including the author). At the same time, its undesirable consequences are also exaggerated by its opponents. For that matter, the critics of merit pay frequently misrepresent the factual situation. For example, they often assert that teachers have no confidence in the evaluation procedures, hence salary determinations based upon them are harmful to teacher morale. Aside from the fact that the lack of confidence, if it exists, may be due to unjustified criticisms of the procedures, the reality is that some teachers do not want fair and objective evaluation procedures. They want procedures that do not jeopardize their jobs or, preferably, no evaluation procedures at all. One would never suspect that such teachers exist, to read the objections to merit pay.

My own view is this: Whatever may be the dangers of subjectivity and favoritism, they are exacerbated, not reduced, by union participation in the process. Not because teacher union leaders are evil, or because they are more subject to favoritism and bias than school administrators. My reasons are not based upon personality factors but upon role and responsibility factors. School administrators can be assigned the responsibility of identifying and rewarding outstanding teachers. They can be held accountable for how well they carry out this task. There is, however, no feasible way for a school board to hold a union leader accountable for the latter's role in a merit pay plan. In doing what has to be done to protect the union, union leadership may find it necessary to kill an excellent plan for merit pay. Indeed, the better the plan, the more dangerous it is to the union. Unions thrive on deficiencies, not on perfection, in personnel administration.

Educational Specialty Boards

In my opinion, the strongest argument for merit pay is that teachers have no stake in improving their knowledge and skills under single salary schedules. Their salaries are the same, regardless. This point is not affected by the fact that teachers are paid more for additional training under single salary schedules. The teacher's interest is in getting paid more, not in improving performance. Graduate courses that are conveniently scheduled, inexpensive, and not intellectually demanding are taken over courses that would contribute to improved performance.

The unpleasant but inescapable reality is that school districts spend billions of dollars every year for worthless graduate courses. Additionally, hundreds of millions are spent annually for the professors who teach these courses. It is not possible to remedy the situation without facing up to the interests that profit from it. These interests include the large number of teachers, who feel threatened by a change; the administrators (perhaps a majority) and the unions, which oppose a change for reasons they do not always lay on the table; and the institutions of higher education, which offer worthless courses to teachers for salary credit. Anyone who believes that such courses are solely or even primarily in teaching methods is dealing with fantasies, not facts. The situation would not be materially changed if teachers never enrolled in a methods course for salary credit; education departments do not have a monopoly on worthless courses, to say the least.

Notwithstanding the valid reasons for merit pay, it seems apparent that merit pay plans, in which the merit teachers are identified by procedures at the local level, will not be widely adopted. If, however, the designations of merit teachers are to be made locally, there should be clear-cut managerial responsibility for them. The more safeguards that are attached to merit pay, such as advisory committees and appeal procedures, and the more sharing of responsibility for decisions on who received merit pay, the more likely it is that the plan will become top-heavy procedurally. One cannot reconcile merit pay with a popularity contest, or with the lowest-common-denominator approach to decisionmaking.

What about the objection that merit pay is too subjective and leads to favoritism? There is at least one feasible way to avoid this criticism: by not having the designation of merit teachers made at the local level. In medicine, accounting, psychology, and other fields, professionals can become "board certified" without the involvement of the employer. For example, an accountant becomes a CPA by passing an examination prepared and supervised by a national professional association. A physician who seeks to become a "board certified" surgeon must pass rigorous tests of skill and knowledge conducted by the national organization of surgeons. In other words, the widespread assumption that the designation of merit teachers must be made locally is gratuitous; the way some other professions recognize and reward superior levels of performance adequately resolves the conventional objections to merit pay.[20]

The designation "Educational Specialty Boards" has been given to a proposed plan for national nongovernmental boards that would certify teachers as possessing a superior level of competence. Were such a system to be adopted in education, the local district would decide only whether to employ board certified teachers and how much to pay them over the regular schedule. Such a plan would obviate the underlying union objections to merit pay. Inasmuch as the designation of "board certified"—that is, who is meritorious—is not made locally, there would be no occasion for divisiveness at the local level over the designation. Furthermore, the concern that merit pay would be based upon administrative favoritism would be irrelevant; since local administrators would not designate the teachers who are board certified, favoritism by administrators could not become a factor. The teacher unions would still have to bargain on the salary differentials to be paid to board certified teachers, but this should not be a major problem. The unions currently bargain on several kinds of differentials, such as those for advanced degrees or directing extracurricular activities. Bargaining on differentials for board certified teachers should become as routinized as bargaining for other differentials.

Note also that Educational Specialty Boards would have several other advantages over conventional merit pay. For example, a teacher's designation as "board certified" would be portable, as it is in other professions. This would give outstanding teachers more mobility, since they would not lose their designation as board certified if and when they move. Such a plan would also be extremely helpful to school districts trying to recruit outstanding teachers to strengthen a school or department. Instead of relying upon evaluations from other districts, they could employ teachers who are board certified, just as hospitals employ board certified physicians. The examinations could feasibly include actual demonstrations of teaching skills, perhaps videotaped for analysis. Directly or indirectly, the boards could be used to facilitate a career ladder approach to teacher compensation.[21]

In a shift away from a 1983 AFT policy statement on merit pay, AFT President Albert Shanker became the first national educational leader to endorse the concept in July 1985.[22] Initially, NEA President Mary Futrell expressed opposition to it; subsequently, however, NEA Executive Director Donald Cameron unequivocally expressed the NEA's interest in exploring a national board approach to the problem. Both Shanker and Cameron asserted that Educational Specialty Boards would not constitute "merit pay," a disclaimer that illustrates the extent to which union leaders are hostage to union rhetoric.[23]

Paradoxically, AASA Executive Director Richard Miller expressed opposition to Educational Specialty Boards, albeit for unspecified reasons.[24] Miller's reactions illustrate the posturing on merit pay by management leaders who insist they have always supported merit pay in principle. Faced for the first time with NEA/AFT willingness to consider an approach to merit pay (by whatever label), AASA leadership expressed neither a desire nor willingness to work with the unions and other organizations to resolve the real problems posed by the board concept. With supporters like these, there is hardly any need for union opposition to merit pay.

In any event, merit pay plans in which the designations of merit teachers are made locally are not being and will not be widely adopted. As few as they are, the purported merit plans in existence are largely exercises in cosmetics and semantics; none unequivocally rewards merit on a substantial scale.[25] Currently, the Reagan administration is spending millions to promote merit plans that emphasize "peer review" at the local level and district affiliation with an institution of higher education that utilizes merit pay. Encouraging merit pay this way is like trying to stimulate a corpse with a lethal dose of cyanide.

Teacher Salaries and Entrepreneurial Schools

Clearly, entrepreneurial schools could avoid the crippling effects of existing teacher salary schedules. Indeed, to some extent, their existence might depend upon their ability to recruit teachers whose superiority is evident to parents. Obviously, such teachers could command a salary premium that is not within the realm of possibility in public education.

From a salary point of view, entrepreneurial schools would have enormous advantages over public schools.

1. They would not be locked into a system that is so embedded in law, practice, and ideology that the transition to something different would itself be a major problem.
2. They would be unlikely to face union opposition to new types of salary schedules, for the simple reason that they are unlikely to be unionized or as heavily unionized as public education.
3. The success of entrepreneurial schools will depend heavily upon their ability to satisfy parents. Therefore, the schools will have enormous incentives to recruit teachers who impress parents favorably by their competence and responsiveness. Such teachers will be able to charge a premium for their ability to attract students.
4. Changes in salaries will not require a change in public policy, that is, a decision by a school board that faces all the procedural and political obstacles currently associated with such changes. Instead, salary changes can be made individually and/or collectively as managerial decisions, which are sensitive to market conditions and individual teacher performance.
5. The teacher stake in competence and responsiveness will be direct and critical. Entrepreneurial schools will be under pressure to pay for competence, not for credits or seniority or degrees.
6. Teachers will have common, highly visible incentives not only to improve themselves but to help their colleagues improve and to welcome outstanding new teachers. Teachers are not as likely to resist merit pay if they know that the merit teachers are attracting students who provide a stronger financial base of support for all teachers.

Additional reasons could be cited, but they would be belaboring the obvious. Whatever else may be the advantages and disadvantages of entrepreneurial schools, their greater flexibility in teacher salaries and their urgent need to pay for competence and responsiveness is hardly debatable.

NOTES

1. The most informative materials on this subject are a series of publications by Educational Research Service, a nonprofit organization sponsored by several national educational organizations. See *ERS Publications in Print* (Arlington, Va.: Educational Research Service, 1984).

2. Research Division, NEA, *Estimates of School Statistics 1983-84* (Washington, D.C.: National Education Association, p. 17).

3. National Commission on Excellence in Education, *A Nation At Risk: The Imperative for Educational Reform* (Washington, D.C.: U.S. Government Printing Office, 1983), pp. 22-23.

4. Sheppard Ranbom, "State Efforts to Control Pension Costs Spark Controversy," *Education Week*, March 7, 1984, pp. 1, 19.

5. NEA, *The Teaching Profession* (Washington, D.C.: National Education Association, December 1983), p. 2.

6. *At Nation At Risk*, pp. 22-23.

7. Ibid., pp. 30.

8. Ernest L. Boyer, *High School: A Report on Secondary Education in America* (New York: Harper & Row, 1983), p. 308.

9. *The Cost of Reform: Fiscal Implications of A Nation At Risk* (Arlington, Va.: American Association of School Administrators, 1983).

10. Boyer, p. 308; "Where We Stand," Advertisement paid by United Federation of Teachers, New York *Times*, September 18, 1983, p. D7.

11. AFT, *Incentive Schemes and Pay Compensation Plans* (Washington, D.C.: American Federation of Teachers, n.d.), p. 1.

12. Commission on Precollege Education in Mathematics, Science and Technology, appointed by the National Science Board, *Educating Americans for the 21st Century* (Washington, D.C.: National Science Foundation, September 12, 1983).

13. *Merit Pay For Teachers* (Arlington, Va.: Educational Research Service, 1979).

14. *Merit Pay Plans for Teachers: Status and Descriptions* (Arlington, Va.: Educational Research Service, 1983); and Glenn E. Robinson, *Incentive Pay For Teachers: An Analysis of Approaches* (Arlington, Va.: Educational Research Service, 1984).

15. See Stanley M. Elam, ed., *A Decade of Gallup Polls of Attitudes Toward Education, 1969-1978* (Bloomington, Ind.: Phi Delta Kappa, 1978).

16. AFT, *Incentive Schemes and Pay Compensation Plans*, pp. 2-3.

17. Resolutions 1983-D, 1983-37, NEA Convention, 1983.

18. Information provided by Susan Staub, Concerned Educators Against Forced Unionism; San Ramon Valley Unified School District; Jacqueline Foster-Smith, teacher in the San Ramon Valley Unified School District; and various newspapers in the San Ramon area.

19. *The American Teacher Survey* (New York: Metropolitan Life Insurance Co., June 1984), pp. 43-47.

20. This asumption is evident in American Association of School Administrators, *Some Points to Consider When You Discuss Merit Pay* (Arlington, Va.: American Association of School Administrators, 1983). It also is a glaring weakness of U.S. Department of Education programs to encourage merit pay, and in an otherwise excellent analysis: Henry C. Johnson, ed., *Merit, Money and Teachers' Careers* (Lanham, Md.: University Press of America, 1985).

21. See Myron Lieberman, "Educational Specialty Boards: The Solution to the Merit Pay Morass?" *Phi Delta Kappan*, October 1985; and commentary by educational leaders in the same issue, pp. 103-112. Such boards were first proposed in Myron Lieberman, *The Future of Public Education* (Chicago: University of Chicago Press, 1960), pp. 259-70; and in "National Specialty Boards as a Basis for Merit Pay," *Phi Delta Kappan*, December 1959, pp. 118-22.

22. New York *Times*, July 12, 1985, pp. 1, 11.

23. New York *Times*, July 23, 1985, p. 19; Don Cameron, "An Idea That Merits Consideration," *Phi Delta Kappan*, October 1985, pp. 110-12.

24. Richard D. Miller, "A Counterproposal," *Phi Delta Kappan*, October 1985, p. 112.

25. David K. Cohen and Richard J. Murnane, "The Merits of Merit Pay," *Public Interest*, Summer 1985, pp. 3-30.

4

THE "DUE PROCESS" FIASCO

This chapter is devoted to the way school districts deal with incompetent teachers, or teachers who are no longer required because of budget cutbacks or program changes. The main issue is the extent to which teacher tenure protects competent teachers from being fired unfairly while preserving management rights to fire teachers for good cause.

In the early decades of public education, teachers were subjected to racial, religious, and sexual discrimination, intrusions of privacy, patronage and political obligations, and a host of other arbitrary and capricious regulations and reasons for dismissal. Teachers, like public employees generally, sought protection against these abuses. Such protection usually took the form of state legislation providing that dismissals after a probationary period (usually three years) be permitted only for specified reasons and only if the teachers involved received a fair opportunity to rebut the charges of incompetence or misconduct.

Understandably, as teachers and teacher unions view the matter, teacher tenure exists only to ensure that school districts do not abuse their right to fire teachers. In their view, the tenure laws merely protect teachers from being fired for invalid reasons. Because of the tenure laws, teachers receive "due process" in attempted dismissals; because they receive due process, the invalid reasons cannot withstand scrutiny.

The unions also vehemently deny that they wish to protect incompetent teachers. As the unions view the issue, citizens are entitled to due process in challenging small fines for parking violations; surely, teachers are entitled to it in challenging actions that would destroy their careers. If incompetent teachers are employed, the fault lies with incompetent management for hiring them or for not documenting their incompetence adequately. The fault does not lie with teacher unions for protecting teacher rights to due process.

Regardless of the rationale, there is widespread concern about teacher tenure in both lay and professional ranks. The annual Gallup Poll on public attitudes toward public education reveals persistent concern with the quality of teachers. In one such poll, 45 percent of the parents agreed that some teachers in their district should be fired. Incompetence was the reason most frequently given, by a wide margin.[1]

School administrators have also consistently expressed concern over teacher incompetence. According to a nationwide survey in 1972, more than 85 percent of school superintendents supported abolition of or change in the tenure laws. In a 1977 survey of 1,728 districts, 42 percent indicated that staff dismissals were a serious problem; a majority of the respondents cited incompetence as the primary reason for their concern. Significantly, the administrators responding estimated that 5 to 15 percent of their staff were not performing adequately.[2]

ISSUES IN TEACHER TENURE

Like most educational controversies, teacher tenure is not just a single issue; it is a complex set of interrelated issues. The following are surely among the most important:

- What are the criteria of teacher incompetence and under what circumstances should a school board have the right to fire, or refuse to rehire, teachers?
- Should the standards be different for teachers who have been employed a minimum period of time (1-3 years?) than for newly hired teachers?
- What out-of-school or away-from-school conduct, if any, justifies dismissal?
- What should be the criteria if no misconduct or incompetence is involved—for example, if a school board wishes to discontinue a certain program, to what extent should it be required to justify the discontinuance? To continue to employ teachers regardless of the discontinuance?
- Who should bear the costs of litigating a dismissal?

- How much notice of dismissal is a teacher entitled to?
- Who carries the burden of proof in dismissal cases?
- To what extent, if any, should school districts be able to replace teachers who may be "competent" with better teachers?

One could add interminably to the list, but one fact seems clear enough. With respect to each issue, it is possible to adopt a position that either maximizes the protection and job security of individual teachers, or maximizes the ability of a school board to staff its schools as the board sees fit, and therefore increases the accountability of the board to the community. Thus, in a general way, teacher tenure involves an accommodation between the job interests of teachers and the rights of school boards to manage school affairs in the public interest, at least as they perceive it.

Somewhat surprisingly, there is a dearth of evidence on many important tenure issues, such as what constitutes incompetence. Only two tenure statutes (Alaska and Tennessee) include a definition of it. Teacher incompetence seems to be one of those things that can't be defined but can be recognized when you see it.

Regardless of the dearth of statutory definitions of incompetence, any enterprise that cannot effectively terminate incompetent employees, or employees not needed and not useful to the enterprise, is in danger. The danger is not so apparent in public employment because the costs of incompetent or unnecessary employees are shared by the entire public. For this reason, they are less visible and less of a threat to the existence of the enterprise. Inefficiency in the private company jeopardizes the company's existence; inefficiency in the schools is more likely to result in waste of tax dollars rather than the elimination of public schools. By the same token, the fact that inefficiency is not so threatening to a public agency as it is to a private company renders its existence more likely in the public sector.

Ideally, teacher tenure protects the public interest by protecting competent teachers. To the extent that it actually protects incompetent teachers, the waste of public funds is only part of the harm done. Pupils learn less, are more disruptive, vandalize more school property, and so on; consequences such as these, not simply some tax dollars lost, should constitute our main concern in this area.

From one standpoint of individual teachers, tenure provides job security as long as a teacher performs adequately. Job security provides assurance that a teacher can plan his or her personal life and professional career, free from the fear of an arbitrary or capricious or discriminatory termination of the teacher's employment. This is obviously an extremely important benefit to teachers.

Tenure is likewise a critical issue for teacher unions, as it is for unions generally. Job security is a paramount employee concern; the union that cannot protect job security for its members is apt to find itself in deep trouble. In short, teacher tenure is a subject that affects the fundamental interests of all the parties in tenure disputes.

SOURCES OF TEACHER TENURE

Legally speaking, there are three major sources of protection against dismissal for teachers: protections arising out of the Constitution of the United States; protections arising out of the state teacher tenure laws; and protections arising out of collective bargaining agreements between teacher unions and school boards. On their face, these protections do not protect incompetent teachers, or teachers who have engaged in a grave misconduct, or require school districts to employ teachers who are no longer needed. The rhetoric notwithstanding, however, tenure protections frequently lead to these results. To see how and why this happens, we must examine these protections in more detail.

The Constitutional Rights of Public School Teachers

We begin with the constitutional "due process" rights of teachers. The concept of "due process" is an extremely important one throughout our social institutions. According to the Fourteenth Amendment, no person can be deprived of life or liberty or property without "due process of law." Students cannot be expelled from school without due process. Government cannot exercise the right of eminent domain in the absence of due process for the property owner. And so on.

The landmark case on the due process rights of public employees is *Perry* v. *Sindermann* (1972) 408 U.S. 593. Sindermann had been an instructor at Odessa Junior College in Texas for ten years. Faculty did not receive tenure no matter how long they had been employed. In 1968 Sindermann was fired without any statement of reasons. Therefore, he had no opportunity to rebut the reasons. Sindermann sued, alleging that his constitutional rights had been violated. His argument was that as a result of his ten years of service, he had acquired an "expectancy" of reemployment. This "expectancy of reemployment" was asserted to be a property interest that had been taken from him without due process of law. The U.S. Supreme Court upheld this argument.

From a constitutional point of view, what should the college have done to fire Sindermann properly, that is, so that he had no legal recourse? In Sindermann's case, it appears that the college should have provided the following elements of due process:

- Reasonable prior notice of any proposed action that would deprive an employee of a property interest.
- A written statement of the proposed action and reasons for it.
- Right to be represented by counsel at a hearing on the merits.
- Right to examine and cross-examine witnesses.
- A written record of the proceedings.
- A written decision on the merits.
- Some type of court review.

In practice, the constitutional requirements of due process vary somewhat according to the circumstances. For example, a public employer would find it easier to meet the requirements of due process for a probationary employee than for an employee who had "an expectancy of reemployment." In any event, the upshot of the Sindermann case is that public employers who wish to fire employees are held to standards that do not apply to private-sector employers. In the private sector, an employer can fire an employee "at will"—any time, anywhere, and for virtually any reason not prohibited by law. The employer cannot fire someone on account of race or religion or age or sex (unless these things are bona fide requirements of the job). Nor can the employer fire someone contrary to an individual or a collective bargaining agreement. Otherwise, however, there is no constitutional or statutory limitation on the employer's right to fire. There is some sentiment in academic circles to weaken the "at will" doctrine in the private sector, and some recent federal court decisions appear to be moving in this direction. Generally speaking, however, a private-sector employer can fire veteran employees at will. The private-sector employee may have an "expectancy" of reemployment but such expectancy is not protected by constitutional due process in termination.

Thus even in the absence of a tenure law or a collective bargaining contract, public school teachers have a constitutional right not to be fired arbitrarily or capriciously. In effect, the Supreme Court decisions require public employers to observe procedural standards in dismissals that do not apply to private-sector employers. Desirable or not, this fact does limit a school board's right to fire incompetent teachers. Indeed, many public school teachers, even in the absence of a collective bargaining agreement or a tenure law, have more protection than some private-sector employees with bargaining rights or even with union contracts.[3]

Consider the following situation. A school district employs a principal who does not evaluate teachers effectively. Being afraid of confrontations with teachers, and eager to be "a good guy," the principal fails to document the case for firing certain teachers. Eventually, the principal is replaced by someone who promptly recommends that the incompetent teachers be fired.

Immediately, the teachers involved point to their previous evaluations to show the recommendation is not justified. For years, their evaluations were satisfactory; suddenly, they are not, even though the teachers have not changed. Enough doubt is raised so that the court or hearing officer concludes that termination is too harsh under the circumstances. Teachers with many years of satisfactory service must be provided more advance notice and opportunities to correct their deficiencies, that is, they must be accorded "due process."

What is the point of the example? Only to illustrate how due process can limit a district's right to fire incompetent teachers. Just as due process will enable some criminals to escape conviction, so due process will enable some incompetent teachers to avoid dismissal. Nevertheless, I am not contending that we should do away with due process. Instead, my objective is to explain how the concept is actually used or applied in dismissals. "Due process" as an abstract ideal is one thing. As a concrete reality, it may or may not be consistent with the ideal. As with so many issues discussed in this book, we must be willing to compare the rhetoric with the reality.

Due Process and State Tenure Laws

Although significant, the constitutional protections against wrongful dismissal are not the major obstacle to firing incompetent teachers. The major obstacles are the state tenure laws and collective bargaining agreements. First let us consider the tenure laws, which are summarized in Table 4.1. At one extreme, a few states have no statewide tenure law. In these states, job security for teachers depends upon their constitutional protections and negotiated agreements (if any) that provide job protection. In at least one state (Texas), tenure may be provided by local action. At the other extreme, there are states

Table 4.1 Summary of Teacher Tenure Laws

Number of States	Specifications
Duration of Probationary Period	
	Years before Tenure Granted or Eligible
1	Less than 1
2	1
11	2
34	3
1	4
2	5
Cause for Dismissal or Nonrenewal	
41	Cause(s) defined statutorily
9	Cause(s) not defined statutorily
Notice Requirements	
All states require employee to be notified of the cause(s) for dismissal or nonrenewal	
Hearing Requirements	
13	Hearing required automatically
18	Hearing open or closed, employee option
10	Hearing officer or panel required
5	Hearing officer or panel, employee option
2	Hearing officer or panel, board option
Appeal Procedure	
30	Appeal to courts allowed
18	Appeal to state official or agency
23	Appeal confined to hearing record
20	Appeal de novo allowed

Source: Statutory Requirements of Teacher Contract Laws (Olympia: Washington State Senate, December 1976).

with extremely strong tenure laws. "Strong" means that the tenure statute sets forth a heavy procedural and substantive burden on districts seeking to fire teachers. Between these extremes, tenure laws differ widely on virtually every criterion. Some tenure laws are essentially "continuing contract" laws; the teacher must be notified by a certain date if the district does not wish to employ the teacher. If not notified of termination by the specified date, the teacher is automatically reemployed for the following year. This is perhaps the weakest form of tenure and can hardly be regarded as a serious problem from a management point of view.

Although some states lack statutory tenure protections, the states that have the strongest tenure laws tend to be the more heavily populated ones, such as California, Ohio, New York, Illinois, Michigan, and Pennsylvania. Thus the proportion of teachers covered by strong job security is higher than one might suspect merely from the number of states with strong tenure laws.

Additionally, some of the tenure laws apply to reductions in force due to fiscal emergencies or program cutbacks. In these situations, a school district may have valid reasons for terminating competent teachers in the fields being eliminated or reduced. Nevertheless, in order to do so, it may have to meet complex statutory requirements designed to provide job security for teachers. The fact that the tenure statutes often provide job security strictly on the basis of certification presents additional problems. In practice, a teacher certified to teach English may never have taught the subject. Yet according to most tenure statutes, such a teacher would have to be retained to teach English ahead of a teacher who has been teaching it full time, but who has less seniority in the school district. One can debate the merits of such legislation, but it clearly accords a higher priority to job security for teachers than to good education for pupils.

Even more serious problems arise out of the fact that tenure laws were enacted to meet situations different from those in which the laws are applied. The tenure laws were drafted on the asumption that individual teachers would be challenging dismissal. Consequently and understandably, the laws provided elaborate due process rights for the teachers involved. Subsequently, however, these rights became applicable in strike situations, where they are clearly inappropriate.

Under labor law generally, employers are allowed to replace striking employees, permanently if necessary. Under the tenure laws, however, school boards can be required to conduct a hearing for each striking teacher whom it seeks to terminate. The legal problems are usually insurmountable. The larger the school district, the safer the strike; a school board is not going to conduct 20,000 hearings or 2,000 or 200. It is extremely unlikely even to conduct a much smaller number, even if it were of a mind to discipline the leaders responsible for an illegal strike. Thus the upshot of the tenure laws in some states is to enable teachers to strike with little or no risk, even though teacher strikes are theoretically illegal. This fact greatly increases the power of teacher unions to force school boards to make concessions sought by the union. Again, the rhetoric of due process is one thing; actual practice is often quite another.

Due Process in Collective Bargaining

In general, the same arguments used to support teacher tenure laws are used to support job security in teacher bargaining. Nevertheless, the bargaining process differs from the legislative process in several critical ways. Once achieved, legislation is more difficult to amend than a negotiated agreement. Another factor is that bargaining power varies widely among school districts. If unions are strong where school boards are weak, the union may achieve a high degree of job security. Where unions are weak and school boards are strong, the unions may achieve little or no job security. Leadership changes more rapidly and more erratically in bargaining than in the legislative process, adding to the greater unpredictability of the former. Overall, job security in negotiated agreements varies even more than it does in tenure laws.

In collective bargaining, union strategy in negotiating job security is dominated by the appeal to due process. The unions try to negotiate the maximum procedural advantages for teachers. These procedural advantages are then used to block adverse evaluations, or adverse action based upon adverse evaluations. Regardless of whether dismissal proceedings are pursuant to the tenure law or the negotiated agreement, the teacher tries to show that management has failed to observe due process—hence it must not be allowed to take any adverse action against the teacher. Perhaps the classroom observations of teachers were only 48 minutes instead of the contractually required 50. The principal might fail to complete all the items on the evaluation form. The notice of dismissal might be a day too late or the school board meeting that approved the dismissal might have been technically deficient. Such deficiencies are almost always construed strictly against the school board—all in the name of due process, of course.

Figure 4.1, which is an actual union proposal concerning evaluation, illustrates this point. As a matter of fact, the proposal in Figure 4.1 was initially prepared by state unions and disseminated to hundreds of their local affiliates to be used in bargaining. Therefore, we are not discussing an off-the-wall proposal by local unions out of the mainstream; on the contrary, Figure 4.1 reflects mainstream union thinking and bargaining on the subject.

The union proposal in Figure 4.1 would, if accepted, destroy teacher evaluation. An analysis of just a few of its implications will illustrate

Figure 4.1 Union Proposal on Teacher Evaluation

1. It is understood and agreed by the parties that their principal objective is to maintain or improve the quality of education in the District. It is further understood and agreed that this objective can be more readily achieved by a manifest willingness on the part of the District to assist all certificated employees, but especially less experienced employees, in improving their professional skills.

2. The District accepts as a fundamental premise for a successful evaluation program the necessity for mutual respect and confidence to exist between the evaluator and those evaluated.

3. *EVALUATION PROCEDURE*

   A. Every probationary certificated employee shall be evaluated by the administration in writing at least twice each school year, the first occurring no later than December 1.

   B. Every permanent certificated employee shall be evaluated by the administration in writing every other year, no later than December 1 of the year in which evaluation takes place.

   C. No later than the end of the seventh school week of the year in which the evaluation is to take place, the evaluator and the certificated employee shall meet and mutually agree to the elements (Stull Bill requirements) upon which evaluation is to be based. These elements shall be subject to change by irregularities such as class size, intellectual abilities of the learners, availability of support personnel, the learning environment provided, and other pertinent factors. Failure to reach agreement on any of the elements and/or components of evaluation shall necessitate that the evaluator and the certificated employee designate a third party, or parties, agreeable to both, to mediate the disagreement. Resolution of the disagreement shall begin at the earliest possible time that disagreement becomes apparent, but no later than the end of the seventh school week.

   D. During the course of the evaluation period, mitigating circumstances may arise which require modification of the evaluation parameters.

   E. Each evaluation shall be based upon at least one observation, lasting either 30 minutes or one full period and shall be preceded by an evaluation conference in which the evaluator and the certificated employee shall review the observation(s) and what is to be incorporated into the written evaluation. At least three observations shall take place prior to any negative comments or judgments being included in the summary evaluation. Such summary shall be submitted to the employee 30 days prior to the end of the school year.

   F. Such observation(s) shall be arranged by the evaluator and the certificated employee at least two days in advance of the observation.

(*Figure 4.1 continues*)

Figure 4.1 (*continued*)

    G. Any certificated employee who receives a negative evaluation shall, upon request, be entitled to a subsequent observation, conference and written evaluation, as prescribed above. Such entitlement shall continue after each written evaluation until the problems cited in the evaluation are rectified.

    H. The certificated employee's evaluator shall take affirmative action to correct any cited deficiencies. Such action shall include specific recommendations for improvement, direct assistance in implementing such recommendations, and adequate released time for the certificated employee to visit and observe other similar classes in other schools.

    I. If subsequent remedial action eliminates the negative evaluation and/or the identified deficiencies, the evaluations citing such deficiencies shall be removed from the evaluatee's file after a period of eighteen (18) months.

    J. No certificated employee shall be held accountable for any aspect of the educational program over which he has no authority or ability to correct deficiencies.

    K. Non-administrative certificated personnel shall not be required to participate in the evaluation and/or observation of other non-administrative personnel nor shall they be required to assess their own performance.

    L. Should a certificated employee choose to assess his or her performance, such employee shall be notified before revealing the substance of such self-assessment that the matters contained therein may adversely affect his or her job security, and that such employee is not required to reveal such self-assessment.

    M. The evaluator shall not base his/her evaluation of a certificated employee on any information which was not collected through the direct observation of such employee. Hearsay statements shall be excluded from written evaluations.

    N. The District shall release certificated employees who are chosen to serve on the Commission on Professional Competence in accordance with Education Code Section 44944. Such service shall be considered a professional responsibility and the rights and duties of the certificated employee rendering such service shall be those contained in Education Code Sections 44944 and 45047.

4. *PERSONAL AND ACADEMIC FREEDOM*

    A. The District shall not inquire into, nor predicate any adverse action upon a teacher's personal, political and organizational activities or preferences.

    B. It is recognized and agreed that the welfare of students is served through the introduction and open exchange of ideas.

    C. The District shall not interfere with a teacher's freedom of speech or use of materials in the classroom unless such speech or materials constitute a clear and present danger to the students of the District.

(Figure 4.1 continues)

Figure 4.1 (*continued*)

5. *PERSONNEL FILES*

    A. The District shall not base any adverse action against a teacher upon materials which are not contained in such teacher's personnel file. Moreover, the District shall not base any adverse action against a teacher upon materials which are contained in such teacher's personnel file unless the materials had been placed in the file at the time of the incident giving rise to such materials and the teacher had been notified at such time that such materials were being placed in the file.

    B. Unless otherwise agreed to by the involved teacher, a teacher's personnel file shall not include ratings, reports or records which (1) were obtained prior to the employment of the teacher, (2) were prepared by identifiable examination committee members, or (3) were obtained in connection with a promotional examination.

    C. A teacher shall be provided any negative or derogatory material before it is placed in his/her personnel file. He/she shall also be given an opportunity during the school day and with compensated release time to initial and date the material and to prepare a written response to such material. The written response shall be attached to the material.

    D. Upon written authorization by the teacher, a representative of the Association shall be permitted to examine and/or obtain copies of materials in such teacher's personnel file.

    E. The person or persons who draft and/or place material in a teacher's personnel file shall sign the material and signify the date on which such material was drafted and placed in the file. The employee shall have ten (10) days to attach a response.

    F. The contents of all personnel files shall be kept in the strictest confidence.

    G. Negative or derogatory material in a teacher's personnel file shall be destroyed after remaining in the file for a period of two (2) years.

    H. The District shall maintain the teacher personnel files at the District's central office. Any files kept by the teachers' immediate supervisors shall not contain any material not found in the District's files.

---

this point. (Numbers below correspond to paragraph numbers in the union proposal.)

1. Flowery language such as this is intended to persuade arbitrators that the school district is adopting a "punitive" approach when it tries to fire a teacher. Inasmuch as quality education is facilitated by dismissing incompetent or marginal teachers, the union's proposed language should be rejected.

2. A teacher could veto every evaluator merely by declaring that the teacher had no "respect and confidence" in the evaluator. In short,

the clause would give individual teachers the right to select their own evaluators. The proposal that the union have equal power to determine training programs for management personnel is absurd on its face.

3C. This would give the teachers a veto power over the criteria to be used in evaluation. The proposal to refer disputes over the criteria to a mediator could be used to cripple evaluation completely. Suppose, for example, that every teacher wanted mediation of disputes over the evaluation criteria. Aside from the fact that there aren't that many mediators around, the proposal could tie up principals for months, while the disputes with each teacher were being resolved—if they ever were resolved.

3E. The requirement that there be "at least three observations" before any negative comments could be included in the final evaluation would by itself preclude most negative comments. Not because teachers would improve, but because principals simply would not have the time to make the required number of observations. Suppose, for example, that the principal observed some important deficiencies near the end of the school term. These deficiencies would have to go unreported if the principal could not make the additional observations.

3F. This proposal assumes that the deficiencies can and will be corrected, an assumption that would be unrealistic in many cases. In any event, there comes a time when school districts have to say to some teachers: "You've had your chances and we've given you all the help we can, but you just don't make the grade." A district would never be able to make this decision if it agreed to this clause.

3G. Again, there comes a time when dismissal, not continued assistance, is the only appropriate management action to be taken.

Without any difficulty, I could list dozens of additional valid objections to the union demands in Figure 4.1. Acceptance of even a small number of them would destroy effective evaluation. Instead of pursuing this issue, however, let me point out some aspects of the proposal that are typical of union proposals generally on the subject:

1. The absence of concern over the retention of incompetent teachers.
2. The way every issue is resolved in favor of the employee, and against the educational needs of the district.
3. The enormous time and record-keeping burdens on the district. Again, bear in mind that the proposal illustrates the union's version of "due process." If a district violated any of these provisions, the union would contend that any adverse action against the teach-

er should be null and void because the evaluation did not provide "due process." When termination (that is, "capital punishment" in labor relations) is involved, arbitrators tend to interpret contract language strictly against the employer.

Still, is there anything really to be concerned about? After all, a district need not accept this proposal—not even one sentence of it. This reaction, however, overlooks the dynamics of the bargaining process. First of all, the union is proposing detailed restrictions on management on every issue: transfers, assignments, hours of work, leaves of absence, and so on. Psychologically, it is difficult for school boards to keep saying, "No, no, no." They are pressed to make concessions to show "good faith." Board members often believe that their counterproposals must include some elements of the union's initial proposals to show "good faith." Furthermore, many items in the union's proposal would seem innocuous to some boards and administrators. It becomes very tempting to make concessions on "non-economic items," especially if the district cannot provide a substantial salary increase.

Above and beyond these considerations the union proposal is not just a one-shot effort. A year or two later, the contract expires and the union is back, pressing for concessions again. (The provisions cited in Figure 4.1 have been proposed four times over an eight-year period.) As the union achieves some concessions in each contract, it eventually achieves a formidable array of job security clauses—and a corresponding management inability to terminate incompetent teachers.

THE FREQUENCY OF TENURE CASES

How often are teachers fired for incompetence? In view of the tremendous number of teachers, only a minuscule number are fired, at least according to the research on this issue. The following data demonstrate the nationwide nature of the problem.

1. Bridges found that only 86 cases of dismissal for incompetence reached the courts or a hearing officer from 1939 to 1982. Obviously, tens of millions of teachers were employed over these 43 years.
2. In Florida, only one teacher lost a teaching certificate because of incompetency in the 1977-78 school year.
3. From August 1975 to December 1979, an average of ten cases a year contesting dismissals for incompetency went to formal hearing pursuant to the Illinois tenure law.

4. Based upon a search of California's employment records from 1933 to 1973, no teacher was dismissed for incompetence during that period.
5. A 1979 study of teacher dismissals in Pennsylvania revealed that from 1971 to 1976, only 11 cases of dismissal for incompetence were appealed to the Pennsylvania secretary of education. Inasmuch as formal dismissals in Pennsylvania are usually appealed, and the secretary is the last step in the appeal process, it appears that 11 cases were a small number, to say the least. Only 5 of the 11 cases solely involved incompetence; one of the 5 may have involved insubordination also (refusal to comply with a school board order to shave off a beard). Excluding this case, therefore, it appears that only two teachers in Pennsylvania were formally dismissed for incompetence during this five-year period.[4]
6. In New York, teachers were dismissed pursuant to a formal hearing approximately 24 times in 1983; in most of these cases, the charges were moral turpitude or some basis other than incompetence.[5]

Tenure cases appear to be litigated more frequently in New Jersey than in other states. The New Jersey tenure statute (N.J.S.A.18A) spells out a review procedure in which the state commissioner of education initially decides whether a school board has sustained dismissal charges. The commissioner's decision can be appealed to the State Board of Education and then to the courts. The number of tenure decisions made by the commissioner in recent years were as follows:

1983	63
1982	48
1981	48
1980	56

Prior to 1982, tenure cases in New Jersey were frequently settled by agreement upon a lump-sum payment. Inasmuch as charges had already been filed, the approval of the state commissioner was required but such approval was routinely given usually after the payment was made. In 1982, however, the commissioner announced that settlements could not be implemented without his approval, and that lump-sum payments would be scrutinized carefully to prevent payments contrary to the public interest. These charges will probably reduce the number of buyouts, since the basis for the buyouts must now be a matter of public record, and must not be unreasonable or excessive.[6]

Is the number of legal cases, including formal hearings, an accurate guide to the frequency of dismissals for incompetence? In my opinion, they are. One reason is that the teacher unions normally litigate dismissals if requested to do so by the teachers involved. In view of the union position that its role is only to ensure due process for teachers facing dismissal, it would be difficult for the unions not to litigate dismissals. Such refusal would be tantamount to saying the teacher is not entitled to due process. Legally and practically, the teacher unions cannot afford to be in this position. It is not true, as they sometimes assert, that they are legally obligated to contest every dismissal. Nevertheless, if a teacher desires to challenge dismissal, and has even the semblance of a defense against it, the unions typically feel they must litigate the dismissal in order to maintain credibility with their membership.

In at least some states, and I believe a majority of them, union representation in dismissals, including legal counsel, is routinely provided. To the extent this is true, we can expect teachers to take advantage of this assistance and to litigate dismissals. As noted earlier, in a 1977 nationwide poll of school superintendents, they frequently estimated that 5 to 15 percent of their teachers were not performing adequately. If we use the lowest figure, we could assume, for example, that 5 percent of California's 230,000 teachers (11,500) were performing incompetently in 1980. Be that as it may, it is very unlikely that formal charges of teacher incompetence were filed ten times during the year. As a matter of fact, insofar as legal records are concerned, no tenured teacher was fired solely for incompetence in California until 1983.[7]

Forced Resignations

School boards and school administrators frequently reveal some ambivalence in discussing teacher tenure. On the one hand, they often believe that tenure laws are a major obstacle to dismissing incompetent teachers. On the other hand, they are sensitive to allegations that their schools retain incompetent teachers. To maintain their criticisms of the tenure laws, while avoiding its implications for their schools, they frequently assert that management has been able to persuade incompetent teachers to resign rather than face charges of incompetence. Undoubtedly, this does happen, so that dismissals of tenured teachers occur more often than the number of court cases involving this issue.

For several reasons, it is practically impossible to ascertain the frequency of forced resignations. Teachers who resign are unlikely to concede that they did so because the teacher feared the outcome of a tenure hearing. Also, since the real reason for a forced resignation is not the reason that appears on the records, management's assessment of its frequency is highly suspect. For a superintendent to say, "I persuaded X to resign instead of facing charges," when X's record shows a resignation for some other reason and no basis for incompetence charges would be risky. It also raises some serious questions about the ethics of administrators in these situations. Imagine the reactions of school districts that employ teachers who have supposedly been pressured to resign because of incompetence. Inasmuch as the records of such teachers do not reflect this fact, forced resignations may simply result in incompetent teachers moving from one district to another.

The frequency of forced resignations is suspect for still another reason. School administrators do not have many ways to exert pressure on teachers to resign. This is especially true if the teacher is covered by a comprehensive collective bargaining contract, as so many are. In that case, teacher load, hours of employment, transfers, extra duty assignments, and other personnel policies are spelled out in the contract. Therefore, managerial discretion to pressure teachers is correspondingly reduced. If the contract emphasizes seniority, managerial discretion is reduced even more. Any administrative action to pressure an incompetent teacher to resign is likely to be a violation of the contract, hence not available to management.

The Frequency of Tenure Cases: A Diagnosis

Let us see why the frequency of formal charges is so shockingly low. One reason is that attempted dismissals are frequently litigated and tenure litigation is very expensive. One estimate ranges from $7,000 to $20,000 per case, but one recent case was estimated to have cost the district $100,000.[8]

Although the estimates do not factor in the "gains" or "savings," they substantially understate the costs. The reason is that they do not usually include the time of regular school staff, such as the time devoted by administrators to tenure cases. Also, school districts sometimes have reason to minimize public awareness of the costs. School districts lose almost two out of every five tenure cases that are litigated. The more a district spends on such a case, the greater its public embarrassment if it loses. Inasmuch as tenure cases can be lost for many reasons having no relationship to teacher competence, districts are naturally reluctant to publicize the full costs involved.

In most cases, the teacher is represented by the state affiliate of the NEA or the AFT. The union attorneys are highly experienced on the subject of teacher dismissals. In contrast, school board attorneys, especially in smaller districts, may litigate only a few cases or none for several years. Although some attorneys handle cases for several districts, and thus acquire an expertise on the subject comparable to union attorneys, school board attorneys not experienced in dismissal cases are naturally reluctant to let such lucrative cases be referred to other attorneys.

Although costs vary, usually several witnesses have to be interviewed. The attorney has to review all the backup material such as observation reports, evaluations, parental complaints, and so on. The teacher will have witnesses also, and these must be discredited. Frequently, the teacher will try to show that some personal crisis, such as a divorce or death in the family, adversely affected the teacher's performance. The idea, of course, is not just to gain sympathy but to convey the idea that the teacher does a good job when there is no crisis. If the hearings require several days, as often happens, the hearing costs go up accordingly. Also, a hearing usually ties up at least a few administrators for several days, especially if preparation time is included.

Sometimes cases never get to a hearing—and the teacher is not fired—because the administrators fear that the litigation would put them in a bad light. A tenure hearing is not just a trial for the teacher involved. The administrator(s) are also tested by a tenure hearing. If the teacher wins because an administrator has not followed proper procedures, the implications are that the administrator was incompetent or biased, or both.

Additionally, the tenure statutes usually place the burden of proof on the school board to show the dismissal was justified. It is not ordinarily incumbent on the teacher to show that the dismissal was unjustified. In the private sector, an employee can sue an employer to void a dismissal allegedly based upon discrimination: racial, religious, sexual, age, or national origin. Although such legal protections against discrimination are important, they are not involved in most dismissals. Even when they are relevant, the procedures are not as favorable to the employee as tenure statutes often are. An employee who alleges that he was fired as a result of illegal discrimination still has the burden of proof in such lawsuits. The employee tries to establish a prima facie case, and thereby shift the burden of proof to the employer. The latter must then show a valid basis for the dismissal. Suppose, however, that employees in the private sector had a tenure law, so that the employer was routinely required to litigate dismissals based upon incompetence. Unquestionably, the impact of such a law would be to keep more incompetent employees in their jobs. There is a world of difference between requiring employers to bring charges *before* a dismissal can be effectuated; and requiring the employee who has been fired to file a lawsuit and bear the burden of proof to show that the firing was unjustified.

Additionally, the tenure statutes typically provide a tight time schedule for tenure hearings. This is an important advantage over the private-sector employee trying to void a dismissal allegedly based upon illegal discrimination. The teacher must receive notice of dismissal by a certain date or period of time after the board decision to dismiss. The tenure statutes typically provide so many days for the teacher to respond, so many days until a hearing, so many days for a hearing officer decision, and so many days for each side to appeal. Of course, if the decision is appealed and the issue is in the judicial system, it can take quite a while to get a decision, as in litigation generally. On the other hand, some tenure laws make the state superintendent of public instruction or the state board of education or a hearing officer the ultimate decisionmaker in tenure cases.

Most of the debate over teacher tenure is confined to ideal laws and hypothetical situations. Relatively little attention is devoted to the actual consequences of tenure statutes. In principle tenured teachers charged with incompetence are entitled to prompt notice, specific charges, right to counsel, and all the other elements of due process. If the only effects of the tenure statutes were to provide due process, it would be foolish to challenge them. Unfortunately, the tenure laws have much broader consequences.

Perhaps an analogy will help. Our criminal justice system operates on the principle that some who are guilty may avoid conviction as the price we pay for avoiding conviction of the innocent. The tenure calculus is this: How many incompetent teachers do we accept in order to avoid firing any competent teachers? The data previously cited indicate that we are tolerating too many incompetent teachers in order to prevent unfair treatment of competent ones. Statistical precision in this area is not feasible, but it seems clear that the public interest in protecting competent teachers has evolved into excessive protection for incompetent teachers.

One reason may be the uncritical acceptance of the idea that due process in tenure cases should be similar to due process in criminal cases. Conviction of a crime should be beyond a reasonable doubt. We do not want to imprison or stigmatize an individual for life in the absence of a strong and persuasive case. The consequences are too serious to permit conviction if there is a reasonable doubt.

The consequences to the teacher charged with incompetence may or may not be as severe. Of course, being fired as a teacher is much more serious than being fined for overnight parking. In addition to the loss in income, the teacher who is fired may lose important health and welfare benefits. Dismissal may affect the teacher's pension and the retirement income of the teacher's spouse. These are important considerations that strengthen the argument for due process in dismissals.

We must, however, look at all the consequences, not just some of them. As tenure statutes allow more and more incompetent or marginally competent teachers to keep their jobs, what is the gain? What is the public benefit from tenure that corresponds to not convicting an innocent person of a crime? Realistically, it is that some marginally competent teachers are not fired. For every such teacher who would have lost a job except for tenure law, however, dozens of incompetent ones have retained their jobs. Although teachers and teacher unions often complain that school administrators evaluate teachers unfairly, most administrators who conduct teacher evaluations are too easily satisfied. In many school districts, there are few, if any, negative evaluations of teachers.

It should be noted that some of the circumstances giving rise to tenure laws no longer prevail. For instance, federal and state laws provide strong protections against discrimination on the basis of race, religion, sex, age, and national origin. In many situations, employees also receive legal assistance from public funds to litigate their claims.

A person charged with a crime has no choice to opt out of the situation. In contrast, the teacher often has the opportunity to resign and start anew, either elsewhere in teaching or in a different field. Granted, starting over somewhere else is not always a practical alternative, but it is frequently. This fact suggests a different approach to balancing the public's need to hire competent teachers and teacher rights to job security. We should not abolish due process, but we might limit its application in two ways. First, we might narrow the category of teachers who are entitled to maximum job security. Teachers might still be tenured after a probationary period, but the nature of the tenure protections might be different, depending upon the duration of their service. A tenured teacher with 15 years of service might receive more protection than a tenured teacher with only four years of service. The older teacher, because of a higher salary, would have fewer opportunities to get a teaching position elsewhere, or to enter a different field. The personal trauma of facing charges of incompetence is also likely to be more severe in the case of an older teacher. Actually, such an approach would not involve any new principles; even now, "due process" for a probationary teacher provides less protection than "due process" for a tenured teacher. Although everyone is entitled to due process, the way the concept is interpreted and applied should vary more than it does at present.

EDUCATIONAL REFORM AND TEACHER TENURE

Thus far, teacher tenure has been considered largely in terms of how it affects the dismissal of allegedly incompetent teachers. Although public opinion tends to focus on this issue, the tenure statutes often provide certain protections for teachers subject to a reduction in force (RIF). Thus regardless of the controversies over teacher incompetence, the tenure statutes constitute an obstacle to programmatic changes. This problem is widely neglected, even though the reform proposals would require school districts to replace many teachers for programmatic reasons.

The reformers agree that public schools, especially secondary schools, do not require enough courses in basic subjects. Instead, public school have allegedly diluted the curriculum with personal service and personal development courses, remedial courses, work experience outside the school, and other courses that divert students from a solid education. As *A Nation At Risk* pointed out, only 31 percent of recent high school graduates completed intermediate algebra; only 16 percent completed geography; only 13 percent completed French I, and only 6 percent completed calculus.

Obviously, increasing these percentages substantially will require changes in the composition of the teaching profession. Suppose, for example, that our objective is to double the proportion of high school graduates who have completed geography, French I, calculus, and the other neglected subjects currently taken by 20 percent or fewer of our high school graduates. It would be impossible to achieve this objective without adding a large number of teachers of these subjects. This raises a question: What happens to the teachers of the nonessential courses? After all, we just cannot add the required teachers to the existing staff—the costs alone would be prohibitive. Do we just fire the existing teachers, with or without severance pay? Retrain them, and if so, at whose expense? Reduce their numbers through attrition?

All of these solutions, including any combinations of them, face enormous obstacles: legal, financial, political, and educational. Nothing galvanizes a union like threats to job security. If the union cannot prevent competent teachers from being fired, it will suffer a severe loss of support among its members. Even in the absence of a collective bargaining law, local, state, and national teacher organizations would wage an all-out attack against any effort to terminate teachers to accommodate changes in educational programs.

For several reasons, replacement through attrition would be the only way most school districts could introduce major changes in the composition of their teaching staffs. The unavailability of teachers needed to implement the changes also points in this direction. If we go this route, however, what happens to reform? The moment school districts indicate that certain courses will be phased out, the attrition rates in those courses will decline precipitately. If certain courses are being dropped throughout the state, the teachers who teach them will not be as likely to get another job. For this reason, teachers who would otherwise resign under pressure will not do so; on the contrary, they will do everything possible to keep their jobs.

Also, bear in mind that attrition rates vary enormously from district to district. In many districts, a substantial number of teachers of allegedly nonessential courses are at the maximum step of the salary schedule. Their level of retirement income and ability to pay their medical expenses is closely tied to their continued employment as teachers. Of course, school boards can expedite attrition in some ways. They might offer early retirement incentives, such as the continuation of medical benefits to retirees. Even so, the pace of attrition is likely to depend on many factors that school boards cannot control, or that would be too expensive to overcome.

The pace of reform, therefore, will depend upon several factors that are conducive to delay. If districts rely upon attrition to replace incumbent staff, reform may become a mirage. On the other hand, efforts to replace competent teachers for programmatic reasons will generate morale and bargaining and political problems of the first magnitude. The teacher unions will support school board candidates who are opposed to the changes. I have seen unions do this to challenge the termination of one teacher or one clerk. In short, any reform that envisages teachers losing their jobs faces intense opposition and heavy odds; any reform that relies upon attrition faces a loss of momentum and the perpetuation of the status quo for many years.

THE COGNIZANCE ISSUE

Whatever valid criticisms can be made of the preceding analysis, I believe that it does point to an inescapable conclusion: Any realistic effort to remove incompetent teachers, or to make significant changes in the subjects to be taught, must take cognizance of teacher tenure. This raises a question: To what extent do the leading reform proposals recognize and deal with the issue? In all candor, the answer is: "Not at all." Let me run down the list briefly:

1. *A Nation At Risk*—The *only* reference to tenure is the following: "Salary, promotion, tenure and retention decisions should be tied to an effective evaluation system that includes peer review so that superior teachers can be rewarded, average ones encouraged, and poor ones either improved or terminated."[9]

For reasons explained in Chapter 3, introducing "peer review" into public education would make matters worse, much worse. Regardless, *A Nation At Risk* does not address the tenure controversy. It does not include any reference to the tenure laws or to the bargaining problems inherent in its recommendations. As a matter of fact, Appendix C of the report lists the 44 commissioned papers that the National Commission considered in making its report. Not one appears directly relevant to the issues discussed in this chapter.

2. *Making the Grade*—The only reference to teacher tenure is the statement that

> the unions and professional associations—to which teachers belong— have protected their weakest members rather than winning rewards for the strongest. . . . The collective bargaining process, moreover, has not only made it more difficult to encourage promising teachers or dismiss poor ones, it has forced many of the best to leave teaching for more financially rewarding work. . . . Because the institutional arrangements and procedures governing the teachers are so well entrenched, incremental changes in federal policy cannot by themselves dramatically improve the quality of instruction.[10]

There is no analysis or documentation of the statements concerning unions or collective bargaining, and no discussion of tenure issues.

These meager references constitute the attention paid to teacher tenure and due process by the reform movement. The following reform documents do not address the issues at all:

3. *Action for Excellence*—The only reference to tenure is the sentence reading: "The system of tenure in most school systems also makes it difficult if not impossible to deal with the problem of ineffective or unmotivated teachers."[11]

4. *High School*

5. *Educating Americans for the 21st Century*

6. *Education for the 1980's and Beyond*

7. *The Paideia Proposal*

8. *A Place Called School*

In fairness, it should be noted that tenure issues were not equally relevant to all of the reform proposals. Paradoxically, however, the most direct reference to the issue was the one just quoted from *Making the Grade*, a reform document devoted to the federal role in public education. Essentially, it says only that federal policies can't change the undesirable effects of teacher tenure. If this is true, however, it does not say much for the reform proposals that have ignored the issue.

Most significantly, legislative efforts to achieve reform also ignore the issue. For instance, Governor Kean of New Jersey outlined his education program to a joint session of the New Jersey legislature on September 6, 1983. This was the first special session in the state's history devoted solely to education. Although Governor Kean's speech emphasized the need to raise teacher as well as student standards, the subject of teacher tenure was not mentioned.[12] It should be noted that New Jersey has perhaps the most serious tenure problems of any state. The reason is that school administrators, including superintendents, have tenure under New Jersey law. A reform program that does not even address this issue must be viewed as a hopeless endeavor, regardless of its fate in the legislature.

THE FUTURE OF TEACHER TENURE

Clearly, there is no national movement to change teacher tenure. Bluntly speaking, there is no constituency for such changes. The reform movement has ignored the issue. Teacher organizations, especially at the state level, would oppose changes that weakened tenure. School administrators and school board organizations are not actively working to change the tenure laws or to restrict bargaining on the issue. In this situation, political leaders have no reason to kick a sleeping dog, especially one that can bite as well as bark.

Teacher Tenure in Public Schools: A Suggestion

Despite the absence of a political constituency able and willing to tackle the issue, a more effective approach to tenure might be achievable, provided we adopt a different approach to tenure issues.

The different approach needed would emphasize the costs of "due process" to the state and to local school districts. The costs are often scattered in school board budgets under legal fees, personnel, consultants, and so on. As a result, the public and the legislatures do not really understand the costs of the fancy rhetoric they are asked to swallow.

More importantly, an effort should be made to characterize tenure cases as economic as well as personnel issues. In 1983-84, teachers averaged about $27,000 a year in salary and benefits. Given the likely increases in the future, the public will eventually be paying from $0.5 to $1 million per teacher who teaches 20-25 years. Should public policies encourage that much public investment in marginal teachers? I believe few taxpayers and parents would support the status quo if the issue were framed in economic terms. Certainly, not many would wish to invest that much in a marginal employee in their own business. Of course, I am not denying that tenure cases involve other dimensions and concerns. My point is, however, that the rhetoric on the issue has obscured the economic realities of it. These realities must be faced if we are ever going to get a handle on the problem.

Along with emphasizing the community's economic stake in dismissals, the possibilities of economic resolution of tenure issues should be carefully considered. For instance, it might be possible to strengthen school board ability to dismiss teachers but tie such measures to automatic buyout provisions. For instance, a school board might have the right to dismiss teachers for incompetence, subject to payment of a stipulated amount. The amount could vary, depending upon the teacher's length of service. A teacher who had taught in the district for 20 years would be entitled to a higher amount than a teacher with only 5 years of service. The teacher could still have the right to appeal, but would lose the buyout by doing so. Districts would be precluded from replacing competent teachers receiving high salaries by new teachers at beginning salaries for two reasons. First, the teacher being fired could appeal and presumably carry the burden of proof. Second, the buyout amounts would be substantial for teachers receiving high salaries.

There are several ways to frame such an approach, and I would be the first to agree it would require further study. It seems unfair to pay an incompetent teacher to resign while competent ones who wish to resign receive nothing; at the same time, if payments are made to the latter, the approach may not be viable. Still, it seems to me that we are trying to make do with arrangements that have outlived their usefulness. Incremental improvements in these arrangements are not to be denigrated, but it may be easier to find a different type of solution to the problem.[13]

Teacher Tenure and Entrepreneurial Schools

Unquestionably, entrepreneurial schools could and would avoid the negative consequences of teacher tenure. Reasons include the following:

1. Teachers in entrepreneurial schools would not be public employees, hence they would not enjoy the tenure benefits of public employment arising out of the U.S. Constitution.
2. Teacher tenure in entrepreneurial schools would not be protected by the state tenure laws, which apply only to public school teachers.
3. Because there would be a much smaller and weaker union presence in entrepreneurial schools, the latter would be much less likely to be deterred from the firing incompetent teachers by union opposition.
4. Teachers in entrepreneurial schools would suffer directly from the incompetence of colleagues. By diminishing parental support, such incompetence jeopardizes the well-being of all teachers in entrepreneurial schools.

    One can easily visualize teachers taking the initiative to fire instead of retain incompetent teachers; under the present system, teacher support for incompetent teachers poses no economic threat to the supporters.
5. The common and highly visible stake in educating students effectively is much more likely to encourage teachers to support managerial policies/decisions that give a higher priority to getting the job done effectively than to job security for teachers.
6. Although job security for teachers overall would be reduced, there would be some job security advantages to teaching in entrepreneurial schools; a school is not likely to fire teachers who attract students—especially if the fired teacher might be employed by a competitor.

Of course, popular teachers are not always competent. One danger is that entrepreneurial schools will overemphasize teacher popularity;

in addition, they may tend to identify competence as popularity and recruiting ability. On the other hand, the promise of entrepreneurial schools is that they will use educational technology, especially computer assisted instruction, much more effectively than public schools. Their "edge" might not be in better teachers per se but a better system of instruction, which reduces dependence upon the qualities of individual teachers. Quite possibly, tenure issues would take a different orientation or fade in importance altogether. A teacher's mastery of educational technology might become a more important dimension of competence than the teacher's popularity with students.

NOTES

1. Stanley M. Elam, ed., *A Decade of Gallup Polls of Attitudes Toward Education, 1969-1978* (Bloomington, Ind.: Phi Delta Kappa, 1978), p. 36.

2. The primary sources are cited in Edwin M. Bridges and Patricia J. Gumpert, *The Dismissal of Tenured Teachers for Incompetence* (Stanford, Calif.: Institute for Research on Educational Finance and Governance, Stanford University, February 1984).

3. For a critique of the "employment at will" doctrine, see Jack Stieber, "Employment At Will: An Issue for the 1980's," Presidential address to the Industrial Relations Research Association, December 29, 1983. Reprinted in *Daily Labor Report*, January 5, 1984, pp. D1-5.

4. Harry F. Finlayson, "Incompetence and Teacher Dismissal," *Phi Delta Kappan*, September 1979, p. 69.

5. See Edwin M. Bridges, *The Management of Teacher Incompetence* (Stanford, Calif.: Institute for Research on Educational Finance and Governance, Stanford University, 1983), and Bridges and Gumpert for the citations and analysis of the data cited in items 1-6 in the text.

6. Data provided by letter from New Jersey School Boards Association, March 21, 1984.

7. The primary sources are cited in Bridges and Gumpert, p. 2.

8. Ibid., p. 20.

9. National Commission on Excellence in Education, *A Nation At Risk: The Imperative for Educational Reform* (Washington, D.C.: U.S. Government Printing Office, 1983), p. 30.

10. Task Force on Federal Elementary and Secondary Education Policy, *Making the Grade* (New York: Twentieth Century Fund, 1983), p. 9.

11. Task Force on Education for Economic Growth, *Action for Excellence* (Denver: Education Commission of the States, June 1983), p. 26.

12. Governor Thomas H. Kean, *Education in New Jersey: A Blueprint for Reform*. Speech before a Joint Session of the Legislature, September 6, 1983 (Trenton, N.J.: Office of the Governor, 1983).

13. A recent study of teacher evaluation by the Rand Corporation illustrates the futility of conventional approaches. Among other things, it recommends that teachers play a more active role in evaluation—without providing any hints on what should happen to teachers who botch the job of evaluating their fellow teachers. See Arthur E. Wise et al., *Teacher Evaluation: A Study of Effective Practices* (Santa Monica, Calif.: Rand Corporation, 1984).

5

SCHOOL GOVERNANCE: NO ONE IN CHARGE

If educational reforms are to be achieved on a broad scale, we cannot avoid consideration of school governance. Who is going to decide what reforms are to be implemented? What are the capabilities of the decisionmakers to carry out the reforms? Do they control the resources and the personnel to get the job done? This chapter is devoted to governance issues such as these.

Simply stated, my argument is that the governance structure of public education constitutes an impenetrable roadblock to educational reform. This argument requires consideration of the federal, state, and local roles in education. Before discussing these roles, however, a few comments about governance structures generally may be helpful.

In analyzing any governance structure, we must avoid two common mistakes. One is to assume that the governance structure is always an accurate guide to power and influence. The other is to assume that the governance structure can be safely ignored because it is not an unfailing guide to the power to change things.

Every major institution has a formal governance structure, which is supposed to reveal who has the authority to do what. Armies, city councils, legislatures, government departments, the courts—all these have a formal structure of some kind. At the same time, however, we know that the actual decisionmaking power often deviates from the formal structure. A strong council member sometimes has more power than a weak mayor. A business subordinate sometimes dominates the decisions of his superiors. Even in the classroom, a teacher's aide with a strong personality sometimes dominates the teacher who is formally the decisionmaker.

Nevertheless, although actual power is not always distributed according to the table of organization, organizational structure can help or hinder the way decisions are made and implemented. Other things being equal, an individual can make decisions more readily than a committee. Overlapping or shared authority leads to more confusion than undivided authority, and so on.

Here, our concern is whether the governance structure of public education provides clear-cut lines of authority and accountability. Unless we know who is responsible for what, we will not know how to proceed to achieve reform.

For example, suppose you are a parent concerned about poor teachers in schools attended by your children. Whom do you visit to bring about improvement? The administrators who recommended the teachers be employed? The school board members who approved the recommendation? The colleges from which the poor teachers graduated? The state department of education for its weak certification policies? The legislators who allowed this situation to develop? The reporters who ignored it? The unions that are overprotective of incompetent teachers? And so on.

As we analyze the governance structure, we must never lose sight of its practical implications. This is especially important for individuals who are, or may wish to be, actors in the educational scene. The governance structure matters, whether you are simply a parent trying to do what's best for your children, or a legislator concerned about issues that go beyond any parental concern.

THE FEDERAL ROLE IN PUBLIC EDUCATION

Education is not mentioned specifically in the U.S. Constitution. For this reason, it has always been regarded as a power reserved to the states and to the people. With only negligible exceptions, such as schools for children of military personnel stationed overseas, the federal government does not administer elementary and secondary schools. Paradoxically, the one governance issue that has received national attention in recent years was essentially a federal one. I refer to the controversy over the establishment and subsequently the disestablishment of the U.S. Department of Education. Its establishment in 1979 culminated an intensive campaign by the National Education Association, whose members accounted for 10 percent of the delegates at the 1980 Democratic Convention. The NEA's main objective in establishing the department was to realign the congressional committees dealing with education, especially the House Labor and Education Committee; it was felt that they were dominated by members of Congress beholden to the AFL-CIO and hence its affiliated teacher union, the American Federation of Teachers.

From a public policy standpoint, the establishment of a separate federal department of education was not important and did not justify the time and effort of the Carter administration. On political grounds, however, the action was an attractive option for President Carter; it enabled him to satisfy a key constituency simply by reorganizing federal activities in the field of education.

Ironically, President Reagan has come under intense pressure from conservatives to abolish the department. From a public policy point of view, there is no more reason for President Reagan to waste his resources trying to abolish the department than there was for President Carter to establish it. At any rate, like so many issues in education, there is less to it than meets the eye. During the 1985 Senate hearings on President Reagan's nomination of William J. Bennett to be Secretary of Education, President Reagan stated that although he preferred to abolish the department, there was insufficient congressional support for such action. While keeping his options open, President Reagan made it clear that he had no intention of abolishing the department "at this time." Regardless, the issue is a peripheral one from the standpoint of educational policy.

FEDERAL REFORM INITIATIVES

Federal opportunities to initiate and implement reforms are largely confined to appropriating funds with strings attached; the strings are doing whatever the federal government decides school districts must do to get the money. In this way, the federal funds can be used to achieve a desired reform.

What are the prospects for achieving educational reform this way in the future? At best, they are minimal. Federal aid to education is currently provided for specific objectives: education of the disadvantaged and the handicapped, vocational education, and so on. There is no movement to shift these funds to objectives sought by reformers. Furthermore, there is no congressional consensus on which initiatives should receive federal support. If and when such a congressional consensus should materialize, any increases in federal aid to education face formidable difficulties. For better or worse, Congress has established income streams to a variety of recipients. Some of these income streams will balloon in the years ahead. The Reagan administration is struggling to limit the increases, but rollbacks to free up substantial funds for education are not going to happen.

There is also a national consensus (which includes most leaders of both the Republican and Democratic parties) that defense expenditures should be increased. There is considerable debate over the size of the increase, but any increase diminishes prospects for increased federal aid to education. In brief, the discretionary area in the federal government cannot provide a large-scale increase in aid to education without raising taxes, increasing the federal deficit, and/or shifting funds from other federal programs with influential constituencies.

The size of the federal deficit is a matter of deep concern to both parties; even if a president were willing to increase the deficit to provide increased federal aid to education, a congressional consensus to do so is lacking. Nor is there a congressional consensus to increase taxes for federal aid to education, or to transfer funds to education from other major federal spending programs. In fact, despite their rhetoric, educators have largely written off the possibility of large increases in federal aid to education. Instead, their strategy is to maintain current levels, adjusted for inflation, and to assume some entitlement programs that the states help to pay for. Such assumption would free up state revenues that presumably would go to education.

As Table 5.1 shows, there has been no major increase in federal spending for education in recent years. In fact, when adjusted for in-

Table 5.1 Federal Appropriations for Education,
Fiscal Years 1981 to 1986
(in billions of dollars)

Fiscal Year	Appropriations
1981	$14.8
1982	14.7
1983	15.4
1985	17.6
1986	15.5*

*President Reagan's proposed FY 1986 budget.
Source: Department of Education Budget Documents.

flation, federal appropriations for education actually declined from 1980 to 1984. Prior to his reelection in 1984, President Reagan's proposed budget for FY 1985 had called for a slight increase over 1984 federal spending for education. Since President Reagan's reelection, however, the pressures to reduce federal spending in order to reduce the federal deficit have increased dramatically. President Reagan's proposed education budget for FY 1986 is about $2.5 billion less than the appropriation for FY 1985. Although the reductions were almost entirely confined to financial aid for students in higher education, the proposed budget simply continued the 1985 dollar level for assistance to school districts. As this is written (fall 1985) the final outcome is far from clear, but it seems safe to say that federal spending for education will not materially increase over 1985 levels.

Given the intense opposition to President Reagan's reelection by public-sector unions, especially the NEA and the AFT, the Reagan administration has no political obligation to maintain federal spending for education at the 1984 level of support. Furthermore, the Reagan administration has emphasized the need to reduce federal regulation and reporting to federal agencies. These objectives also run counter to efforts to use federal aid to achieve educational reform.

THE ROLE OF THE STATES

What are the prospects for reform by state action? To answer this question, we must first review the structure of education at the state level.

Every state has a state department of education, headed by a state superintendent of education. These departments vary enormously in structure, resources, authority, prestige, and just about every other meaningful criterion that can be applied to a governmental agency. In some states, the state superintendent is an elected constitutional officer; in others, the superintendent is appointed by a state board of education or by the governor. The authority delegated to the state superintendent and/or the state board of education varies a great deal, as does the extent of legislative action affecting local school boards and superintendents.

As an example of the confusion that characterizes the governance of public education at the state level, the state superintendent in California is an elected constitutional officer. The state also has a state board of education appointed by the governor for staggered four-year terms. Illogical as it seems (and is), the elected state superintendent is subordinate in some ways to the appointed state board of education (whose members may be from a different political party).

In addition to an elected state superintendent, a state board of education appointed by the governor, three different systems of higher education (each governed by trustees with staggered terms), and a statute that requires collective bargaining between school districts and teacher unions, California statutes regulate every phase of school operations. Let me cite just one example, which reflects a legislative pattern not only in California but in many other states as well.

Prior to enactment in 1975 of bargaining rights for school district employees, the state unions of teachers and nonteacher employees lobbied the legislature for employee benefits. These efforts were often successful. One such statute relates to fringe benefits for nonteacher employees. School districts normally hire a large number of part-time workers; for example, most school cafeteria employees are not needed seven-eight hours a day.

Invariably, one of the issues that school districts had to resolve was what fringe benefits, if any, should part-time employees receive? Eventually, the state unions that represented nonteaching employees were successful in getting enactment of Education Code Section 45136. Among other things, Section 45136 required school districts to prorate leaves and other benefits provided full-time employees. This requirement solved two important problems for the unions. Many of their members were part-time employees who were constantly putting pressure on the union to achieve the fringe benefits available to full-time employees. Also, Section 45136 discouraged districts from assigning work to part-time employees who received fewer benefits than full-time employees.

Whatever the intent, the practical consequences leave something to be desired. If a school district provides 12 days of vacation a year for an eight-hour employee employed twelve months a year, it must provide a pro rata vacation benefit for cafeteria aides who work two hours a day, 175 days a year. Just why such aides need a vacation is not clear, at least if the normal purpose of a vacation is the issue. Or just why the matter can't be left to collective bargaining or local school boards is not clear either.

It is convenient to assume that such ridiculous state laws are exceptional. Such an assumption enables reformers to ignore the subject, and all have done so. Unfortunately, the assumption is erroneous. The state education codes include hundreds of prescriptions and prohibitions that no sane business man would tolerate in his own business.

All that I can do here is refer the reader to a few summaries of the situation and hope that the examples cited in this book adequately illustrate the real world of educational legislation.[1]

Will educational reform legislation improve matters? The reform legislation enacted to date compounds instead of resolves the problems. Inasmuch as California's reform legislation has been widely praised in national media, let me comment briefly on the reforms enacted there in 1983. The reforms were included in an omnibus funding bill, S.B. 813. Inasmuch as S.B. 813 runs to 214 pages, I shall have to resort to examples again.

One item in the bill deals with teacher suspensions. Prior to S.B. 813, school districts could not suspend a teacher in California as a disciplinary measure. Teachers could be suspended pending charges leading to dismissal, but suspension per se was not available as a disciplinary action. As a practical matter, this left school districts with the impractical option of dismissal or simply placing a reprimand in the teacher's personnel file. The first option was too harsh, the second too lenient. So the good news was that S.B. 813 legalized suspensions as a disciplinary measure.

The bad news was this: S.B. 813 required that the procedure for suspending a teacher be the same as for dismissing one. This procedure required a hearing by a Commission on Professional Competence. One member of the commission is appointed by the teacher, one by the school district, and one member is a hearing officer appointed by the State Office of Administrative Procedure. The statutes prescribe very detailed procedures; the parties normally use legal counsel at the hearing. At the conclusion of the hearing, the commission issues a decision by majority vote, and "the decision of the Commission on Professional Competence shall be deemed to be the final decision of the governing board." Also—and get this—

> If the governing board orders that the employee not be dismissed, the governing board shall pay all expenses of the hearing, including the cost of hearing officer, and any costs incurred under subdivision (d) (2) above, and the reasonable expenses, as determined by the hearing officer, of the member selected by the governing board and the member selected by the employee, and the cost of the substitute or substitutes, if any, for the member selected by the governing board and the member selected by the employee, and reasonable attorney fees incurred by the employee.[2]

In other words, a California school district that desires to suspend a teacher for one day must first conduct a formal hearing on the issue before a three-member panel. If the school district does not prevail, it must pay the costs not only of its own representatives but of the impartial chairman and of the teacher-designated panel member, as well as reasonable attorney's fees for the teacher's counsel. Needless to say, this "reform" destroys realistic use of suspension in teacher personnel administration.

Does the example misrepresent the California or the national situation? It is impossible here to review California's reform legislation, let alone hundreds of state laws associated with the reform movement. Nevertheless, the realities of state education legislation suggest that there is little reason to be optimistic about it. Some legislators meet only once every two years. A larger number meet annually but for only a limited time. The range is from 70 days every two years in Wyoming to 300 a year in California; most of the states are near the low end.

Although education is a major state function, most state legislatures do not employ full-time specialists in education. It is not unusual for the staff of the finance committees to be the leading source of educational advice to legislators. Most of the staff who provide the educational expertise are not employed full time in the field of education.

In addition to staff deficiencies, the legislatures themselves find it difficult to devote much time to education. A recent study revealed that a majority of legislatures identified as educational leaders devoted less than 25 percent of their time to education. More than half of the leadership group did not expect to be in office more than two terms. Under circumstances such as these, it would obviously be difficult to sustain the momentum needed for basic reform. In this connection, other research confirms the slow pace of legislative innovations. It takes about ten years for 25 percent of the states to enact a legislative initiative, and 24 years are required on the average before 50 percent of the state legislatures have done so.[3]

The Governance of Higher Education

Some of the most important reforms needed to improve elementary and secondary education, such as improving programs of teacher education, are controlled by institutions of higher education. This fact alone is all but fatal to the prospects for reforms. To see why, it is necessary to consider the policymaking structure and process in higher education.

Public institutions of higher education are usually autonomous institutions or systems that operate under boards of trustees. Sometimes there is a board of trustees that is the governing body for an entire college or university system; sometimes each institution has its own board of trustees. Private institutions of higher education, which also play an important role on reform issues, are typically less subject to public control. Thus a board of trustees for a public college may raise the standards for admission to programs of teacher education. Private colleges, however, would still be free to march to their own drummer on this issue. If they perceive an excellent opportunity to gain students by not raising their standards, or even by lowering them, they are apt to do so.

In practice, most policy decisions in higher education are not made by the trustees. They are made by the faculty and administration, and ratified pro forma (if ratification is required) by the trustees. The decisions are not based upon what is good for our nation, or for education, or for students. They are usually based upon what is good for the institution or department initiating the recommendation. A college faculty that would be decimated if it adopted higher standards is not going to propose such standards. Nor is it going to accept them meekly if and when proposed by others. It is going to oppose them at every step of the way. Over 30 years ago, President Eisenhower's nominee for secretary of defense evoked widespread mirth on the nation's campuses by asserting that "what was good for General Motors was good for the country." Still, in the intervening years, I have yet to meet a professor who did not believe that what was good for his institution—nay, his department or even himself—was not also good for the country.

A Nation At Risk found that

> one-fifth of all 4-year public colleges in the United States must accept every high school graduate within the State regardless of program followed or grades, thereby serving notice to high school students that they can expect to attend college even if they do not follow a demanding course of study in high school or perform well.[4]

Agreed, this is deplorable. Who is going to change it? Not the institutions of higher education. They now have faculty, programs, housing, actually an entire subsystem geared to educating students who are unable or inadequately prepared benefit from higher education. These interests will oppose the change, and they will have some strong allies—such as football coaches who can fill stadiums and get lucrative television appearances because they can recruit players uninhibited by academic considerations.

These comments may seem unduly cynical, but they really understate the obstacles to reform resulting from the governance structure of higher education. Almost invariably, one or more academic interest groups stand to lose from a proposed reform. Neglect of this fact underlies much of the naive optimism about educational reform. For instance, in higher education higher standards are likely to result in fewer students, regardless of whether the higher standards apply to programs or individual courses. Fewer students mean fewer job opportunities, less job security, and smaller budgets. The dynamics of this process are similar at all levels of education. In higher education, however, the interests threatened by reform are more strategically situated to block it. The reason is that "faculty self government" is the accepted system of governance in higher education. For most intents and purposes, higher education is governed by faculty whose welfare interests are directly affected, potentially at least, by decisions about standards, programs, and courses. As long as this is the case—and I see no prospect of change for a long time to come—higher education will support educational reform only insofar as such reform serves professorial interests. Inasmuch as reform is usually adverse to such interests, it can be written off as a lost cause as far as higher education is concerned.

The State Role in School Finance

Among the reformers, there is widespread agreement that our nation must invest more in public education. For example, it has been estimated that the reforms proposed in *A Nation At Risk* would require an additional $13.5 billion over 1982-83 expenditures.[5] What level of government, if any, is going to pay for these reforms? We have seen that the federal government is unlikely to do so. Will state governments provide the substantial increases required, such as for making teacher salaries more competitive with other scientific and professional fields?

Clearly, some states are in a much better position than others to increase state funding. For example, the local/state/federal share of financial support varies enormously from state to state. In 1983-84, the proportion of funds from local government ranged from a low of 0.3 percent in Hawaii to a high of 88.8 percent in New Hampshire. State support varied from a low of 8.0 percent in New Hampshire to a high of 90.0 percent in Hawaii. And the federal share ranged from a low of 2.9 percent in Alaska to a high of 17.8 percent in Mississippi.[6]

Of course, other factors also affect the ability (and the willingness) of state governments to increase their levels of support. Overall, however, it would be unrealistic to expect a relatively higher level of state support for public education. As a rough estimate, the cost of elementary and secondary public education in 1984-85 was $138 billion. The federal government contributed about 6.2 percent, state governments 49.0 percent, and local governments 44.8 percent.[7] Let us assume that the federal share remains at 6.2 percent, an optimistic assumption. If state governments were to finance the reforms in *A Nation At Risk*, state funding for education would have to be increased by about 25 percent, not counting any increases required to stay abreast of inflation. If local sources were to provide the necessary funds, the local share would have to increase even more, again excluding any increases required to keep pace with inflation.

Even in states that have a budget surplus, such increases are simply out of the question. The states that enjoyed a budget surplus in early 1985 are states that were in financial difficulty a few years previously. These states raised their tax rates; the higher rates resulted in higher than expected revenues as a result of the strength of the economy. In at least some of these states, such as Ohio and New York, the state governments are providing increases in state aid, though nothing on the scale proposed by reformers. Tax reductions have a higher priority than any significant change in the level of state support for education.

Another critical factor is that federal aid to the states for other services is expected to decline substantially beginning in FY 1986. The Reagan administration is attempting to eliminate or reduce an imposing array of federal programs, such as revenue sharing, mass transit, and health services. In many cases, making up for the reduction or elimination will receive a higher priority than education from the state and local governments. A recent statement by New York City Mayor Edward I. Koch illustrates this point. Testifying on a new sentencing system for New York State, Mayor Koch stated: "The two top priorities for us are education and law enforcement. If I had to deal with only one, if I had to make a choice, it would be to punish the criminals."[8] Elsewhere, health services, mass transit, or some other public services will undoubtedly receive a higher priority than education in any competition for increased state or local funding.

In some states, it is doubtful whether the state governments would appropriate funds to make up for the anticipated loss of federal aid.

For instance, Mississippi received 17.8 percent of its total education revenues from the federal government in 1984-85. The reason for this high proportion is that almost 50 percent of federal aid is allocated to states on the basis of the number of low-income families. Thus, the same factor that generates the high level of federal support for Mississippi schools renders it practically impossible for Mississippi to replace federal funds from state sources.

The reality is this: In the abstract, there is widespread agreement that public education should have more money. In practice, however, our legislative bodies try to achieve this goal by persuading the other levels of government to provide the additional funds. The widespread legislative opinion in favor of increased spending for public education is really widespread opinion that some other level of government ought to provide the money.

LOCAL SCHOOL DISTRICTS

Historically, education emerged as a function of state governments. Each state government established school boards to carry out this function; at the present time, there are approximately 15,500 school boards in the United States. These boards vary from state to state, and often within a single state, in such important ways as:

1. Their power to raise money independently of approval by other government agencies and officials, and whether their budgets must be approved by another local government agency, such as a city council. School districts that do not have to submit their budgets to other local agencies are "independent" districts; districts that must do so are "dependent" districts. A 1982 Census study showed 14,847 independent and 1,537 dependent school districts, a proportion likely to continue indefinitely.
2. The grade levels covered; there are high school districts, elementary districts, unified (K-12) districts, and special districts (usually for special education or vocational education).
3. The budgetary and fiscal controls exercised by the state, usually by the state department of education. These controls often govern the budget-making process, investment of idle funds, bidding requirements and procedures, limits on the use of consultants, sales of school property, bonding requirements, and a host of other matters of this nature.

4. The nature and extent of state legislation on curriculum, personnel, construction, finance, health, safety, and other aspects of school operations.
5. The proportion of revenue coming from local, state, and/or federal sources.
6. The existence and nature of any collective bargaining legislation covering school district employees.
7. Whether the school board is legally a partisan or a nonpartisan office; the number of board members, requirements to be a board member, duration of term of office, and election schedule. These issues obviously affect citizen efforts to achieve reform.

In the folklore of education, the organization of public schools is supposed to foster local initiative and accountability. In practice, it actually fosters inertia and buck-passing. Suppose, for example, you are a parent actively seeking educational reform. You urge your school board to adopt a number of reforms that require additional funds. In a fairly common scenario, the school board says: "We agree with you, but our hands are tied. Our funds come from the city government and the state—and the amount needed to implement your suggestion is just not there." You go to the mayor, only to be told about the pressing need for more police officers, firefighters, and sanitation workers. The mayoral response is likely to be: "It's not our fault. Blame the legislature, which didn't increase state aid to education as it should have." Needless to say, state legislators have their own explanation of the situation: "We agree with you on the need for more state aid but our hands were tied. The governor said he would veto any tax increase, so we had to limit ourselves to what we already have." Of course, if and when you get to the governor, you learn that he was elected on a platform of no tax increases—and he intends to carry out this pledge.

This a relatively simple runaround; the deluxe models can take you from teacher to principal to superintendent to factions A and B on the school board to various political leaders and groups in city hall and the state legislature.

Controversies over which level of government should fund education have been widely publicized. These controversies, however, are only part of a much larger problem of educational accountability. Virtually all of the reform proposals emphasize the importance of upgrading the text materials used in public schools. This may appear to be a relatively easy reform to achieve, but the appearances would be deceiving, at least in this case.

First of all, textbook selection at the local level is usually regulated by the states. As Table 5.2 shows, complete local control over textbooks prevails in only 11 states. In view of the legal and administrative morass portrayed by Table 5.2, a "simple" change in textbooks may not be quite so simple. In some states, a local school district may never be unable to adopt the textbooks of its choice because the textbooks are never on the state-approved list. Elsewhere, local districts may have to wait three-six years before their preferred texts are approved by the state. In still other districts, school boards may prefer the textbooks provided by the state at no cost to the local district over better textbooks that must be purchased from local funds.

As formidable as they are, the mechanics of the adoption process may not be the sole or the major obstacle to improving instructional materials. When new textbooks are adopted, it may be necessary to conduct faculty orientation and training on their use. This is especially true in subjects like reading and mathematics, where the subject matter is sequentially arranged over several years of instruction. The districts may lack the funds or the instructional leadership required. The teachers, especially those nearing retirement or planning to move, may wish not to be bothered by the changes required. The upshot is that here, as elsewhere, inertia has a great deal going for it.

To the layman, education seems to be characterized by constant change. The overwhelming predominance of the status quo seems inconsistent with their experience. New courses, new programs, new textbooks, new methods—constantly launched from conferences, seminars, conventions, symposia, professional books and journals—emerge on a daily basis. The apparent inconsistency is easily resolved, however, by recognition of a critical fact. Teachers and administrators have a large stake in the appearance of progress. Frequently their stake in the appearance of it is much larger than their stake in its actual existence. For this reason inconsequential cosmetic changes are routinely treated as having important substantive ramifications. On this score, teachers and administrators probably delude themselves as much as they do the public. The gap between reform rhetoric and reality with respect to textbooks illustrates a pervasive weakness of the reform movement. Programmatically, it is firmly anchored in flights of rhetoric that ignore formidable obstacles to change. The very

Table 5.2 State Regulation of Textbooks

Extent of Local Authority	Number of States
Local board can choose, all subjects	11
Local board can choose in some but not all subjects	4
Local board must choose from state approved list, all courses	27
Local board must choose from state approved list, some courses	7
Local board can choose within state standards, all courses	3
Local board can choose within state standards, some but not all courses	6
State regulation of textbook contracts	21

Years Textbook is on State-Approved List before
Review of Continued Suitability

6 years	4
5 years	4
3-5 years	1
4 years	6
3 years	3

In addition, some states provide that:
  (a) Local districts may choose any textbook they wish but the state will pay only for textbooks on the state-approved list;
  (b) The price paid by the state may not be less than what is paid by any other state;
  (c) The copyright date may not exceed a stipulated number of years;
  (d) If there is insufficient funding for state-provided textbooks, elementary pupils are provided free textbooks before secondary pupils;
  (e) Local boards must provide free textbooks to indigent pupils but otherwise retain discretion over charges, if any.

Source: Lawyers Committee for Civil Rights Under Law, *State Legal Standards for the Provision of Public Education, An Overview* (Washington, D.C.: National Institute of Education, 1978), pp. 95-97.

fact that the reformers did not deal with these obstacles justifies the utmost skepticism toward their recommendations.

DECISIONMAKING IN PUBLIC AND ENTREPRENEURIAL SCHOOLS

Of all of the advantages of entrepreneurial schools, probably none is as pervasive as the superiority of its decisionmaking structure. Essentially, this superiority reflects the differences between decisionmaking in an economic instead of a political system. To appreciate these advantages, we need to free ourselves from the mythology of public education.

A major element of this mythology relates to local control of public education. Politicians and educators alike reflexively praise local control of public education. Such control is said to keep public education "close to the people." It is assumed that citizens and parents understand the needs and problems of "their" schools better than "outsiders," whether in state capitols or in the federal government. Accordingly, local control is deemed to be efficient and responsive.

The difficulty with this view is that it ignores the mass of state/federal regulation and restriction upon local school districts. The latter must comply with hundreds of state and federal statutes, bureaucratic rules, and judicial decisions. Such compliance undermines the theoretical advantages of local control of public education. Local school boards simply do not function as a decisionmaking body on scores of important issues; even when they do, the procedures and limitations associated with the decisions often impair the efficiency and responsiveness of the decisionmaking process.

In the normal course of events, economic decisions can be made more expeditiously than formal decisions by public agencies. Any policy adopted by a school board is a public policy and must meet certain legal requirements for enactment. These are likely to include notice to the public, a specified time prior to board meetings, statements of the agenda, opportunities for public comment, and so on. If there are conflicts in public opinion, the procedural requirements for arriving at a broad decision can be extremely time consuming; for example, it is common practice that new policies must be accorded a "first reading," meaning that they cannot be adopted until the next board meeting regardless of board unanimity on the policy.

In many important situations, entrepreneurial schools could act within hours on matters that might require several months or years in a school district—or even never be consummated. For example, consider textbook changes. It appears that students spend about 75 percent of their classroom time and 90 percent of homework time with textbooks. Understandably, changes in textbooks are the most important way the curriculum is changed in public education.[9] Public school parents and teachers may be precluded even from considering textbooks that are not on the state-approved list—and the books on the list may not come up again for review for years. The entrepreneurial school faces no such roadblocks. It can consider any textbook. It could adopt a textbook and order it the same day. This example applies to hundreds of decisions that must be made in operating a school, and points to a major advantage of entrepreneurial schools.

As the textbook example illustrates, the decisionmaking structure of entrepreneurial schools would be more cost-effective and more responsive. The restrictions upon school district action are only one dimension of the public school disadvantage. School districts must meet onerous reporting and regulatory requirements, such as those relating to school budgets and pupil attendance. A wide variety of enactments on matters directly improving upon classroom instruction also add to costs and/or decrease effectiveness. Class size may be limited arbitrarily. For example, a public school district may be prohibited from having more than 32 students in a primary class. When the 33rd pupil shows up, the district is legally required to establish another class. Suppose a group of migrant children or only one child over the statutory limit enrolls in the class. Do you split the 33 students for one-four weeks, then recombine them if someone transfers to another school or out of the district? Do you transfer students within the district? State mandates such as these are virtually certain to do more harm than good, since they do not allow consideration of factors that should influence decisions such as class size. In addition, to the extent that such statutes are based upon research—which is not very often—they cannot be modified easily in light of subsequent research. Even when the statutes allow requests for exemptions, they add to inefficiency. Sometimes the governing statutes, such as those on class size, are so unrealistic that exemptions are requested and approved routinely. Sometimes approval is not so routine. In either situation, the statutes increase inefficiency and decrease responsiveness.

As previously noted, the greater responsiveness of entrepreneurial schools would be reflected immediately in teacher incentives. Teachers would have an immediate and direct incentive to have a successful school. The relationship between school effectiveness and responsiveness on the one hand, and teacher welfare on the other, would be highly visible in entrepreneurial schools. In contrast, as we turn more and more to state aid instead of local support for public schools, teachers have less and less incentive to develop local support. After all, state aid is the same, regardless of how the local citizenry feels about its schools.

Paradoxically, the deficiencies of our educational system are the source of its major protection. An extremely small number of persons at any level, including the university, thoughtfully compare (or are exposed to thoughtful comparisons) of economic and political systems of decisionmaking. The possibilities of converting one to the other are not a systematic part of our educational system at any level. Most citizens, regardless of their formal education, do not adequately understand markets as decisionmaking processes. In view of the fact that education at all levels is currently dominated by a political approach to its problems, the absence of market alternatives is quite understandable. Anyone who undertakes a critical comparison of the diffuse, unaccountable, and nonresponsive system of educational decisionmaking with market alternatives would recognize the inherent superiority of the latter in this context. The problem is overcoming the cliché barrier. When citizens realize that the formal existence of local school boards has little or nothing to do with local control of education, they may be ready to consider alternatives that are outside the parameters of the current reform movement.

NOTES

1. See Myron Lieberman, *Identification and Evaluation of State Legal Constraints Upon Educational Productivity*, Final Report, Project 3-0231, National Institute of Education, U.S. Department of Health, Education and Welfare (1975); and Lawyers Committee for Civil Rights Under Law, *State Legal Standards for the Provision of Public Education: An Overview* (Washington, D.C.: National Institute of Education, 1978).

2. Sections 53-59, S.B. 813, approved by Governor George Deukmejian, July 28, 1983.

3. Susan Fuhrman and Alan Rosenthal, eds., *Legislative Education Leadership in the States* (Washington, D.C.: Institute for Educational Leadership, 1981).

4. National Commission on Excellence in Education, *A Nation At Risk: The Imperative for Educational Reform* (Washington, D.C.: U.S. Government Printing Office, 1983), p. 20.

5. American Association of School Administrators, *The Cost of Reform: Fiscal Implications of A Nation At Risk* (Arlington, Va.: AASA, 1983).

6. Research Division, NEA, *Estimates of School Statistics 1984-85* (Washington, D.C.: National Education Association, 1985), p. 38.

7. Ibid.

8. New York *Times*, February 15, 1985, p. 1. Statements by bipartisan committees of the National Governors Conference also assert that the states cannot make up the anticipated reductions in state aid for various state and local public services.

9. Paul Goldstein, *Changing the American Schoolbook* (Lexington, Mass.: D. C. Heath, 1978).

6

EDUCATION AND
SOCIAL ISSUES

In Chapter 1 we saw that educational achievement declined from the mid-1960s to the early 1980s, culminating in the educational reform movement of the early 1980s. For the most part, the reform movement has focused upon academic issues such as curriculum and standards of admission, promotion, and graduation.

Academic decline is certainly important and deserves to be considered carefully. Nevertheless, many citizens are equally if not more concerned about other dimensions of public education. How do public schools relate to teenage sexual attitudes and conduct? What sort of family life, if any, should schools foster, and what is their actual influence in this area? How do public schools relate to religious values, standards of dress and speech, patriotism, drugs, tobacco, alcohol, crime, respect for law and order—the list of nonacademic concerns is a long one. In what follows, I shall try to show both the wide range of these concerns and how strongly many citizens feel about them. We shall then be in a position to relate these concerns to the main argument of this book.

RELIGIOUS ISSUES IN PUBLIC EDUCATION

Historically, religious issues have generated the most dissatisfaction with public education. Beyond any doubt, public schools in many states were initially characterized by a strong anti-Catholic bias. As a matter of fact, the emergence of Catholic schools was partly due to the Protestant orientation of many public schools. Thus for many years, approximately 90 percent of nonpublic schools were denominational; of these, about 90 percent were Catholic schools.

As shown by Table 6.1, the proportion of nonpublic schools under denominational auspices is lower today, and the religious mix is not so heavily Catholic.

As Table 6.1 shows, private school enrollments increased from 1980 to 1983 despite a decrease in total enrollments.

In and of itself, the existence of denominational schools does not imply any criticism of public schools. If parents want their children educated in a particular religious environment, they are legally free to do so. Such parental decisions, however, should not be regarded as a legitimate criticism of public schools. On the other hand, many parents believe that public schools are undermining their religious beliefs, and the religious beliefs of their children, in an indefensible way. These parents do not expect public schools to indoctrinate sectarian religious views. They believe, however, that public schools should not undermine these views but are doing just that.

For example, some critics believe that public education is dominated by "secular humanism," which they regard as an antireligious philosophy based on the idea that "Man is the measure of all things."

Table 6.1 K-12 Public and Private School Enrollments, Fall 1980, 1983

	Total Enrollment (millions)	Public School Enrollment (millions)	Percent of Total	Private School Enrollment (millions)	Percent of Total
1980	46.2	40.9	88.5	5.3	11.5
1983	45.2	39.5	87.4	5.7	12.6

Private School Enrollments

	Catholic		Other Denominational		Nonsectarian	
	Millions	Percent	Millions	Percent	Millions	Percent
1980	3.4	64	1.1	19	.9	17
1983	3.2	56	1.4	24	1.2	20

Source: National Center for Educational Statistics, *The Condition of Education*, 1983 edition (Washington: U.S. Government Printing Office, 1983), pp. 16, 18; U.S. Department of Education News Release, December 13, 1984.

These critics attribute the decline of public education to the growing influence of secular humanism. The argument is that as an outgrowth of secular humanism, public schools have emphasized the social and psychological adjustment of pupils. This emphasis has allegedly replaced learning of basic skills as the leading priority in education.

To my knowledge, however, no public school has explicitly advocated "secular humanism." Instead, critics have applied the term to a variety of subjects and activities of which they disapprove. Most likely, the teachers accused of secular humanism do not know what it is and would be surprised to discover they are "secular humanists." In this respect, the teachers are no different from some leading political figures, including opponents of secular humanism. On June 6, 1984, the U.S. Senate approved legislation providing $75 million for magnet schools implementing desegregation plans. A section of the legislation under the heading "Prohibition" reads as follows: "Section 509: Grants under this title may not be used for consultants, for transportation, for any activity which does not augment academic improvement, or for courses of instruction the substance of which is secular humanism." The final vote in the Senate in favor of the legislation—which included Section 509—was 86 to 3.

Asked about the prohibition, Senator Patrick D. Moynihan of New York, the sponsor of the appropriation, responded: "I have no idea what secular humanism is. No one knows . . . I thought it was the price I had to pay to get school desegregation money." Even Utah Senator Orrin G. Hatch, who initiated Section 509, could not say what teachers were prohibited from teaching because of his amendment. The upshot was that "with no real guidance from Congress on the definition of secular humanism, the Department of Education last month proclaimed it to mean whatever local school authorities determined it to mean." Needless to say, this legislation was not passed on one of Congress's most outstanding days.[1]

However local school boards handle the issue, the legal definition of religion in the United States does not presuppose belief in a supernatural or supreme being. Since 1961, the U.S. Supreme Court has treated Buddhism, Taoism, Ethical Culture, and secular humanism itself as religions. For this reason, one thoughtful analysis of secular humanism treats it as a nontheistic religion.[2] As the definition of religion has expanded, however, impartiality between theistic religions is no longer an adequate defense against charges of religious indoctrination or of teaching a religion contrary to that of the parents. Indeed, religious neutrality in public education may no longer be possible under some interpretations of the Supreme Court's view of religious belief. As long as religious groups believe that whatever does not support their beliefs actually serves to undermine them, the public schools will face a growing but intractable dilemma on the issue of religious neutrality.

Critics of secular humanism are frequently concerned about what they perceive to be invasions of student privacy. Such invasions are regarded as a means to manipulate the values and attitudes of students. Virtually always, traditional moral and religious values are allegedly the target of the manipulators. One recent interview in a conservative journal asserts:

> Among techniques and practices that "openly beg psychological manipulation and invasion of student privacy" . . . are non-academic personality tests; questionnaires on personal life, views, and family; autobiography assignments pertaining to personalized moral and legal dilemmas; log books used as supplements in language arts and social studies, diaries, journals, compulsory K-through-12 life science curriculum, sociograms, group contact sessions and talk-ins, blindfold walks, isolation techniques, role playing, psychodrama, sociodrama, values clarification strategies, and life/death survival games.[3]

The controversy over evolution and creationism also illustrates concern about the impact of education upon traditional religious views. Many Protestant fundamentalists believe that public school teachers are teaching the theory of evolution in a way that undermines their religious beliefs. In some states the issue led to textbook revisions and legislation ensuring that "creationism" is taught, at least as an alternative theory to "evolution." The issue also emerges in controversies at the local level over various science courses.

Frequently, the alleged undermining of religious belief is based upon school policies or practices deemed indifferent or even hostile to religious faith. Controversies over Christmas carols, crèches, and Nativity scenes illustrate this point. Christian parents sometimes believe that public schools are unnecessarily restrictive in these areas. In their view, music, art, and literature having a religious theme are justified on educational grounds, as part of a cultural heritage. Exclusion of such music, art, or literature on religious grounds is perceived as hostility to religion, inasmuch as there is a secular basis for permitting its inclusion.

In any event, litigation over church-state relations has been increasing in recent years. The issues involved include the right of public bodies to portray Nativity scenes; the right of public schools to use religious music on an equal basis with secular music in its Christmas programs; whether public universities must provide the same access to university facilities for religious groups as they do for nonreligious organizations; whether public secondary school students enjoy the same rights to religious speech and access for religious organizations as are available for nonreligious speech and organizations; whether the establishment clause prohibits secondary students from student-sponsored and student-conducted prayer and Bible study on public school campuses during the regular school day; and whether the Internal Revenue Service could deny tax exemptions to universities that prohibit students from interracial dating.[4]

Controversies over prayer in public schools illustrate the fact that dissatisfaction over nonacademic issues often arouses citizens more than academic issues. Constitutional amendments to allow voluntary prayer in public schools were rejected in the U.S. Senate in March 1984. Opponents contended that the amendments were unnecessary and would have injected teachers and administrators into religious issues. When the constitutional amendments were defeated, their supporters immediately raised the issue during the 1984 elections—an outcome opponents often alleged to be the underlying purpose of the amendments in the first place. In any event, the issue has activated many groups on both sides and has evoked editorial comments in such influential publications as the *Wall Street Journal* and the New York *Times*.

The critical point here is not the merits of particular positions in these controversies. It is the existence of a broad, ongoing controversy over the relationship between public education and religious groups. Such controversy reflects a significant element of dissatisfaction, justified or not, over the role of public schools vis-a-vis religion. It thus also reflects a weakening of the prestige of public schools, and an erosion of support for it as a social institution.

Resort to litigation to force a public agency to act in a certain way usually reflects a breakdown in the legislative and political process. We do not ordinarily sue agencies regarded as supportive or friendly. On the face of it, citizens who believe that public schools unnecessarily "exclude God" are not likely to be supporters of public schools. With a president effectively articulating the view that "God should never have been expelled from our children's classrooms," the outlook is for increased pressure on the public schools to accommodate religious activities. Such pressures will lead to increased controversy over religious issues, and increased dissatisfaction with the public schools, no matter what they do about the issues.

CRIME AND SECURITY

In many schools, crime and violence have become a paramount consideration. Some idea of the dimensions of the problem are evident from a National Institute of Education study conducted from 1974 to 1977 at the request of Congress. Some of the major conclusions of the study were as follows:

1. *Every month*, 6,000 teachers were robbed, 125,000 were threatened with bodily harm, and 1,000 required medical care. In a 1983 report by the Departments of Justice and Education and the Office of Management and Budget, 60 percent of the teachers who were victims of an attack thought that their principals had not taken appropriate action.
2. In secondary schools alone, 282,000 students were physically attacked each month and about 7 percent of all junior high school students reported that they were assaulted within the month preceding the study; a slightly higher percent reported that they were robbed during this brief period of time.
3. It was estimated that 2.4 million thefts of personal property occurred each month in secondary schools.
4. At one time or another, approximately 20 percent of all students feared physical assault or harassment at school.
5. Most school crime was committed by students, not outsiders.
6. The cost of school property stolen or damaged every year was over $200 million. Twenty-five percent of all public schools experience vandalism every month.[5]

Interestingly enough, the NEA has estimated that 110,000 teachers were "physically attacked" by students in school in 1978-79. Notwithstanding the facts that the association did not define "physical attack" and that it had an obvious interest in having the problem presented in a way to stimulate action on it, the figure is extremely high.[6]

In a recent study of outstanding middle schools (grades 6-9), students indicated that their major concern was mistreatment by fellow students. Approximately 25 percent of the students in 50 middle schools deemed "top notch" by educators identified "bullies, vandals, [and] thieves" among their fellow students as their major concern.[7]

Whatever the national averages, data on particular school districts sometimes reveal an all but impossible educational environment. In December 1983 a Boston "Safe Schools Commission" reported that (1) half the teachers and almost 70 percent of the students were victims of crime in 1982-83; (2) 3 of every 10 students carried weapons to school at one time or another in the school year; and (3) almost 40 percent of the students "often felt afraid for their safety while at school or avoided such places as hallways and bathrooms at school."[8]

Undeniably, many school districts have adopted stringent security measures to maintain law and order within their schools: identification is required to enter the building, halls and toilets are constantly patrolled, lunchrooms and parking lots are heavily monitored, police cars are constantly in the vicinity to discourage troublemakers. Nevertheless, despite these and other measures the public appears to be convinced that school efforts along this line are inadequate. In 1969 the annual Gallup Poll on public attitudes showed that 39 percent of the public thought that schools were "too lax" in their discipline. By 1978 the proportion had increased to an astonishing 84 percent. In fact, every year since 1972, "lack of discipline" has been the problem confronting public schools cited most often by the public.[9]

One reason for the high level of public concern may be the ambivalence of public school authorities toward publicizing their crime and security problems. On the one hand, school officials want action to improve the situation. On the other hand, they are concerned about bad-mouthing public schools, which need all the support they can get. The result is that crime and security data tend to be interpreted according to which purpose is uppermost at the time. If there is a perceived danger of losing public support, then even the most negative data are interpreted in Pollyanna fashion.

DISCIPLINE AND AUTHORITY

Students who commit crimes are not doing just that and nothing else. They are also engaged in antisocial, educationally disruptive behavior. Insubordination, absenteeism, and denigration of teachers and school authorities are only a few elements of this larger pattern. Declining standards of dress and language also reflect declining school authority. Foul language in classrooms, punk hair styles, see-through blouses, shirt-tails out, and risqué T-shirts hardly reflect much respect for the institution that tolerates, or is forced to tolerate, them.[10]

The changing attitudes toward smoking illustrate the way schools have accepted conduct they formerly prohibited. Many schools that formerly suspended students for smoking now have smoking sections. In fact, if this were the only change for the worse, the vast majority of school authorities would be euphoric. The grim reality is that smoking among secondary school students goes far beyond the use of tobacco. In 1981 about one out of every ten high school students smoked marijuana every day; about 50 percent used it during the year. In grades 8-9, 29 percent of the students had smoked marijuana during the year; even in grades 6-7, 8 percent had done so.

Marijuana smokers vary widely in their use and in their ability to function despite their habit. It should be noted, however, that marijuana is widely available to young people, as it is in our society generally. Frequent use of marijuana appears to have negative effects on both academic skills, such as reading comprehension, and psychological factors, such as ego development and goal orientation. It should also be noted that frequent users of marijuana are also much more likely to use cocaine, amphetamines, heroin, and other drugs whose adverse effects are beyond dispute.

The decline in school authority among pupils is in part a reflection of the decline in the status of teachers. In an earlier era, standards of teacher conduct, speech, and dress were indefensibly rigid, but the rigidity reflected the conviction that teachers were important role models for pupils. Be that as it may, school authorities today have a difficult time requiring teachers to dress conservatively, refrain from smoking or using foul language in school, or otherwise conduct themselves as desirable role models, at least by conventional or conservative standards; paradoxically, however, the greater freedoms achieved by teachers are associated with a decline in their status. For example, the percentage of New York City parents who said they would be pleased if a child became a teacher declined from 75 in 1969 to 48 in 1980. As teachers decline in community respect and support, they are bound to have a more difficult time maintaining an appropriate educational environment.[11]

ALCOHOLISM

Alcoholism among youth does not receive as much publicity as drug abuse, but it is a major problem nevertheless. A 1978 study showed that over 20 percent of 10th-12th graders drank more than once a week (a "drink" being 12 ounces of beer, 4 ounces of wine, or

1 ounce of distilled spirits). Over 8 percent reported drinking three-four times a week, and almost 2 percent reported drinking every day. Whereas 51 percent of 10th-12th graders were either abstainers, infrequent drinkers, or "light" drinkers (once a week at most or three-four times in small amounts), 49 percent were moderate, moderate/heavy, or heavier drinkers. A substantial number of youth were moderate to heavy drinkers by age 15.[12]

The costs of excessive drinking among teenagers is staggering. To cite just one item, 5,000 fatalities annually result from teenage drunken driving—the largest cause of fatalities among teenagers. Of course, public schools do not encourage student use of alcoholic beverages. On the contrary, insofar as they deal with the issue, they undoubtedly encourage abstinence, at least prior to the age of majority. Thus the increase in student drinking is seen as a symptom of the decline in school authority, and hence school effectiveness.

FOUL LANGUAGE AND CENSORSHIP ISSUES

Many parents believe it is undesirable to expose students to foul or obscene language, or at least what they regard as such. That is, the objections are not necessarily religious or ideological. "We don't want our children to use foul language, and not exposing them to such language will help to achieve this goal." This is the argument.

Regardless of whether it has merit, the argument illustrates another dimension of parental concern. School libraries include many books and magazines objectionable to some parents on "good taste" grounds. To the extent that public schools make such books available to students, they risk criticism from parents who believe that their availability violates school responsibilities for encouraging good taste and proper language. In perhaps the most widely publicized recent case of its kind, the Island Trees (New York) Board of Education voted (1976) to remove the following books from the school library:

The Fixer, Bernard Malamud
Slaughterhouse Five, Kurt Vonnegut
The Naked Ape, Desmond Morris
Down These Mean Streets, Piri Thomas
Best Short Stories by Negro Authors, Langston Hughes, editor
Go Ask Alice, anonymous
A Hero Aint Nothin But A Sandwich, Alice Childress
Soul On Ice, Eldridge Cleaver
A Reader for Writers, Jerome Archer, editor

The removal was based upon several grounds, including the view that the books were not conducive to desired standards of expression. Subsequently, the community split over the issue, and legal action was initiated to keep the books in the school library. The issue eventually reached the U.S. Supreme Court, which divided 4 to 4 on whether the school board had the right to remove the books under the circumstances.[13]

To say the least, the public school position on these issues is frequently weak, politically as well as educationally. For example, teachers sometimes defend their use of obscenities as essential to establish rapport with students who use obscenities constantly. Similarly, teachers sometimes justify toleration of "Black English" as a distinct language or a cultural difference that should be tolerated if not encouraged. Efforts to teach pupils to use standard English are viewed as the wrongful imposition of "middle class values" on poor minorities. Needless to say, many black as well as white parents do not share or support this attitude.

Regarding censorship, public school personnel usually invoke "academic freedom" as their defense. In my view, this defense is justified in situations where the disputed reading assignment is essential to achieve the educational objectives. Generally speaking, however, a wide variety of instructional materials can be used to achieve an educational objective. In such cases, offensive materials should be avoided, as long as their avoidance does not encourage vigilantism or require a major expenditure of district time and resources.

SEX EDUCATION AND ABORTION

Controversies over sex education and abortion often have a religious origin, but they also involve public policy issues independently of religious considerations. For this reason, they are discussed separately from religious issues, even though they are frequently involved in the controversies over public education and religion.

A few statistics on these issues may help to demonstrate their importance. Leaving aside questions as to what is cause and what is effect, the following facts are illustrative:

1. There are about 29 million teenagers in the United States. About 12 million (7 million males and 5 million females) are sexually active.

2. Over 1.2 million female teenagers become pregnant every year. Over half of these pregnancies lead to live births.
3. About 30,000 females age 13-14 become pregnant every year.
4. Approximately 6 of every 10 teenage pregnancies end in live births; 3 in 10 are aborted, and 1 in 10 is terminated by miscarriage.
5. The consequences of teenage pregnancy upon the mothers are likely to be negative:
   a. Pregnancy is the most frequent cause of female dropouts from high school; four of five pregnant teens do not graduate from high school. Teen fathers are also less likely than others to complete high school.
   b. The rate of pregnancy complications, miscarriage, and even death is significantly higher for pregnant teenagers than for older women.
   c. The divorce rate for teen marriages is two to three times the rate for other marriages.
   d. Teen mothers are more likely to be unemployed and/or welfare dependent.
6. The children of teenage mothers have a much higher incidence of illness and of mental and physical retardation than children of older mothers.
7. The costs of teenage pregnancy are staggering. For a family unit with one dependent child, Aid to Families with Dependent Children (AFDC) is about $3,500. About $4.7 billion of direct and indirect AFDC payments goes to family units in which the mother had a child as a teen. Also, it has been estimated that the total costs of government services per child of a teenage mother is about $300,000.[14]

Paradoxically, the above data are cited by opponents as well as proponents of sex education to support their position. Many parents object to sex education (which is often included in courses with other titles, such as "health education," "family living," or "values clarification") for one or more of the following reasons:

• Premarital sexual intercourse in sex education courses is treated as an individual preference, without any social, moral, or ethical dimension. On the other hand, many parents believe that sexual attitudes should be established in a moral, ethical, and/or religious context. Treating premarital sexual intercourse as merely a student personal option, apart from such a context, is abhorrent to these parents.

- Public school curricula treat homosexuality and unisex marriage as acceptable life-styles.
- Sex education is not an appropriate school subject. On the contrary, education on sexual issues is a parental responsibility.
- Sexual issues should be taught in a religious context. Inasmuch as public school teachers cannot or should not teach from a denominational standpoint, public schools should avoid involvement in sex education.
- Although sexual abstinence is the only sure method of avoiding pregnancies, abstinence is not taken seriously as a meaningful option in sex education curricula. While abstinence receives only pro forma mention, sex education courses include explicit discussions and exhibits of contraceptive techniques and devices. This latter emphasis inevitably downgrades abstinence as an option.
- Sex education (by whatever title) is usually introduced and advocated as means of reducing the incidence of pregnancies, abortions, and births among teenage students. Nevertheless, there is no evidence that it is successful in this regard; if anything, it appears to be having the opposite effect.

Before considering these arguments directly, let us consider the closely related issue of abortion. Dissatisfaction with sex education courses is often based partly upon their treatment of abortion. For example, it is frequently presented to students as a last resort to avoid pregnancy. Obviously, any such teaching is anathema to opponents of abortion.

In recent years, abortion issues have affected federal aid to education as well as state and local legislation. A major controversy has arisen over the so-called squeal rule in student abortions. In many school districts, guidance counselors or teachers have been informing pregnant students where and how to secure abortions. Such information is typically given without notifying the parents of the pregnant students. School administrators and teachers defend nondisclosure on the grounds that students would not confide in teachers or counselors if the school personnel had to inform parents about the referral. It is also thought that disclosure to parents would be a violation of the professional-client relationship that should exist between teachers/

counselors and students. Essentially, the typical public school position is that requiring disclosure to parents would discourage students from seeking assistance, thus leading to more students giving birth to more unwanted babies.

On the other hand, parents frequently believe that school personnel have no business advising pupils about abortions without the consent of the parents. In their view, notification to parents is essential to the primacy of the family. Public school personnel who help students get an abortion without notifying the parents are viewed as trying to usurp the role of parents in this sensitive area. For school personnel to get involved in abortions without notifying such parents obviously weakens the latter's confidence in the schools.

Although the impact of parental notification cannot be determined precisely, such notification would undoubtedly deter many teenagers from using abortion services. According to Planned Parenthood, about 25 percent of the teenagers using "family planning services" would not do so if their parents were notified.[15] Although not all of these teenagers were using abortion services, probably most of them were.

Understandably, therefore, parental notification has been the subject of legislative controversy at the federal, state, and local levels. Supporters of parental notification have tried to cut off federal and state funds to school districts that do not notify parents when a pupil is informed about agencies or physicians providing prescription contraceptives or abortions. In contrast, public school administrator, teacher, and parent organizations have consistently opposed notification requirements. The issue was partially resolved in favor of notification by the regulations implementing the 1981 amendments to the Public Health Service Act. These amendments required the U.S. Secretary of Health and Human Services to establish regulations that "shall encourage family participation" in family planning projects authorized by Title X of the act. Pursuant to these amendments, Secretary Richard Schweiker promulgated regulations that required that:

a. a parent or guardian of an unemancipated minor be notified within ten days following the provision of prescription contraceptives to the minor by a Title X grantee;

b. state laws imposing parental notice and consent requirements be complied with by Title X grantees; and

    c. family income be considered in most cases when determining fees to
      be charged to unemancipated minors. (48 Fed. Reg. 3614 [1983].)

These regulations were challenged in federal court by Planned
Parenthood and other family planning agencies. When two federal
appellate courts held the regulations to be contrary to the congressional intent, the Reagan administration did not appeal the decision
to the U.S. Supreme Court.[16]

PUBLIC SCHOOLS AS INSTRUMENTS OF SOCIAL REFORM

At mid-century, the idea that public schools could be powerful
instruments of social reform was very popular in the teaching profession. More than a decade earlier, one of the nation's best known professors of education had written a book entitled *Dare the Schools
Build a New Social Order?*[17] Needless to say, the author answered his
question in the affirmative. So did a host of others, in and out of
prestigious institutions and organizations all over the nation. Indeed,
a group of educational philosophers calling themselves "social recon-
structionists" latched on to this idea and urged the public schools to
banish racial discrimination, poverty, war, and a host of other negatives associated with human existence.[18] This was indeed heady stuff;
education was a more exciting and more significant enterprise because
it could lead the way.

The notion of using public schools as instruments of social reform
peaked in the 1960s. Its apogee was the educational legislation in
President Lyndon B. Johnson's Great Society. Once they received an
equal and presumably better education, black citizens would eliminate
the earnings gap between whites and blacks. Racial segregation and
discrimination would gradually disappear as the ripple effects of better
education spread throughout our society. Likewise, a host of other
social problems were expected to disappear as the result of a benefi-
cient system of public education.

Today, the futility of such an optimistic outlook is manifest;
everyone realizes that schools are not going to usher in Utopia. Nevertheless, the idea that schools can contribute to the resolution of specific social problems is far from dead. Some citizens believe that public
schools not only can but do make such contributions. Others, often
with the same problems in mind, believe that public schools are creating or adding to the problems involved.

Regardless of whether schools are perceived as responsible for a problem, their efforts to remedy them may lead to widespread criticism of public education. For example, few citizens hold schools responsible for drunk driving among teenagers. On the other hand, school efforts to reduce the incidence of drunk driving among teenagers seems to be ineffectual. Such ineffectiveness may result in criticism, just as a failure to make any effort along this line would do.

Of course, citizens often lack information, or are guided by misinformation, on either the social problem or school involvement or both. Nevertheless, public opinion, even when it is in error, can be a political fact of enormous significance. Criticism of public schools for failure to solve problems they did not create, and cannot be expected to influence, may be unfair, but the criticism may nevertheless become the basis for changes of one sort or another. Indeed, for present purposes, the existence of the criticism, not its validity, is often the more important fact. This is why I have not tried to assess some criticisms of public education that may well be unjustified.

On the other hand, we should not overlook the possibility that even good-faith efforts to remedy a problem may actually exacerbate the problem.

To illustrate, if you teach someone to drive, you run the risk of being associated with the accidents that befall your student. As a matter of fact, this is precisely the situation with respect to driver education. All over the nation, school districts offer this course in the belief that it leads to safer driving; students who take driver education have a lower accident rate than drivers who do not. Although teachers of driver education accept this evidence as Holy Writ, some critics are not impressed by it. A few even allege that driver education actually increases the incidence of accidents among teenagers. The reason is that as a result of the availability of driver education courses, students begin to drive sooner (and, therefore, experience accidents sooner) than they otherwise would. Ergo, driver education courses are (or may be) contributing to the very outcome they seek to avoid.

Of course, each effort to solve a social problem through the public schools must be judged on its own merits. Because the effort to solve one problem fails, we cannot assume that efforts to solve others will also fail. In terms of rationale and feasibility, each school program must be evaluated in terms of its own specifics. Nevertheless, a closer look at one such program may provide some clues to the effectiveness of others that are intended to guide student conduct away from school or after leaving school. Accordingly, a modest critique of sex education concludes this discussion of the influence of public schools on non-academic conduct and attitudes.

SEX EDUCATION: THE PROBLEM OR THE SOLUTION?

An analysis of sex education controversies illustrates several fundamental points about public education. First, it illustrates the futility of most controversies between "liberals" and "conservatives" on educational issues. Second, it underscores the paralysis that characterizes the governance structure of U.S. education generally. In addition, these controversies illustrate the fact that self-preservation, not "educational statesmanship" or "educational leadership," dominates the actual course of events on educational issues.

Let us begin with a point of agreement. Both proponents and opponents of sex education agree that the teenage birthrate in the United States constitutes a social disaster. The negative consequences of such pregnancies upon both the teenage mothers as well as the children themselves are beyond dispute; furthermore, it can hardly be desirable to have a substantial number of fathers without any significant legal or social responsibility for the children they have fathered.

The harmful consequences notwithstanding, a recent study revealed that the teenage birthrate in the United States is much higher than in England (including Wales), France, Canada, Sweden, and the Netherlands—all countries similar to the United States in economic development, general cultural background, and level of teenage sexual activity. As a matter of fact, the rate of teenage pregnancies and abortions, as well as the teenage birthrate, is much higher in the United States than in these six countries, all of which regard teenage childbearing as undesirable. It should also be emphasized that although the rates for black teenagers in the United States are higher than for white teenagers, the latter have a much higher rate of pregnancies, abortions, and births than do teenagers in any of these six other countries. Even more striking, although the U.S. rates are higher at every age level, they are especially high among the younger teenagers. For example, the U.S. birthrate for girls aged 14 is more than five per 1,000 girls; this is about four times the rate in Canada, the only other country with at least one birth per 1,000 girls aged 14.[19]

Theoretically, most public schools could follow one of the following policies: encourage chastity until the parties are able to accept the responsibilities of parenthood; offer sex education; avoid sex education altogether; or in schools of sufficient size, offer parents and/or students all three options.

The proponents of sex education are concerned about teenage venereal disease as well as teenage pregnancies, abortions, and birthrates. They are also very concerned about the widespread ignorance of young people about sex, including ignorance about the availability and effectiveness of contraceptive measures. In general, proponents believe that advocating abstinence would be futile or would have no effect upon a large proportion of teenagers. Consequently, they view sex education as a means of fostering "responsible decisionmaking" by teenagers in sexual matters. As part of the process, they deem it essential to discuss contraception. For such discussions to be effective, however, teachers must avoid moralizing about teenage sexual activity. Instead, they should discuss the subject in a nonjudgmental manner, in order to encourage pupils to participate in the program.

As we have seen, the opponents of sex education cite a variety of reasons for their opposition. Before assessing these reasons, let us first clarify the goals to be achieved through sex education. One possible goal is to reduce the level of teenage sexual activity. Another possibility is a reduction in pregnancies, abortions, and/or the teenage birthrate. Ostensibly, these goals do not necessarily conflict, since reducing the level of teenage sexual activity is virtually certain to reduce the teenage pregnancies, and hence teenage abortions and birthrates as well. Nevertheless, the goals do conflict, and the conflict lies at the heart of many disputes over sex education.

To understand why the goals conflict, it will be helpful to cite some data from the AGI study. One of its most critical conclusions is that other countries with substantially similar levels of teenage sexual activity are characterized by substantial differences in teenage pregnancies, abortions, and births. Inasmuch as differences relating to abortions and births are highly correlated with differences in the pregnancy rate, the latter appears to raise the critical question: Why are there substantial differences in teenage pregnancy rates between countries with similar levels of teenage sexual activity?

Although more than one factor is involved, the main reason appears to be that the countries with the lower pregnancy rates have the more comprehensive programs (not necessarily sex education in secondary schools) for teenagers in the use of contraceptives. This fact underscores the importance of defining the goals of sex education. If reducing the level of teenage sexual activity is the goal, the schools should foster abstinence. If, however, school efforts to foster abstinence are ineffective, but that is the main thrust of the sex education program, the latter will also be ineffective in reducing the level of teenage sexual activity. It would hardly be feasible to include education about contraception in a program intended to encourage abstinence; such an inclusion would only weaken the credibility of the effort to foster abstinence.

On the other hand, if schools assume that a considerable amount of teenage sexual activity is inevitable, efforts to educate teenagers about contraception, albeit with parental consent and as part of a broader program intended to foster "responsible decisionmaking," might lower the incidence of teenage pregnancies.

What is the likelihood that schools will try to encourage abstinence among teenagers until they are prepared to accept the responsibilities of parenthood? The chances that more than a handful of public school districts will make such an effort are remote. Regardless, those that make such an effort are virtually certain to be unsuccessful. Even if they are successful with some teenagers, they are likely to be ineffective with a much larger proportion of them. The public schools cannot be expected to overcome the influence of television, film, and advertising, three powerful media that are conducive to teenage sexual activity. In addition, neither the teachers nor the materials for such an effort are in place, or even in sight. Significantly, in the other countries mentioned that also seek to minimize teenage pregnancies, there is no explicit public policy of discouraging teenage sexual activity. Instead, a certain level of such activity is taken for granted; programs of sex education, in and out of school, aim at effective contraception, not the encouragement of abstinence. On this issue, therefore, the proponents of sex education have the stronger argument.

As might be expected, the instructional materials widely used in sex education courses adopt a nonjudgmental point of view. For example, the introduction to one text intended for use in grades 7-12 states:

> We have included questions and concerns about which there are no right answers, only opinions. We have written activities that encourage you and your classmates to share your opinions with each other. Whenever you do this, it is important to respect opinions of others, even if you disagree.
>
> We believe that each person has the right to think, feel, and act as he or she wishes while respecting the rights of others. Thus, we have tried not to tell you how to think, feel, and act. Some of you may be disappointed that we have not told you what decisions to make about your

sexual behavior. This we cannot do. These decisions are yours, although you will probably be influenced by your family and your friends.[20]

Modern Sex Education is another major text used in health classes.[21] In it, abstinence is discussed as a method of birth control; the text, however, devotes only four and one-half lines to abstinence but four and one-half pages to contraception. Likewise, family planning emphasizes the prevention of pregnancy, and abortion is presented simply as a contraceptive technique. Needless to say, many parents and taxpayers object to such a limited view of abortion.

On the other hand, if sex education is to be made available, school authorities should face up to the evidence concerning its effectiveness. Such evidence supports the view that only clinical programs of sex education have any effectiveness in changing adolescent sexual conduct. Indeed, a recent five-year comprehensive study of this issue concludes that nonclinical programs have no impact on the sexual behavior of adolescents.[22]

In fact, it is readily understandable how courses in sex education may lead to the very consequences they are intended to avoid. Although sex education courses may lead to greater use of contraceptives by teenagers, the courses also tend to increase teenage sexual activity. Teenagers previously inactive may become active, thinking that sexual intercourse is "safe" because of the contraceptives. Those already active tend to increase their level of activity, for the same reason. In practice, however, teenagers are frequently ineffective users of contraceptives, because of their immaturity, tendency to accommodate the impulse for immediate gratification, and noninvolvement in a permanent relationship with their sexual partners. Thus it is entirely possible, as critics contend, that sex education courses are actually counterproductive, in terms of their effects upon unwanted pregnancies.

Supporters of sex education contend that bad as the situation is, it would be worse if it were not for school programs in sex education. One problem with this argument is that the effectiveness of the programs is assured no matter what happens outside of school. If teenage pregnancies decrease, supporters of sex education take credit for this development. If pregnancies increase, the supporters contend: "Not as much as if our program did not exist." One can concede the possibility that the argument is valid, but it is not persuasive educationally or politically. Insofar as public schools continue to teach subjects that are so vulnerable politically, they are courting adverse public reaction when the public, rightly or wrongly, deems the subjects to be ineffective in achieving their stated purpose.

The emphasis upon personal decisionmaking in sex education courses seems naive, in view of the dynamics of teenage sexual liaisons. Such liaisons are often spur-of-the-moment decisions. Spontaneous or not, however, a teenage decision to be sexually active is not responsible unless the teenager is fully prepared to avoid conception. This point has far-reaching implications for programs of sex education. Preparing teenagers to avoid conception requires clinical programs as well as conventional lectures or discussions. That is, instead of merely discussing sexual issues and options, effective programs (in terms of reducing unwanted pregnancies) actually train students in the use of contraceptive devices and techniques. Sex education programs that do not provide this clinical level of instruction simply do not affect adolescent sexual conduct.

Recognition of this reality would lead to a moment of truth for both proponents and opponents of sex education. Some proponents might flinch at the prospect of public schools providing such training. At the same time, opponents of sex education would lose one of their strongest arguments against it, to wit, that sex education is ineffective at best and counterproductive at worst. Many opponents of sex education would have a difficult problem choosing between sex education programs that clearly reduce teenage pregnancies or no program at all.

The reality is that we could probably raise the level of educational achievement more by raising the age level of mothers than by compensatory education—and raising teacher salaries substantially. Granted, such an emphasis wouldn't help children already born, but the remedial programs aren't helping them very much either.

At any rate, the research on the relationship between the age of mothers and the subsequent well-being of their children raises some serious questions about the notion of "responsible decisionmaking." Should teachers encourage teenagers to make a decision without any moral or public policy implications: "Whether you have sexual intercourse and run the risk of a pregnancy that will be undesirable for you, your child, and our society as a whole is merely a personal decision"? Or should teachers let students know in no uncertain terms that although teachers cannot control or monitor what students do in this regard, the latter have no moral right to risk adding to the number of disadvantaged/handicapped and/or retarded children, merely to indulge in personal gratification? Or should teachers avoid the issue altogether?

Whatever the right answer, perhaps the most basic weakness of most sex education programs is their assumption that teenagers view pregnancy, contraception, and abortion as deliberate decisions within the control of the teenagers themselves. Of course, the assumption is realistic as applied to some teenagers. With many, however, it is not. Many teenagers feel that they exercise little control over their future. They have very limited time horizons, and do not understand or appreciate the relationship between present conduct and future well-being. They regard even unwanted pregnancy as inevitable and do not view contraception as an option. Discussion of responsible decision-making in this context is frequently irrelevant. Teenagers who do not perceive themselves as having a choice or making a decision are not likely to be influenced by appeals to make the decision responsibly. Proponents of sex education may contend that it is intended to change this fatalistic outlook, but classroom approaches to it have failed to achieve this result.

Arguably, the facts justify educational policies that encourage abstinence, not "responsible decisionmaking." Even if the issue should be presented as a matter for individual decision, programs of sex education fail to emphasize the adverse personal and social consequences of teenage sexual activity. On this issue, as on so many others, the critics of public education probably have a better case than they know. When choices have to be made and priorities set, as is always the case, school courses intended to develop "responsible decisionmaking" are marginal at best. Significantly, liquor manufacturers and tobacco companies emphasize "responsible decisionmaking" as the answer to the problems of teenage alcohol and tobacco abuse. What they fear, of course, are effective measures, such as legislation or regulation, that would limit their freedom to sell to the teenage market.

For similar reasons, most school administrators, even those who support sex education, are not going to carry "responsible decisionmaking" to its logical educational conclusion. From their standpoint, sex education of any kind is a constant threat to their job security. To most school superintendents, proposing the introduction of clinical programs, even as a parent option, would be tantamount to a kamikaze mission. Most are unaware of the probability that clinical programs could reduce the teenage birthrate, but even those who are cannot be expected to raise the issue. Job security is a paramount consideration among school administrators; typically, the status quo reflects a political balance that is better left undisturbed from this standpoint.

In this connection, it should be noted that any effort to introduce clinical programs involves not just one but a series of problems: Persuading the school and the community to adopt a program, finding the appropriate physical facilities, employing a competent staff, purchasing appropriate supplies and equipment, and so on. Inertia alone would often be sufficient to preclude such action. Even where it is not, most superintendents would not regard the introduction of clinical programs as an act of educational statesmanship. From their point of view, it would be more like shooting themselves in the foot.

Given the very real dangers the subjects pose for school administrators who would have to provide the leadership, it is unlikely that schools will confront the underlying issues. As serious as the problem is, avoidance will continue to be the typical public school reaction to it. By "avoidance," I mean avoidance of the underlying issues, not avoidance of sex education per se. In the absence of improved medical approaches to the problem, we can expect a continuation of it, at least until its staggering costs force an agonizing reappraisal of the issues. Such reappraisal might well lead to the conclusion that whatever the solution, if any, public schools will not play a significant role therein.

In many respects, the reasons why sex education in the United States has been ineffective apply to other school efforts to solve social problems. Teachers can observe, monitor, control, assess, and reward academic performance. They can foster responsibility by insisting upon it in areas they control: school attendance, timely completion of schoolwork, cooperation in keeping schools clean and attractive, avoidance of disruptions, and insistence upon respect for the rights of others in the day-to-day school routines. With sex education, however, the schools are attempting to influence how students will conduct themselves away from school, in bedrooms, on living room couches, in backseats of cars, whatever. Teachers are not present to observe or monitor such activities and to use instant feedback as performance unfolds. Also, they do not control the reward and punishment system associated with out-of-school conduct. In addition, they are seeking to guide behavior heavily influenced by the mass media, by peer groups, and by a host of unpredictable and fortuitous factors that arise constantly. Under these circumstances, it is not surprising that school efforts to guide sexual conduct have failed dismally, as have similar school efforts to solve social problems.

Examples abound:

1. Schools teach the harmful consequences of smoking. If, however, our objective is to reduce smoking by school-age pupils, we need to limit tobacco advertising, make it more difficult for pupils to buy or possess cigarettes, tax cigarettes more heavily, and/or penalize businesses that sell cigarettes to young people.
2. Schools try to teach children to be more effective consumers by courses in consumer education. The impact of these courses, especially in light of the enormous advertising campaigns that affect students when they actually purchase goods and services, is marginal at best. As with sex education, it is impossible to justify such courses on the grounds that they lead to "responsible decision-making."
3. Schools teach the dangers of drunk driving, but the need is to raise the age limit for legal drinking, prosecute sellers of liquor to minors more vigorously, and make it more difficult to get and keep a driver's license. The incidence of problem drinkers among school-age children and of automobile accidents and fatalities caused by drunk school-age drivers has clearly increased despite courses in driver education and alcohol education; the reasons for their ineffectiveness are similar to the reasons why courses in sex education are ineffective.

Finally, school efforts to ameliorate social problems have overwhelmingly failed to overcome one other pervasive objection. The case for school involvement must demonstrate more than some improvement in the situation. To be feasible, the case must show, or anticipate, cost effective improvements.

For instance, let us suppose that students who enrolled in courses in driver education experienced fewer accidents than other students; that students who enrolled in sex education courses experienced fewer pregnancies and abortions than others; and that students who enrolled in alcohol education were less often problem drinkers than other students. Let us even make two additional assumptions, in order to present the strongest possible case for these courses. We shall assume that the outcomes are not affected by differences between the students who enrolled in these courses and those who did not; and that the outcomes supportive of school efforts were actually due to those efforts. For example, we shall assume that students who enroll in driver education courses drive more safely than other students as a result of the courses.

In the vast majority of cases, we do not have evidence that would support these assumptions. Even if we did, however, it would leave unanswered a critical threshold question: How much improvement is needed to justify how much school expenditure to achieve it? If valid comparisons show that the accident rate among students who have taken driver education courses is 20 percent, and among others it is 21 percent, is the 1 percent difference sufficient to justify the recruitment of teachers, the costs of teacher salaries and benefits, the costs of instructional materials, and so on? What if the same dollars spent in other ways could reduce teenage accidents by 10 instead of 1 percent? Unfortunately, school authorities rarely raise, let alone answer, the question of how much improvement is achieved for how much in school costs. It is difficult to avoid the conclusion that raising such questions would be damaging to the programs involved; otherwise we would be flooded with studies showing that formal instruction is a cost-effective way to achieve social goals. Clearly, the absence of such studies is not due to any lack of resources to conduct them.

One last observation. The public school community frequently falls back on the argument that schools must provide certain services because no other organization will meet the need. This argument is rarely persuasive. Consider Figure 6.1, an advertisement from a high school student newspaper in my own community. Let us ignore the issue of whether the advertisement is appropriate in a high school paper read by hundreds of 13- and 14-year-old students. Regardless, the advertisement illustrates the availability of nonschool resources for sex education. Similarly, the private sector can meet our driver training needs and students would probably be better off with a subscription to Consumer Reports than a course in consumer education. Wherever one looks, the educational landscape reveals a mindless commitment of public school resources to the solution of social problems that are beyond their influence. In the long run, the waste of resources, substantial as it is, may be less important than the loss of respect for public schools engendered by such misguided efforts.

SOCIAL ISSUES AND ENTREPRENEURIAL SCHOOLS

Dissatisfaction over social issues will be important to entrepreneurial schools in at least two ways. First, such dissatisfaction obviously helps to generate a market for entrepreneurial schools. Second,

Figure 6.1 Advertisement in *Knight's Herald*, Downey High School, Modesto, California, January 22, 1982

entrepreneurial schools will have enormous advantages over public schools in meeting parent demands in this area. Quite possibly, their superiority in nonacademic areas will encourage their development more than any other factor.

It hardly needs to be argued that dissatisfaction over social issues will increase the market for entrepreneurial schools. Although we can only speculate on the issues, my guess is that it may be very large indeed.

First of all, many parents unhappy about the nonacademic role of public schools do not have a viable alternative to them at the present time. To repeat, almost two-thirds of private school enrollments are in denominational schools. On the other hand, about half the U.S. adult population regards itself as nondenominational. Parents dissatisfied with their public school may be unwilling to send their children to a denominational school, or one of a different persuasion, even if the latter has a more satisfactory approach to social issues. Actually, about 11.1 percent of the students in Catholic schools in 1983-84 were non-Catholic.[23] Undoubtedly, in some cases these students enroll in spite of, not because of, the Catholic auspices of the school. A private school that fulfilled parental wishes concerning discipline, homework, dress, language, and manners but without the denominational dimension would be even more attractive to at least some parents.

What about the effectiveness of entrepreneurial schools in demanding and inculcating desirable attitudes and habits concerning dress, punctuality, language, civility, avoidance of drugs, and other nonacademic dimensions of development? On this issue, entrepreneurial schools would have one overriding advantage over public schools. The latter are severely restrained by state and federal constitutions, statutes, and judicial decisions when they act in these areas. Frequently, they are unable to act effectively because of these restraints. A private school can insist upon the right to search student lockers simply without notice or reasonable grounds for expecting to find illegal drugs. The private school can take such action merely as a deterrent, so long as it informs parents and students that acceptance of such searches is a condition of enrollment in the school. Public schools cannot legally adopt such a posture; as state agencies, they cannot conduct searches merely to deter illegal possession of drugs. In many states, insistence upon dress codes and avoidance of foul language is legally risky in public education. A child advocacy or a civil rights organization may challenge the action as discriminatory or unreasonable or lacking a rational relationship to education. Again, private schools can legally insist upon whatever standards they wish and can get parents to accept.

NOTES

1. New York *Times*, February 22, 1985, p. 12. Congress repealed the ban against secular humanism without debate in October 1985.

2. Elmer J. Thiessen, "Religious Freedom and Educational Pluralism," in *Family Choice in Schooling*, ed. Michael E. Manley-Casimir. (Lexington, Mass.: Lexington Books, 1982), pp. 57-69.

3. "Parents Decry Mind-Bending Courses," *Human Events*, April 14, 1984, p. 6. See also Onalee McGraw, *Secular Humanism and the Schools* (Washington, D.C.: Heritage Foundation, 1976); Phyllis Schafly, ed. *Child Abuse in the Classroom* (Alton, Ill.: Pere Marquette Press, 1984).

4. See *Lynch* v. *Donnelly*, 79 L.Ed.2d 604 (1984); *Florey* v. *Sioux Falls School District*, 49-5, 619 P.2d 4311 (9th Cir., cert. denied, 449 U.S. 987 (1980); *Widmar* v. *Vincent*, 454 U.S. 263 (1981); *Lubbock Civil Liberties Union* v. *Lubbock Independent School District*, 669 F.2d 1038 (5th Cir.), rehearing denied, 680 F.2d 424 (July 16, 1982), cert. denied, 103 S. Ct. 800 (1983): *Bender* v. *Williamsport Area High School*, 563 F. Supp. 697 (M.D. Pa. 1983), May 12, 1983; *Bob Jones University* v. *U.S.*, 76 L. Ed.2d 157 (1983).

5. *Violent Schools—Safe Schools*: *Safe School Study Report to Congress* (Washington, D.C.: National Institute of Education, 1978). See also National Opinion Research Center, *Discipline, Order and Student Behavior in American High Schools* (Washington, D.C.: National Center for Education Statistics, 1981).

6. NEA Research, *Nationwide Teacher Opinion Poll* (Washington, D.C.: National Education Association, 1979), pp. 17-18.

7. James Keefe, Donald C. Clark, Neal C. Nickerson, Jr., and Jerry Valentine, *The Middle Level Principalship, Vol. II* (Reston, Va.: National Association of Secondary School Principals, 1984).

8. New York *Times*, December 4, 1984, p. 86.

9. Stanley M. Elam, *A Decade of Gallup Polls of Attitudes Toward Education, 1969-1978*, (Bloomington, Ind.: Phi Delta Kappa, 1978), and subsequent September issues of the *Phi Delta Kappan*.

10. An excellent discussion of the declining authority of public schools, and its practical effects, can be found in Paul Copperman, *The Literacy Hoax* (New York: William Morrow, 1978), especially pp. 145-81.

11. Gerald Grant, "The Teacher's Predicament," *Teachers College Record*, Spring 1983, pp. 593-609.

12. Secretary of Health and Human Services, *Fourth Special Report to the U.S. Congress on Alcohol and Health* (Washington, D.C.: U.S. Government Printing Office, January 1981), p. 32.

13. *Pico* v. *Island Trees Board of Education*, 457 U.S. 853 (1982).

14. Data are from flyers published by Planned Parenthood of San Francisco.

15. *Fact Sheet, Teens and Family Planning* (San Francisco: Planned Parenthood, Alameda/San Francisco, January 1983).

16. *Planned Parenthood Federation of America* v. *Heckler*, 712 F.2d 650 (D.C. Cir. 1983); *New York* v. *Heckler*, 719 F.2d 1191 (2d Cir. 1983).

17. George S. Counts, *Dare the Schools Build a New Social Order?* (New York: John Day Company, 1932).

18. See the books by Theodore Brameld, such as *Toward a Reconstructive Philosophy of Education* (New York: Dryden Press, 1956).

19. Elise Jones et al., "Teenage Pregnancy in Developed Countries: Determinant and Policy Implications," in *Family Planning Perspectives*, March/April 1985, pp. 53-63. Inasmuch as the study was sponsored by the Alan Guttmacher Institute, it is referred to hereinafter as "the AGI study."

20. Peter Kelman and Burt Saxon, *Modern Human Sexuality* (Boston: Houghton Mifflin, 1976), p. v.

21. Cloyd J. Julian, Elizabeth N. Jackson, and Nancy S. Simon, *Modern Sex Education* (New York: Holt, Rinehart, Winston, 1980).

22. Douglas Kirby, *Sexuality Education: An Evaluation of Programs and Their Effects* (Santa Cruz, Calif.: Network Publications, 1984).

23. Estimate provided by Research Department, National Catholic Education Association, August 22, 1985.

7

THE LEADERSHIP GAP

INTRODUCTION

The most depressing fact about our educational situation is the leadership failure that it reflects. Educational and political leaders at every level of education and of government are dominated by conventional hortatory approaches to reform. These approaches have failed in the past and will fail in the future.

At the school level, most public school teachers and administrators do not regard their own actions and policies as a cause of decline. Instead, educational decline is attributed to social changes that are having a negative effect upon educational achievement and student conduct. Some examples are:

- The tremendous increase in single-parent families, and the consequent decline in parental supervision of school-age children. Parental support for school tasks is also believed to have declined as a result of the increase in single-parent families.
- The erosion of the authority of teachers and school administrators as the result of judicial decisions and greater state and federal regulation.
- The migratory, transitory status of large numbers of children, especially in large urban centers and areas employing large numbers of migrant farm workers. In some school districts, it is not unusual for classes to experience a complete turnover of pupils during a single school year.

• Social and community pressures that have forced public schools to accept a variety of noneducational functions. Even when the costs are defrayed by state and/or federal agencies, the activities tend to weaken the educational focus of the public schools.

To illustrate, consider the school response to children who come to school without breakfast. Not surprisingly, such children are unable to concentrate upon their schoolwork. Consequently, school districts began to provide breakfasts in order to carry out their educational mission. Over time, and with considerable help from agricultural and dairy interests eager to dispose of their surpluses, the schools became large-scale feeders of the young. Today, in many schools, their role goes beyond merely eliminating the lack of food as an obstacle to school performance. Instead, the school system is being used to solve the broader problem of malnutrition among young people. Regardless of how one views the situation, however, it points to an obstacle to educational achievement that schools did not create but are struggling to overcome.

Change in the School Population

Another line of defense relates to changes in the school population, especially at the secondary level. The United States enrolls a much larger proportion of its youth in school, especially secondary schools and colleges, than any other nation in the world. In 1975, 86 percent of our population between the ages of 5 and 19 was enrolled in school; less than two-thirds of this age group in Europe and the Soviet Union were so enrolled.

About 75 percent of our total adolescent population remains in school through the final year of secondary school. The only nations that come close are Japan (70 percent), and Russia and Sweden (at least 65 percent each). Finally, we send about half of our high school graduates on to college. No other nation comes close to this figure; in the Soviet Union, only one in ten secondary school graduates enters an institution of higher learning.[1]

In the early 1900s the high school curriculum in the United States was overwhelmingly oriented to college admission requirements. Consequently, American high schools catered overwhelmingly to pupils from the upper middle classes. Most students did not complete high school; of those who did, only a minority went to college. Over time, however, our educational policies began to emphasize the needs and interests of pupils who dropped out of school under a selective approach to secondary and higher education. This new emphasis led to retention in school of millions of students who were not as likely to do well in school. Some simply did not have the ability to profit from additional years of schooling. Many were not interested in continued schooling because they were not cognizant of its importance to their own life chances. Many were from low-income families, characterized by low expectations and minimal or no home support for success in school.

Retaining such pupils in school required several adjustments to maintain pupil interest in continued schooling. For example it was deemed imperative to add to or change the college preparatory curriculum. Students not going on to college had different needs from the college preparatory students; it would have been unfair and undemocratic to meet the needs only of the latter. Furthermore, it is impossible to predict precisely who will and will not benefit from high school and/or college. Thus the public schools in the United States deliberately avoided selectivity, that is, high standards in order to emphasize equality of educational opportunity. Needless to say, this becomes very expensive, especially since the per pupil costs of education increase as the grade level increases.

Among educators at least, these arguments help to explain both our comparatively poor international ranking in educational achievement and the declines in educational achievement over the past 20 years. In the United States, education is extremely important to an individual's career opportunities and prospects. To avoid the stratification of our society, or allowing socioeconomic status to be severely limited by educational opportunities, our public schools have retained a higher proportion of young people in school than any other nation. As they view it, however, they have been unfairly and even ignorantly accused of "diluting" or "watering down" the curriculum as a result.

On the whole, however, the contention that adverse social changes are largely responsible for the decline in academic achievement is a weak one. Granted, certain changes, such as the growing toleration of drugs and alcohol in our society, do have a tendency to affect educational achievement adversely. Nevertheless, the declines in academic achievement simply cannot be explained on this basis. The declines are too pervasive and affect too many students who appear to be unaffected by adverse social change. Sometimes the adverse effects are exaggerated, as in the case of single-parent families. There is little evidence to show that this fact plays an important role in educational achievement.

Likewise, there is little merit to the notion that social change has placed new demands upon public education, thereby splitting its resources and confusing its purposes. Over the years, scores of courses that are supposed to meet a need or respond to a social change have been added to the public school curriculum, especially at the secondary levels. Some examples are: health education, consumer education, conservation education, alcohol education, drug education, energy education, sex education, family life education, driver education, and distance education.

With few if any exceptions, these efforts are educational fiascos. The specifics vary, but the underlying reasons are much the same. Such courses constitute efforts to guide student conduct away from school, sometimes many years in the future. Unfortunately, the conduct involved relates to matters on which school influence is a negligible factor. Such courses continue to exist, but not because they are successful. They exist for the same reason many bureaucracies continue to exist; once established as part of a school program, the teachers of these subjects strive to maintain their positions, regardless of the evidence concerning the *raison d'être* for the course.

Furthermore, the picture of an educational community reluctantly acceding to outside pressures to take on new functions is simply inaccurate. Sometimes, an outside interest group will initiate the effort to add a function, such as encouraging abstinence from alcohol or tobacco. More often, the educational community is the initiator or at least the willing accomplice in the effort. Certainly, it is rare for school districts to say: "We are having enough trouble teaching reading, writing, and arithmetic and other fundamentals, and don't really need or want any more diversionary functions."

Realistically, given the structure of American education, we cannot expect school administrators to adopt such a posture. Regardless of their "nonpartisan" legal basis in most states, school boards are political entities. If a community is upset about drunk driving or venereal disease or drug abuse among its teenagers, it is likely to demand that the school system do something about the problem. After all, the schools are the only public institution that can conveniently reach the overwhelming majority of youth; there is a certain plausibility in using schools to carry out certain noneducational functions. In any event, school administrators do not oppose such efforts very vigorously, if indeed they oppose them at all. In this connection, we should not minimize the problem of achieving specific educational goals through 15,500 school boards subject to various pressure to deviate from them.

Let me turn next to the demographic argument that purportedly explains our educational decline. It seems reasonable to assume that if other nations maintained as large a proportion of their youth in school as does the United States, the academic achievement levels of their high school and college graduates would decline; comparisons of highly selective to highly nonselective educational systems must take this probability into account. Unfortunately for the argument, however, our decline and our low international ranking characterize even those levels of education not significantly affected by increases in retention rates during the past 20 years. Granted, our educational system looks worse than others partly because our schools deliberately retain students who, for a variety of reasons, would not be retained in other nations. Nevertheless, public education itself has been a significant causal factor in our academic decline, as evidenced by the following:

1. Grade inflation has been increasing while achievement has been declining. It is therefore difficult to accept the argument that declines in achievement were due to external factors over which schools had no control. Educators have used the grading system to cover up the decline in achievement, when the former could (and should) have been used to publicize the latter. The implications go far beyond the academic dimensions of education. Teachers have rewarded students more for less work and less achievement. This hardly fosters respect for the school or for education.

2. Opposition to testing, especially external testing as a basis of evaluation, pervades the entire education enterprise. In my view, testing may be regarded as analogous to the market system; with all of its imperfections, it still provides a corrective discipline to poor performance. The avoidance of frequent external testing has forced school authorities and the public alike to rely on the subjective judgments of teachers for evaluating student progress, and consequently of teacher and school performance. The upshot has been rampant grade inflation along with a significant decline in academic achievement. Minimally, the educational community is responsible for the absence of an understandable and effective system for evaluating student progress. Paradoxically, teachers give tests and grades and make much of their inviolability—but strongly oppose tests by external agencies.

3. Schools are willing to blame external factors for negative out-
    comes, but are first to take credit for positive outcomes that are
    also due to external factors. This is understandable politically, but
    the argument that adverse social conditions are to blame for nega-
    tive developments is often more of an afterthought than a care-
    fully studied argument.
4. In their relationships with pupils, public schools are excessively
    oriented to pupil rights and liberties. There is inadequate emphasis
    upon pupil responsibilities to respect the rights of others, espe-
    cially in day-to-day school operations.

Certainly, if our educational decline was really due to social and
demographic factors, public school personnel were foolish to conceal
the fact by their opposition to testing and by tolerating grade inflation.
Regardless, it seems indisputable that the policies governing public
education have played an influential role in the decline.[2]

State Aid Formulas and Educational Decline

Policies governing state aid to local school districts illustrate how
state educational legislation unwittingly fosters undesirable outcomes.
School districts typically receive a significant proportion of their
operating funds, often more than 50 percent, from the state government. In allocating funds to local school districts, states typically use
formulas based upon "average daily attendance" (ADA as it is commonly referred to in educational circles). Although formulas based
on ADA vary, their common denominator is that school districts receive more state aid for each day of attendance (of a specified duration) by each pupil.

Beyond any question, this is one of the most important and most
widely neglected facts about American education. In effect, the states
have given school districts a strong economic interest in retaining
pupils in schools. Typical ADA formulas provide more state aid for
secondary than for elementary school students, so the school districts
have an even greater stake in retaining secondary than elementary
school pupils.

The significance of this fact can hardly be overestimated. Teachers
and administrators are aware of the fact that their own salaries and
benefits are dependent to some extent upon ADA. The higher the
ADA, the more state aid and hence the more funds that become available for salaries and benefits. True, higher ADA also requires higher
costs but the increased income is virtually always greater than the

increased costs. If a teacher has 15 students, adding five more may increase ADA by $7,500 but would not increase school costs by this amount.

Question: What do teachers and school officials tell youngsters to encourage them to stay in school? Not, of course, "Please stay in school so the school board can pay us higher salaries." To be persuasive, the reason has to relate to the welfare of pupils. How about: "It's a jungle out there, and you can't hack your way through it without a high school diploma." Or: "If you don't stay in school, you won't amount to anything. Employers won't hire you. People will look down upon you. And you'll be missing out on all these exciting stimulating courses we have arranged for you, to hold your interest and keep up your morale."

Of course, it did not take long for the public school lobby to believe its own propaganda. As Pareto observed, it is easy to convert one's interests into principles. States could have allocated state aid in a way that maximized teacher welfare by minimizing student attendance, or that ignored student attendance as a factor, but this did not happen. In any event, public education is committed to a vast, stay-in-school-at-all-costs ideology, nonetheless harmful because it is so naively and sincerely accepted by those who propagate it.

The public education lobby is fond of asserting: "We have solved the problem of quantity. Now we must solve the problem of quality." What they should be saying is this: "We have created the problem of quantity. By doing so, we have made it all the more difficult to solve the problem of quality. Not because there is anything 'elitist' or anti-democratic about selectivity based upon standards of performance. The reason is that there are limits to how much even a wealthy nation like the United States can spend to perpetuate a fiction."

Perhaps the most remarkable aspect of the reliance upon ADA is the virtual absence of any critical attention to it within the educational community. To be sure, a great deal of attention is devoted to it, but such attention focuses upon refinements in ADA formulas, not upon the harmful consequences of basing school revenues upon average daily attendance.[3]

One additional comment seems appropriate. Undeniably, some factors not controlled by educators have rendered it more difficult to educate children. At the same time, however, little, if anything, is said about the factors conducive to a higher level of achievement than in the past. Presumably, we know more about how to educate today than we did 20 or 30 years ago. If we do not, we ought to be raising some hard questions about the hundreds of millions spent for educational research and development. School buildings and equipment are better today. There is a much larger, more varied, and better tested supply of teaching aids of all kinds, including technological aids that did not exist or were seldom available in the past. Of course, it is impossible to estimate precisely how much improvement we should expect from these things. My point is, however, that the pervasive neglect of them weakens the arguments made by the public education community. Clearly, it has searched much harder to defend itself than it has to reach an objective judgment about its role in the educational decline.

THE EDUCATIONAL REFORM MOVEMENT

To be fair about it, the educational reform movement has not tried to absolve public schools from all responsibility for our educational decline. As we have seen, however, its own programs and strategies are also inadequate. Let us review the reasons briefly, before turning to their implications.

1. The reform movement does not recognize the fact that many groups can block reform, and have a strong reason to do so, whereas no agency has the power by itself to achieve reforms. The existence of over 15,000 school boards, overlapping control between local school districts and state governments; the independence of higher education on critical reform issues; the fragmentation of state authority between governors, legislatures, state boards of education, state superintendents of public instruction, state departments of education, independent textbook commissions; staggered terms for governing boards at every level of education—these and other obstacles to reform have been ignored by the reformers. They rely upon a massive voluntary effort, coordinated by some unseen hand, to get the job done. While wishing reformers good luck, we should not blind ourselves to the facts they have ignored.
2. The reform movement has largely ignored the impact of public education upon religious views, sexual attitudes, dress, language, and many other nonacademic areas of concern.
3. The role and influence of interest groups opposed to reform are consistently ignored or underestimated. Reform strategy also fails to take into account the fact that the benefits of reform are widely diffused, and it is often impossible to assess the benefits or even

identify the beneficiaries in the early stages of reform. In sharp contrast, the opponents of reform are often faced with immediate and substantial loss if reform is implemented. Thus the opponents of reform are frequently better organized and more highly motivated than its supporters.

4. The reform movement pays little or no heed to an imposing list of legal obstacles to reform, such as tenure laws, collective bargaining, and state aid based upon average daily attendance. For this reason alone, reform programs are fatally flawed, conceptually and programmatically.

5. The importance of inertia is simply ignored, although it is a negative in the reform situation. Much of the action needed to achieve reform is voluntary, that is, the individuals who must act if reform is to be achieved will not suffer any adverse personal consequences if it is not achieved. Quite frequently, life is so much easier and more pleasant if the status quo is left alone. Doing nothing is especially easy because agreement on reform is often agreement on vague generalities that are interpreted differently at the action level. For this reason, support for reform is easily overestimated, as is its actual occurrence.

6. The reform movement does not relate public education to either higher education or the mass media in ways adequate to the task at hand. The relationships between public education and higher education are viewed much too narrowly; media treatment of education is not discussed at all. On the contrary, the sponsors of each reform document concentrated solely upon achieving adequate media coverage of their document, including its alleged impact. For this reason, media vulnerability to being used by the reformers explains more about the reform movement than any actual change in the schools.

A recent statement by former Secretary of Education T. H. Bell illustrates the preceding point. Commenting on developments during the year following release of *A Nation At Risk*, Bell asserted:

> The Administration has taken a number of actions in response to the commission's report. Some of them include:
>> Submitting an education budget that would be the largest in history, if enacted, for the 1985 budget.
>> Increasing state bloc grant funding by 52 percent and focusing the Department of Education's discretionary funds on activities to promote excellence.

Launching an initiative aimed at diminishing and ultimately eradicating adult illiteracy.

Creating the Secondary School Recognition Program to recognize the nation's outstanding high schools.

Raising public awareness of the close relationship between discipline and learning. . . .

When the commission issued its report, it hoped it would serve as a clarion call for improvement. Fortunately for our nation, that hope is rapidly becoming a reality. We are witnessing a tidal wave of reform, unprecedented in its breadth and support, that promises to restore excellence as the hallmark of American education.[4]

Secretary Bell's statement illustrates how media are manipulated to substitute the appearance of reform for its substance. Thus the administration was "submitting" the largest education budget in history; the facts that it was submitted in an election year, was the largest by the slimmest of margins, and was to be followed by substantial reductions in the FY 1986 education budget were, of course, not mentioned. Similarly, the administration "is launching an initiative" to reduce illiteracy. This is merely another way of saying it has no concrete progress to report. It is "raising public awareness of the close relationship between discipline and learning"—even though the Gallup Poll on education revealed that the public has considered the need for more discipline as the top priority in schools for over ten years. Reliance upon such weak evidence of reform confirms the argument of this book that reform is not taking place, and that our political and educational leaders often have a vested interest in fostering the belief that it is taking place.

In my opinion, competent media treatment of *A Nation At Risk* when it was released would probably have consigned it to oblivion. Throughout this book I have pointed out its glaring deficiencies, such as its failure to deal with collective bargaining and teacher tenure laws. Significantly, the national commission that sponsored the report deliberately avoided several issues in order to have a unanimous report. There would be nothing necessarily wrong with this if the commission had informed the American people of this important fact. Minimally, its failure to do so reflects a lack of candor. In submitting the report, the commission said in effect to the American people: "This is what we believe is wrong about public education and what should be done about it." What it should have said is this: "This is what's wrong with American education, and what should be done about it, *insofar as we can achieve unanimity among the commissioners. However, we have omitted any discussion of several critical issues because it would have been impossible to achieve unanimity on them. Readers should decide for themselves how these omissions affect their conclusions about what's wrong and what should be done about it."*

The important point here is not, however, the commission's lack of candor. It is the media failure to pursue some obvious questions about the report. For example, in view of the fact that a majority of the American people appear to support tuition tax credits/vouchers, why was this issue not addressed in the report? What other important issues (and there were others) were not discussed because the commissioners could not achieve unanimity on them? Or for any other reason? If implementation of the commission's report depends partly upon the resolution of issues on which there was not unanimity, what is the value of the report? Questions such as these could and should have been raised when *A Nation At Risk* was released. If such questions had been raised, educational reform would have been greatly enhanced.

EDUCATIONAL REFORM AND POLITICAL LEADERSHIP

Not surprisingly, there is more support for basic changes among political than among educational leaders. The latter are too likely to have their careers hostage to the status quo. On the other hand, although faced by the need to "do something" about education, political leaders are not so tied to any particular institutional arrangements. They are limited mainly by a political calculus: What changes will my constituents accept and how will this affect my political fortunes?

Viewed in this light, the 1984 presidential election may have provided the best opportunity for educational reform since the 1960s. One reason is that President Reagan was overwhelmingly reelected despite opposition from the interest groups opposed to changes in the governance structure of education. For example, the NEA, the AFT, and other unions of public employees supported former Vice-President Mondale in the Democratic primaries and the 1984 elections. Their support illustrates the fact that political conservatives generally, including the Reagan administration, are not burdened by political obligations that would cripple their ability to enact drastic reform measures.

Paradoxically, however, the conservatives have failed to deal with, or even recognize, many of the underlying problems of public education. This failure reflects the fact that the fallacies that conservatives share with liberals outweigh their differences. In this case, the two share a common failure to understand or address the major obstacles to reform. In some instances at least, the conservative failure is especially puzzling since conservatives have more to gain politically by raising the issues.

For example, during the 1984 elections, Democratic candidates repeatedly charged that the Reagan administration supported policies that were unfair to the poor and minorities. These charges certainly had a significant effect, since about 90 percent of the black vote went to Mondale-Ferraro. Indisputably, however, at least some of the policies that are unfair to the disadvantaged receive their primary political support from the Democratic Party. For instance, unemployment among black teenagers is almost twice as high as among white teenagers. Virtually every reputable economist concedes that our minimum wage laws are a primary cause of this situation. One reason is that minimum wage laws tend to make it unprofitable to employ unskilled labor, an outcome that inevitably is more harmful to black youth.

At the present time, considerable emphasis is placed upon reducing the dropout rate and/or raising educational achievement levels among minority students. On the other hand, relatively little attention is paid to the excessive licensing requirements in many fields. Whenever a state unnecessarily requires a high school diploma or a college degree or some sort of formal training to work at certain jobs, its actions are especially harmful to disadvantaged minorities; the latter are much less likely to meet the irrelevant educational requirements. Nevertheless, the conservative neglect of licensing requirements, not only in education but in a host of other fields as well, illustrates their frequent failure to raise important issues, many of which would be advantageous to them politically.

Perhaps the most outstanding example along this line is the conservative failure to make an issue of how education, especially higher education, is financed in this country. The funding for higher education comes largely from regressive state taxes, such as state sales taxes. The student beneficiaries of higher education are largely from the upper middle class. As Milton and Rose Friedman assert, "the present use of tax monies to subsidize higher education seems to us one of the great suppressed scandals of our day. *We doubt that there is any other government program that so clearly and so massively transfers income from relatively low- to relatively high-income classes.*"[5]

Perhaps conservatives are reluctant to raise the issue for fear that their own constituency is a primary beneficiary of this public policy debacle. Whatever the reason, the issue is neglected by both political parties.

The conservatives also suffer from both myopia and a failure of nerve with respect to higher education and the philanthropic foundations. To illustrate, the conservatives rightly perceive that certain institutions of higher education are essentially liberal propaganda centers. Instead of meeting the problem head on, however, the conservatives merely set up conservative propaganda centers in other institutions of higher education.

Wealthy conservatives who don't know what else to do with their money are just as naive as wealthy liberals: they give it to colleges and universities. If 1 percent of the money flowing to higher education were devoted to a center of criticism of it, the results might be astonishing. Unfortunately (or perhaps not so unfortunately), it is easier to make money in our society than it is to give it away intelligently.

Like liberals, conservatives are also prone to emphasize minor issues, thereby wasting resources needed to deal with important ones. One example is the conservative effort to eliminate the U.S. Department of Education. As a substantive issue neither its establishment nor disestablishment matter very much. The Reagan administration may simply let it starve to death, which is probably the best political solution consistent with its philosophy of reducing the federal presence in public education.

The attention conservatives devote to a constitutional amendment allowing voluntary prayer in public schools also illustrates their preoccupation with symbolic instead of substantive issues. One can justify the attention as a political tactic to arouse certain conservative constituencies; such tactics do not happen to be my style of politics but that is irrelevant. Political leaders in both major parties and all levels of government raise pseudo-issues to generate support.

Perhaps instead of opposing the school prayer amendment, its opponents should have agreed to it for a specified time on one condition. The condition would be that school prayer be studied immediately by an unimpeachable research group, to ascertain its effects, if any, on academic achievement or student conduct. If the practice turned out not to have any effects on learning or conduct, the sponsors of the prayer amendment would be publicly accountable for stirring up religious controversy over a policy that had no educational benefits. If school prayer somehow did result in more learning or better conduct, it would then have a beneficial *secular* impact and would therefore be a perfectly appropriate public policy.

What matters is not whether disestablishment of the Department of Education or the school prayer amendment are merely political ploys. What matters is this: Assuming they are merely political ploys, what kind of educational policy/program changes do the conservatives have that will get the job done after they are elected to office? Except for tuition tax credits and/or vouchers, they have none. Clearly, one would look in vain among the conservative media for a reform program that identified and dealt realistically with the problems raised in this analysis.

Despite some differences, such as over federal aid and federal regulation of public education, conservatives accept the conventional wisdom on educational reform. For example, except for its failure to discuss tuition tax credits/vouchers, conservatives applauded *A Nation At Risk*. Practically, this means that if tuition tax credits and/or voucher plans are not enacted, we cannot expect meaningful educational reform from either the Democratic or the Republican Party. By "meaningful reform," I mean reform that has the potential for effectuating basic improvement in education. I do not mean to imply that the overall consequences of tuition tax credits/vouchers are certain to be beneficial. They may be, but everything depends upon the specifics of the enabling legislation.

EDUCATIONAL REFORM AND BUSINESS LEADERSHIP

Although this book argues that business leadership is our most likely source of educational reform, the argument is not based upon the educational views of most business leaders in the United States. As is evident from Appendix A, business leaders were frequently among the sponsors of reform proposals. As a matter of fact, the Committee for Economic Development (CED), the nation's most prestigious business organization, sponsored the most recent reform proposal to receive nation-wide attention.[6] Inasmuch as the group sponsoring the CED report was composed overwhelmingly of chief executives of major U.S. corporations, the report can fairly be said to reflect the views of the U.S. business establishment.

Despite some insights and emphases not to be found in other reform proposals, the CED report is perhaps the most disappointing of them all. Like the others, it ignores the concrete obstacles to reform, such as the inefficient governance structure of public education. It appeals for the benefits of competition but does not even consider family choice policies that would foster it. The report includes the ritualistic appeals for more spending for public education, although its own data showed that increased expenditures had not resulted in greater educational achievement in the past. Furthermore, the report deliberately avoided any discussion of the role of educational technology, despite the fact that the labor-intensive nature of education is a major cause of its pervasive inefficiencies.

Essentially, the CED report severely limits the role of private enterprise in educational reform. It suggests business participation in a number of cosmetic improvements, such as teacher recognition days, while simultaneously failing to suggest meaningful changes in the funding, governance, or delivery of educational services. The timidity of the report is illustrated by its statements on contracting for educational services. The report recommends that this be done, but only for vocational educational services where public schools lack the resources for a high-quality program—and then only on a "limited trial" basis, "where appropriate." Fortunately, some CED members, as well as business leaders not associated with CED, do not share such a narrow view of the possibilities for business leadership to bring about educational reform.

EDUCATIONAL REFORM PROPOSALS: A CASE STUDY

To conclude this chapter, I shall review a single reform document from the perspective just outlined. The document to be reviewed is the study directed by Ernest L. Boyer, the president of the Carnegie Foundation, entitled *High School: A Report on Secondary Education in America.*[7] Like *A Nation At Risk, High School* was launched with prestigious sponsors and enormous publicity; it is clearly one of the most influential reform proposals.

Significantly, the index to *High School* does not include "union," "collective bargaining," or "American Federation of Teachers." The only reference to the National Education Association merely cites a 1913 study sponsored by the NEA. Nevertheless, of all the reform documents, *High School* is the one most avidly supported by teacher unions. The reason is not difficult to understand. Essentially, *High School* recommends much higher teacher salaries for less work by teachers. Furthermore, by its total neglect of unions and bargaining, *High School* fosters the impression that teacher unions contributed nothing to the decline and do not present any problem in remedying the situation—a point of view that the unions find congenial to their interests. A brief discussion of some of the specific recommendations in *High School* will illustrate these points.

In common with other reformers, Boyer laments the low salaries paid to teachers. He asserts:

Teachers' salaries should be increased. When teachers' salaries are compared to those of other professionals, the contrast is depressing. For many teachers, moonlighting has become essential. Salaries for teachers must be commensurate with those of other professions, and with the tasks teachers must perform.

As a national goal, the average salary for teachers should be increased by at least 25 percent beyond the rate of inflation over the next three years, with immediate entry level increases.[8]

Other recommendations from the report are as follows:

A two-week Teacher Professional Development Term should be added to the school year, with appropriate compensation. This term for teachers would be a time for study, a period to improve instruction and to expand knowledge. The planning of such a term should be largely controlled by teachers at the school or district level.

Every school district should establish a Teacher Travel Fund to make it possible for teachers, based on competitive application, to travel occasionally to professional meetings to keep current in their fields.

Every five years, teachers should be eligible to receive a special contract—with extra pay to match—to support a Summer Study Term. To qualify and compete for this extended contract each teacher would prepare a study plan. Such a plan would be subject to review and approval both by peers and by the school and district administrations.[9]

Like other reformers, Boyer says nothing about the fact that fringe benefits for teachers are about 22 percent of salaries, a figure that is much higher than the average for employees generally. Unlike most other reform proposals, however, Boyer glosses over the fact that teachers work only about 180 days a year, compared to 220-240 in other occupations. In other words, their rate of pay reflects the 25 percent increase that Boyer proposes. To discuss paying teachers as much as other occupations while requiring them to work substantially fewer days is not seeking "equity" or "comparability" but a status far more advantageous than these other occupations. It isn't going to happen, but even to propose it illustrates the fatuousness of Boyer's proposals.

In this connection, Boyer echoes the theme that teachers often must work at other jobs, supposedly to earn enough to support themselves and their families. The picture of the dedicated teachers who would rather be inspiring children but are forced to pump gas or clerk at supermarkets during the summer is a staple reform theme, but it is misleading and inaccurate. No doubt, many teachers would prefer to work another month or two at their school rate, instead of a lower one. Many, however, would not. In my area, for example, teacher couples are a common phenomenon. Their children have left the nest, and each spouse is at maximum on a salary schedule. Jointly, they are making about $60,000 a year plus benefits for 180 days. Typically, they are eager for the school year to end and have no interest in extending it, even at a per diem rate. This attitude is shared by many single teachers and teachers supporting families. One need only look at AFT and NEA travel brochures to see that hundreds of thousands of teachers are quite able to travel to various countries of the world during their vacation periods. As a matter of fact, the NEA probably sponsors more travel packages than any other organization in the world not primarily in the travel business.

The reality is that higher salaries would have very little effect on teacher moonlighting. College professors make much more than teachers (certainly 25 percent more, on the average). Nevertheless, a tremendous number of professors moonlight. In fact, the best paid professors—that is, those at Harvard, the University of California, Yale, Stanford, Chicago, Texas, and Big Ten universities—undoubtedly moonlight a great deal more, as well as more lucratively, than their counterparts at institutions that are not so well funded. Some teachers would not moonlight if they were paid more for only one reason: Their after-tax income from the additional work would be less, so moonlighting would be economically less attractive. The notion that with their material needs adequately met, teachers would happily concentrate upon inspiring children belongs in the realm of fiction.

Similarly, Boyer's recommendations on in-service training for teachers ignore the most elementary facts about teacher salaries and teacher unions. The vast majority of teachers are paid pursuant to salary schedules that provide more pay for additional training. Most teachers have taken at least an additional year of graduate work *after* they become teachers; as a matter of fact, over half of the nation's teachers have a Master's degree. As a result, a substantial part of the costs of teacher salaries, perhaps as much as 25 percent, currently is paid for the training that teachers have received *after* initial employment.

What in-service courses do teachers take when teachers themselves decide the issue as Boyer recommends? Let me cite two news items to answer this question. Recently, *Education Week* reported an in-service credit scheme providing fraudulent units for salary credit in

1981. As a result 94 teachers, 50 from the Los Angeles Unified School District, were shown to have received salary credit for courses they had not attended. Some teachers received as much as $10,000 in salary increases for courses they did not attend.[10]

The second item goes back a few more years, but its implications for Boyer's recommendations are even more devastating. In 1980, as a result of its investigations into fraudulent credit for college athletes, the McClatchy Newspapers Service got interested in the problem of in-service credit for teachers. Its investigation revealed the following:

- Thousands of California teachers have raised their salaries—at a cost to taxpayers of millions of dollars—by attending the same dubious college extension programs that have sparked a nationwide scandal in college athletics.
- Courses conducted by two small colleges in Kansas and one in Montana enrolled several thousand California teachers who received salary credit for courses requiring no written work or outside reading.
- Some courses were simply a series of unrelated lectures on everything from solar energy to the value of competition.
- In one college program, 900 students were enrolled during the summer. Of these 900, 16 were undergraduate athletes seeking fraudulent credit to be eligible for intercollegiate athletics. The rest were teachers seeking credit that could be used to increase their salaries.
- Another college based in Kansas nevertheless conducted extension courses for salary credit. Over 3,000 (more than 1,000 at the Sacramento site) were enrolled in these extension courses in California, Kansas, Indiana, Texas, Florida, and Wisconsin. The courses were arranged by educational entrepreneurs who received a commission on each student enrolled in a course.
- Because school districts normally pay teachers solely on the basis of their years of experience and the number of credits they have earned, school districts in California were paying teachers millions of dollars every year for having taken worthless courses.[11]

These news items illustrate why it is unrealistic to let teachers decide what courses should receive salary credit. The problems go much deeper than salary credit for worthless courses. In many instances, teachers take courses intended to prepare them to leave teaching, yet demand that districts pay higher salaries for such training and even for the costs of the courses. Districts must insist that since they will be paying indefinitely for the advanced training, they have the right and responsibility to make sure the money is spent to meet district needs. Apparently, Boyer believes that when teachers or "peers" decide such issues, professional improvement will be their guiding criterion; when administrators paid to make such decisions decide, through ignorance or malice, the decisions will not reflect the best interests of the district. It is tragic that such cheap shots and easily demolished assumptions are portrayed as bold new recommendations to lead us into the educational promised land.

Note that Boyer's recommendations are essentially gratuitous. On the one hand, he proposes to add two weeks with pay as "a time for study, a period to improve instruction and to expand knowledge." Precisely what teachers would or could learn that is not already available, especially from scores of institutions of higher education offering thousands of in-service courses, is not made clear. In any event, if what would or could be learned in these two weeks would be so valuable, why not include it as one of the in-service courses teachers take to increase their salaries? After all, the school districts compensate teachers for such courses not just once, as Boyer proposes, but every year thereafter in which the teacher is employed. In short, the problem is not whether to superimpose another layer of in-service costs on teacher salary schedules. It is how to get school districts to recognize the financial and training implications of these enormous ratholes.

Boyer's recommendations concerning principals provide another glaring example of his neglect of collective bargaining. He states: "Principals should also have more control over the selection and rewarding of teachers. Acting in consultation with their staffs, they should be given responsibility for the final choice of teachers for their schools."[1][2]

This recommendation raises the question of where Boyer has been since 1963. He says nothing about union contracts that vacancies be filled by seniority. Inasmuch as Boyer emphasizes how much his recommendations are based upon practical experience and discussions with teachers/administrators in the trenches, one can only speculate where he got the idea that unions would be willing to drop seniority in filling vacancies, or on other personnel issues. The notion that most unions would accept this, at least without a protracted struggle, is naive, if indeed Boyer ever considered the issue. Certainly, anyone familiar with teacher unions realizes that they would strongly oppose bargaining with individual principals, or relying upon their discretion.

Within a brief time, different principals would apply different criteria to personnel decisions, and the unions would feel imperiled by allowing such subjectivity to run rampant. Granted, such "subjectivity" is "essential flexibility" in the eye of the reformer, but few school boards would hold out for it against the adamant union opposition certain to emerge to any such proposal.

Similarly, the teacher unions are and will be adamantly opposed to according principals more authority over rewarding teachers. Most likely, the denial of such authority would be a life or death issue to many, perhaps most, teacher unions. They are opposed to basing compensation on any criterion involving judgment or discretion. It is unrealistic to assume that the unions would accept, let alone embrace, a system of compensation that maximizes discretion, not merely by a superintendent but by a number of principals.

For that matter, Boyer's proposals reflect fundamental inconsistencies in his approach to personnel relations, quite apart from collective bargaining. At one point he states: "The evaluation of teacher performance should be largely controlled by other teachers who themselves have been judged to be outstanding in the classroom."[13]

Thus on the one hand, principals are to be deprived of the major responsibility for evaluation; whether because of incompetence or bias or lack of time, Boyer does not say. Yet only a few pages later, he proposes that these same principals "should be given the responsibility for the final choice of teachers for their schools." Just how and why principals, who are not allowed to control teacher evaluation, should be accorded more control over teacher rewards escapes me.

Boyer's recommendations that support the union line are as unrealistic as the ones that are opposed to it. Thus he recommends: "Teachers should be exempt from routine monitoring of halls, lunchrooms, and recreation areas. School clerical staff and parent and student volunteers should assume such noninstructional duties."[14]

In collective bargaining with teacher unions, they routinely submit proposals to relieve teachers of "noninstructional duties." Such proposals are characterized by at least two fallacies. One is that the "professional" or skilled dimension of the work teachers do is always the actual teaching. An analogy may help to explain the fallacy. If a person has a broken leg, the "professional" work to be done is not diagnosis. It is repairing the leg. On the other hand, with certain illnesses, the diagnosis is the difficult part. The action required by a correct diagnosis may be easily performed by an aide, for example, giving the patient a pill.

By the same token, "instruction" is not always the work demanding the highest skill level of teachers. Sometimes effective teaching requires simple drills that can be carried out by aides. At times, educational diagnosis requires the highest skills, but a correct diagnosis requires only routine instructional tasks that an aide can perform. Thus we cannot, or should not, regard "instruction" as always denoting the skill dimension to teaching. Sometimes it does, sometimes it does not.

The second fallacy is more applicable to Boyer's recommendation. The fallacy is that it is always desirable to relieve a skilled employee of tasks that do not require the employee's highest skills. This recommendation is plausible but neither realistic nor conducive to productivity. In general, it is desirable to have persons work at their highest skill level. There are, however, many exceptions. It is always necessary to consider the total costs of replacing the skilled employee for intermittent or temporary unskilled duties.

For instance, I once taught extension courses at the University of Oklahoma. When I met the extension classes, hundreds of miles from the campus, it was necessary for me to enroll the students. Would it have made sense for me to argue that because I was a professor, I should confine myself to "instructional" duties, and require the university to hire an additional person to be present to handle the clerical work? I doubt it very much. Skilled and unskilled work may be so related at the workplace that it is highly inefficient to restrict a skilled worker only to tasks requiring the highest skill levels.

Teacher unions will undoubtedly cite Boyer's recommendations to justify contractual proposals that rigidly divide work functions, but such proposals will reduce, not enhance, educational productivity. Interestingly enough, the Japanese automobile manufacturers who open plants in the United States have refused from the beginning to accept the rigid separation of work characteristic of United Auto Workers' contracts with U.S. automobile manufacturers.[15] Teacher unions may protest ad infinitum that "teaching is different," but on this issue there is no difference in principle.

It is impractical to review every recommendation made in *High School*. I doubt, however, whether comprehensiveness is necessary. If the criticisms set forth are not persuasive, adding to them is unlikely to be either.

At this point, readers may be more perplexed than convinced of the unrealistic nature of the reform proposals. On the one hand, the analysis of the proposals may appear to illustrate their deficiencies.

Nevertheless, something appears to be missing from the analysis. The sponsors of the reform documents constitute an impressive group of leaders. It is easy to understand how some of these leaders might have signed their names to unrealistic reform proposals. Even so, when the number of prestigious sponsors is taken into account, the situation appears to be baffling indeed. It is not credible that all of these sponsors were not aware of the tenure laws, the opposition of teacher unions, the difficulty of overcoming vested academic interests, and so on. Thus an issue arises. Assuming that the reform proposals fail to take cognizance of the obstacles to reform, this is still not the same as asserting that the individual sponsors were not aware of these obstacles. Why, then, do the proposals not reflect this knowledge? In other words, how can we reconcile the reputations and expertise of the sponsors with the highly negative conclusions about their reform proposals?

To be candid, this question was a concern throughout this book. The reform proposals consistently ignored the most obvious difficulties of achieving reform, yet it seemed incredible that their sponsors were unaware of these difficulties or deliberately set out to mislead the American people on the issues.

In my opinion, Paul Peterson has provided the most credible explanation for the situation.[16] Peterson, the director of Government Programs at the Brookings Institution, himself served with the Twentieth Century Fund Task Force Report on federal educational policy. Subsequently, in an article highly critical of the reform reports, he raised the same issue that had disturbed me as it must have many readers: How could so many presumably well-informed, competent, and conscientious sponsors produce such a futilitarian series of reform proposals?

Peterson's analysis emphasizes two factors that vitiate the reform documents. One is the social situation of the group members that come together to sponsor the proposals. The individuals are employed elsewhere at full-time positions. Usually they have a limited amount of time in which to put together a report. Merely getting to know the other members of the group can require a considerable amount of time. The meetings are typically held in first-class accommodations that encourage socializing and a vacation-like milieu. The process emphasizes conviviality; it is not conducive to intellectual confrontations and hard questions that might shatter the camaraderie of a distinguished group getting acquainted with each other.

Another factor is perhaps even more influential. The members of the reform commissions and task forces typically have no responsibility in their own jobs for implementing their reform proposals. They can be "good guys" and let others worry about the problems of implementation.

On this issue, Peterson compares the reform groups to the joint congressional committees on social security reform. The members of this latter committee were aware of the fact that they personally would have to face the consequences of failure to formulate a practical solution. They could not blithely ignore the unpleasant realities of the problem. If the joint committee did not resolve the problem, the members would have to face the problems again as members of Congress. So would their congressional colleagues who were looking to them for solutions.

In contrast, the reform sponsors were not accountable in their full-time positions for any deficiencies in their recommendation. They could afford to be generous, since they did not have the responsibility for coming up with the resources required to implement their recommendations. Nor were they required to face up to the obstacles to reform; these mundane tasks could be left to others. Additionally, the emphasis upon unanimity and the pressures of time intensified the tendency to avoid instead of confront the underlying issues.

To this observer, Peterson's analysis is persuasive. Unfortunately, it discourages the hope that public school reform can be achieved by political and/or educational leadership. Peterson does not say so, but his analysis underscores the importance of nontraditional sources of educational reform. I shall return to this issue in Chapter 9; first, however, let us consider the major proposals to achieve reform by strengthening family choice in education.

NOTES

1. Barbara Lerner, "American Education: How Are We Doing?" *Public Interest*, Fall 1982, pp. 59-82. See also a criticism of Ms. Lerner's article and her rebuttal in Richard M. Wolf, "American Education: The Record is Mixed," and Barbara Lerner, "Facing the Unpleasant Facts About Achievement," *Public Interest*, Winter 1982, pp. 124-29, 129-32.

2. For a good brief summary, see Brigitte Berger, "The Centrality of Parents in Education," *Journal of Family and Culture*, Spring 1985, pp. 39-59.

3. Perhaps the best recent criticism of reliance upon ADA, and the most interesting proposal to replace it, was developed outside of the educational community and publicized in the *Wall Street Journal*. See National Center for Policy Analysis, *The Failure of Our Public Schools: The Causes and a Solution* (Dallas: National Center for Policy Analysis, University of Dallas, 1983), and John C. Goodman, "Why Public Schools Fill Desks First, Minds Second," *Wall Street Journal*, January 18, 1984, p. 28.

4. New York *Times*, April 28, 1984, p. 8.

5. Milton and Rose Friedman, *Tyranny of the Status Quo* (San Diego, Ca.: Harcourt, Brace, Jovanovich, 1983), p. 159. Emphasis in original. Also, the Reagan administration is trying to reduce federal financial assistance to students in higher education for the same reason.

6. Committee for Economic Development, Research and Policy Committee, *Investing In Our Children: Business and Public Schools* (New York: Committee for Economic Development, 1985).

7. Ernest L. Boyer, *High School: A Report on Secondary Education in America* (New York: Harper & Row, 1983).

8. Ibid., p. 308.

9. Ibid., p. 310.

10. "Teachers Charged with Obtaining Phony Credit," *Education Week*, March 17 (1982), p. 1.

11. "Shady courses force costly teacher raises," *The Modesto Bee*, January 22, 1980, p. A7.

12. Boyer, *High School*, p. 316.

13. Ibid., p. 311.

14. Ibid., p. 307.

15. For example, the contract between the UAW and the GM-Toyota facility at Fremont, Ca. reduced the number of work classifications from 80 to 4. A. J. Raskin, "Labor's Grand Illusion," *New York Times Sunday Magazine*, February 11, 1985, p. 54.

16. Paul E. Peterson, "Did the Education Commissions Say Anything?" *Education and Urban Society* (February 1985), pp. 126-44.

8

FAMILY CHOICE PROPOSALS

The previous chapters have converged upon a basic conclusion: Conventional approaches to public education will not result in any fundamental educational improvements; for this purpose, changes in the governance structure of education are essential. Obviously, this conclusion raises some critical questions. What changes in the governance structure of education are being proposed? What are the prospects for their enactment? How would they bring about improvement if enacted?

We can answer the first question easily. Tuition tax credits and vouchers (hereinafter referred to as "family choice" proposals) are the only proposals to change the governance structure of education under serious consideration at this time. Paradoxically, however, such proposals are largely ignored in the reform documents. In most, family choice issues are not even mentioned, nor is there any explanation for this fact. In some instances, the absence of any reference to family choice seems peculiar, to say the least. President Reagan has consistently supported tax tuition credits. His support for such credits was well known, long before the National Commission on Excellence in Education submitted *A Nation At Risk* on April 26, 1983. Thus we have a situation in which a national commission, appointed by the secretary of education with support and encouragement from President Reagan himself, completely ignores the major educational reform supported by the Reagan administration. In conjunction with other basic issues ignored by the commission, it appears that it deliberately avoided making any recommendations that would activate political opposition to President Reagan's reelection. In any event, tuition tax credits/vouchers are not in the mainstream of the debate over how to improve public education.

AFT President Albert Shanker has provided an interesting confirmation of this point. In his 1983 address to the AFT convention, Shanker stated:

> We must ask ourselves with respect to each and every decision and action that we take, "Is what we are doing going to help bring tuition tax credits about?"
>
> Each and everything we do will either help to push to tax credits, and undermine support of public education, or it will build support for our nation's public schools. It is going to be hard to get used to doing that, but it is something that we must do.
>
> Second, these reports reject tuition tax credits or vouchers either implicitly or explicitly. They recognize that we can't have both tuition tax credits and necessary, massive overhaul of our public education system.[1]

Essentially, Shanker's reference to the fact that some reform proposals "implicitly" rejected tuition tax credits/vouchers is another way of saying they ignored the subject. Perhaps one reason is that such proposals are widely regarded as intended to strengthen private but not public schools. Whatever the reasons, it is essential to consider family choice proposals and their prospects for improving education.

At the outset, let me restate the context for the analysis. First, it is based upon the assumption that our underlying objective is a well-educated citizenry, achieved with minimal cost or interference with other social objectives. Whether we should foster public or private schools, or a combination or mixture of them, is a means question. The fact that individuals define "well educated" differently does not affect this point. The legal status of schools and the financial arrangements relating thereto are not ends in themselves but are to be assessed in terms of their overall effects upon our social objectives.

Second, even if it be assumed that changes in the governance structure of education are essential to achieve our underlying objectives, we cannot assume that every proposal to change the governance structure is ipso facto a constructive one. Sometimes "reforms" in any field make matters worse instead of better. Sometimes "reforms" solve certain problems but only by creating other more harmful or more difficult ones. Therefore, the basic posture toward family choice adopted here is not so much support as it is an inquiry into the conditions under which family choice policies would be desirable. We also need to consider whether these conditions will be met in the family choice plans actually enacted.

Family choice issues are usually discussed in a context limited to public and private nonprofit schools. The discussion here has an additional dimension. As noted in Chapter 1, it regards profitmaking schools as the most promising route to educational reform. From this perspective, most analyses of family choice issues are either deficient or incomplete. My objective here, therefore, is not simply to assess these issues from the conventional perspective, that is, one that assumes nonprofit private schools will continue to be the major alternative to public schools. It is also to consider the implications of family choice for profitmaking schools. As we shall see, such consideration challenges some traditional arguments for limiting family choice proposals to public and nonprofit private schools.

Before doing so, certain caveats must be emphasized. One is that the following analysis does not discuss all the important issues and arguments raised by family choice proposals; for that purpose, a separate book would be required. Second, the specifics of family choice proposals vary a great deal. Quite often, supporters of family choice prefer no family choice proposal to specific proposals with objectionable features. More importantly, valid arguments against a specific proposal do not necessarily apply to other proposals.

Finally, it should be noted that most of the research on family choice has been conducted by partisans on the issue. For this reason, their research and policy conclusions must be interpreted very cautiously. Quite frequently, the selection of research issues is itself subject to a policy bias. Supporters of family choice tend to conduct research on issues likely to turn out favorably for their position; opponents of family choice do the same. There is nothing unique about this tendency, but it is a factor in the debate over family choice; the "experts" differ sharply in their factual conclusions as well as their policy recommendations.[2] Because this situation arises frequently, the following discussion is mainly an effort to clarify the basic issues. The hope is that readers will be better prepared to assess the various proposals that have been made and that will be made in the years ahead.

THE RATIONALE FOR FAMILY CHOICE IN EDUCATION

Legally speaking, parents are free to enroll their children in nonpublic schools. Practically, their ability to do so is usually limited by financial considerations; parents enrolling their children in private schools receive minimal assistance from government. Tuition tax credits and vouchers would strengthen parental choice by reducing the financial burden on parents who send their children to nonpublic schools. Just how this can or should be done are highly controversial issues to be discussed shortly, but let us first attempt to answer a prior question: What is the case for strengthening parental choice this way?

Typically, supporters of family choice cite one or more of the following reasons:

1. *Equity*. Parents who send their children to private schools are overtaxed for exercising this right. They pay their share of taxes for public education but must pay again for exercising their rights to an education in private schools. This argument is frequently emphasized by parents who send their children to private schools for religious reasons. Public schools, perhaps unavoidably, often adopt policies and programs that conflict with the religious views of parents and pupils. In fairness to such parents and pupils, they should not be forced either to attend public schools in which their religious views are weakened, or absorb all of the costs of attending a nonpublic school. The same rationale sometimes applies to nonreligious objections to public schools; that is, some parents prefer to transfer their children out of public schools for ideological reasons not based upon religion.

2. *Consumer choice*. Parents differ on the kind of education they want for their children. At the same time, consumer choice is an important value in our society. This value is reflected in our economy and in legislation prohibiting or limiting monopolies. It would seem, therefore, that public policy should foster a diversity of schools that could respond effectively to the diversity in parent preferences. Family choice measures would facilitate this objective by strengthening parental financial ability to enroll their children in the type of school preferred by the parents.

3. *Competition*. If parents have more options, public and private schools alike will have to be more responsive to consumer preferences; that is, be more competitive for parental support. If parents want their children to attend a school that emphasizes academic excellence, strong discipline, and traditional family values, they presumably will send their children to such schools if they can afford to do so. Family choice proposals increase the affordability

of this option. Furthermore, if some schools introduce effective educational innovations, competitive pressures will force others to do so. Thus strengthening parental choice is seen as fostering a competitive or market dimension to education. This dimension would stimulate the introduction and dissemination of better techniques, practices, and technological aids.

One objection to this argument is that the benefits of competition are based upon experience in the profit-making sector of our economy. On the other hand, the overwhelming majority of private schools are nonprofit enterprises. I shall return to this issue in the next chapter, but it illustrates the uncertain factual basis of arguments for and against family choice proposals.

4. *Tax reduction.* Most likely, tuition tax credits/vouchers would result in lower tax burdens. This would depend on several factors, but utilization of private instead of public schools must be considered from a tax standpoint. Significantly, the National Taxpayers Union, which virtually always supports legislation that would reduce taxes, supports policies that would strengthen parental choice in education. The tax savings would result from the fact that government assistance, whether by tax credit or voucher, would be less than the cost of educating pupils in public schools. Thus the loss of revenues needed to implement family choice would be exceeded by the savings resulting from lower public school enrollments.

5. *Economic efficiency.* Private schools can define their purposes and clientele more easily than public schools. As a result, the former can devote less of their resources to conflict management, more to implementing their goals.

6. *Racial integration: the "dumping ground" issue.* Tuition tax credits/vouchers are advocated as a means of fostering racial integration in education. This may surprise many persons because attempts have been made to use tuition tax credits and vouchers to perpetuate racial segregation in education. Furthermore, policies to strengthen parental choice have been attacked for many years as measures that would lead to public schools becoming a "dumping ground" for minorities, the handicapped, and the poor. The issue is, therefore, one on which supporters and critics of parent choice are deeply divided.

The foregoing rationale for family choice raises many questions of fact, law, and policy. Clearly, some elements of the rationale are not based upon the argument of this book. For example, consider the argument that parents who send their children to private schools are being unfairly subjected to "double taxation"—that is, they are being taxed to pay for public schools but must pay again to send their children to private schools. On this view, it is important to eliminate the inequity, even if doing so renders public schools less efficient. Of course, most supporters of tuition tax credits/vouchers believe that family choice will improve the efficiency as well as the fairness of public schools. Nevertheless, some arguments for or against family choice are based upon ethical or value judgments that are not likely to be changed by factual considerations.

Even when factual considerations are paramount, however, it is extremely difficult to assess them with a high degree of confidence. This will be evident from a brief review of how family choice plans are supposed to work.

Tuition Tax Credits

In the literature on the subject, tuition tax credits are sometimes referred to as "educational tax credits." This reflects the possibility of providing tax credits for educational expenses other than tuition. This broader meaning is more useful, hence "tuition tax credits" will be regarded here as any legislation that provides tax credits or tax deductions for the expenses of elementary and/or secondary education.

Tuition tax credits can be enacted by federal or state action or both. In the most widely discussed versions they provide a tax credit for the costs of sending children to school. For this reason, they are even more attractive to taxpayers than deductions against income. The amount of the tax credit would be set forth in the legislation; obviously, the larger the credit, the more parents are likely to use it.

Although the educational aspects of tuition tax credits are likely to be uppermost in the minds of parents, the fiscal aspects are likely to dominate the political and legislative controversies on the subject. For this reason, it is necessary to consider the impact of tuition tax credits upon tax revenues.[3] This impact would depend upon several factors but primarily the following:

1. *The amount of the credit, and whether it is available for expenses other than tuition.* If the credit is not substantial and applies only to tuition, it is less likely to stimulate transfers to private schools. Parents who must still pay tuition and the other costs of attend-

ing private schools, such as transportation, are not likely to transfer their children because of a credit that covers only a small fraction of their total costs. Furthermore, if private schools raised their tuition as the result of tuition tax credits, the effect of the latter would be to enhance private school revenues without decreasing the costs to parents.

2. *Who is eligible for the credit*? For example, are parents of public school pupils eligible for it? Parents at all income levels or only those below specified levels of income? Is the credit limited, as has been suggested in some quarters, to parents of handicapped students or students who are not performing adequately in the public schools? Clearly, eligibility for the credits will directly affect the revenue outcomes.

3. *What proportion of tuition costs are covered by the credits*? The answer to this question affects the value of the credit to parents and the possibility that private schools might raise their tuition charges if tuition tax credits are enacted.

4. *Is the credit refundable as a credit to parents who do not pay enough in taxes to use the credit*? Obviously, the answer to this question affects the value of the credit to low-income families and the cost of the credit to the government.

5. *The number of children who transfer from public to private schools as a result of the credit.* This number would also be a critical factor affecting the revenue gains from tuition tax credits.

In practice, the revenue losses would depend upon the interaction of these five factors. The revenue gains from tuition tax credits would depend largely upon the number of pupils who transfer to private schools and the cost of educating children in public schools. Table 8.1 illustrates this. It assumes that a school district enrolls 1,000 pupils at an average cost of $2,000 per pupil. In the same district, 100 pupils already attend private schools without tuition tax credits. The table further assumes that the tax credit is $500 and that as a result of the credit, 10 percent of the public school pupils transfer to private schools.

Table 8.1 greatly oversimplifies several issues; nevertheless, it illustrates the fiscal rationale for tuition tax credits. Using the tax credit and average cost per pupil in the table, revenue gains and losses would be virtually equal if 34 pupils transferred to private schools as the result of the tax credit. The revenue loss would be $67,000 ($50,000

Table 8.1 Tax Consequences of Tuition Tax Credits

Tax Expenditures	Tax Savings	Net Tax Savings
100 pupils in private schools	100 transferees to private schools	$200,000 gross tax savings
100 transferees	$2,000 cost per pupil in public school	$100,000 total revenue loss from tax credits
200 pupils		
$500 tax credit per pupil	$200,000 tax savings	——————
$100,000 tax expenditures		$100,000 net savings to taxpayers

in tax credits to parents of pupils already in private school, plus $17,000 in credits to new transferees). The revenue gain would be $68,000 (34 transferees X $2,000, the average cost per pupil in the public school). Obviously, each additional pupil over 34 who transfers to a private school would increase the savings to government.

Because the number who transfer and the impact on tax revenues would be affected by so many variables, it is impossible to make firm estimates of these matters. In the example just given, 34 transferees were 3.4 percent of public school enrollments. Both supporters and critics of tuition tax credits expect a higher proportion to transfer to private schools if tuition credits are enacted. Initially, the proportion may be very low, since it will be subject to the availability of space and teachers in private schools. Over time, however, the credit is likely to be increased. At some point, it will be large enough to stimulate the development of additional facilities to enroll pupils who could not be accommodated in existing facilities. We cannot predict what this point would be, but there is widespread agreement among both supporters and critics of family choice that the initial credit (or voucher) is likely to be increased within a few years.

In a 1981 poll by *Newsweek*, 23 percent of parents of children in public schools expressed a likelihood of transferring if Congress enacted tax credits of $250 to $500 a year. Edwin G. West, one of the leading scholars on the subject, has argued that if only 1 percent of public school students transferred under a $300 credit, there would be no revenue loss to government in toto. The federal government would lose revenues due to the credits and the states would gain due to the decline in the number of students educated in public schools, but overall gains and losses would be about equal. Elsewhere, West has estimated that "a tax credit based on one-half of the current average operating expenses per student in the private sector will begin to generate substantial gains after 5 percent of the public school population has transferred to private institutions."[4] In arriving at this conclusion, West also estimated that average expenses for private schools are about one-half of the average in public schools.

In the example used, I have not said whether the tax credit was by federal or state law. If the federal government provided the credit, it would not receive any corresponding gain from the transfers to private schools; however, the states and school districts would benefit, since they would have fewer pupils to educate.

Table 8.1 does not show any revenue loss from parents who continue to send their children to public schools. Inasmuch as legislation providing tuition tax credits may provide such credits, there may be a revenue loss from the parents of public as well as private school pupils. Undoubtedly, revenue loss per student in public school will be much less than the revenue loss per pupil in private school. On the other hand, many more parents would receive a tax credit if it applies to the expenses of education in a public school.

Politically as well as legally, making tuition tax credits available to parents of public school children strengthens the case for such credits. It also raises the possibility that if tuition tax credits are enacted, the federal government may eventually assume a much larger portion of the costs of public education. As we have seen, tuition tax credits may be enacted to cover various costs associated with public education: transportation, books, supplies, athletic fees, and so on. Consequently, public school districts may begin to charge parents for services or supplies currently paid from public funds. Insofar as the parents receive a dollar credit for every dollar spent for public education, the result would be to allocate the costs from local school boards or states to the federal government, using the parents as a pass-through.

The more pupils who transfer to private schools, the more we can reduce expenditures for public schools; of course, the costs of private as well as public schools will affect the savings that result from transfers to private schools. Clearly, however, the costs of public schools would not decrease in the same proportion as the decline in their enrollment. We pay teachers the same, regardless of whether they teach 27 or 28 pupils. It costs as much to heat a building with 250 pupils as one with 260 pupils. Nevertheless, as Table 8.1 shows, the impact of tuition tax credits will depend upon the costs of public and private schools and the specifics of the legislation providing the credits.

Voucher Plans

Although many critical issues relating to tuition tax credits have not been discussed, let us consider voucher plans briefly.[5] Under such plans, parents receive vouchers that are used to defray the costs of education. In some voucher plans, the amount of the voucher would be the average cost of educating a child in a public school; however, most voucher plans envisage lower amounts. The vouchers could be used at any school on a state-approved list of schools, that is, those schools that meet whatever standards a state wishes to set. The amount of the voucher, like the amount of the tax credit, would be extremely important and would be established by the legislation.

It is widely thought that voucher plans would be more difficult to administer than tuition tax credits. Although this is debatable, some private school leaders are opposed to voucher plans for this reason. They fear that voucher plans will lead to more state regulation of education, an outcome they regard as a more serious threat than the absence of public support. They are also wary of vouchers providing large amounts of assistance; the larger the amount of the voucher, the more likely it would increase government regulation. Partly for these reasons, tuition tax credits are more likely to be enacted than vouchers, at least at the federal level.

This conclusion is supported by recent developments concerning Chapter I of the Equal Educational Opportunity Act of 1981. Chapter I is the largest federal aid program for pupils from disadvantaged families. In 1983, the Reagan administration was considering a proposal to allow the states to voucherize Chapter I funds. The proposal would have allowed states and local school districts to distribute Chapter I funds to parents as educational vouchers that parents could use to defray the costs of attending a private school. Significantly, the U.S. Catholic Conference declined to support the proposal, ostensibly on the grounds that the proposal would shift funds away from successful programs for the disadvantaged. Similarly, a California voucher initiative did not receive enough signatures to qualify for the 1982 state elections; one reason was that the initiative would have provided a voucher equal to 90 percent of the cost of a public school education. Many supporters of family choice declined to support the initiative because of its high payout, which was seen as ensuring closer government regulation of private schools. This fear existed even though the specific language of the initiative precluded any postelection additional regulation of private schools.

It must be emphasized that both vouchers and tuition tax credits can vary in many ways besides the dollar amounts involved. For example, each type of plan could apply to some but not all pupils; for example, handicapped or low-achieving students but not others might be eligible. There could be differences on the extent of school regulation, or what happens if the pupil moves, or what kind of schools must be attended to receive the tax credit or the voucher. Because the objections to a particular plan are not necessarily applicable to other plans, the importance of specifics cannot be overemphasized.

For the most part, the rationale for voucher plans is similar to the rationale for tuition tax credits. The major differences appear to be the issues of equity, ease of administration, and flexibility.

Voucher proponents contend that tuition tax credits would not help children from poor families who often need help the most. In order to take advantage of tuition tax credits, parents must have a certain level of income. Many parents, however, could not use tuition tax credits because their income is too low; they could not offset the tax credits against income because they lack the income. On this issue, voucher supporters tend to agree with opponents of family choice generally that affluent and middle class parents are much more likely than poor ones to use tuition tax credits. If this happens, the upshot will be a public school system drained of much of its middle and upper income support. Because a much higher proportion of white families are in the middle and upper income categories, the proportion of white students in public schools will drop, thereby exacerbating racial segregation in public schools.[6]

Educational vouchers are thus advocated as a means of enabling all parents to exercise the right to choose the kind of education deemed to be in the best interest of their children. Nevertheless, whether greater equity is an inherent advantage of voucher plans is debatable. Tuition tax credits might provide a cash rebate to parents who lacked the income required to take advantage of tuition tax credits. A rebate of this kind was included in the Packwood-Moynihan Bill, which passed the House of Representatives but not the Senate in 1978. The bill would have refunded any unused credit up to $500 per student to taxpayers. Such refunds, however, have not been included in the legislation sponsored by the Reagan administration, nor does it appear likely that they will be included in the near future.[7]

Because the impact of family choice legislation will depend so much upon its specifics and the circumstances in which they are applied, it is difficult to assess its impact upon racial segregation in education. It is easy to visualize legislation that would encourage integration, legislation that would encourage segregation, legislation that would have little effect in either direction, and legislation whose effects would be purely speculative at this time.

Interestingly enough, public opinion polls indicate that black citizens support vouchers more heavily than the population as a whole, and the reasons are not difficult to ascertain. By and large, black children are not doing very well in public schools. Their parents can hardly be blamed for believing that the public schools bear some responsibility for this situation. In large urban districts, black parents see fierce resistance to assigning the more experienced teachers to schools enrolling their children. Schools attended mainly by disadvantaged minorities are more often staffed by inexperienced teachers, substitute teachers, and/or teachers with only an emergency credential; meanwhile, pursuant to union contracts, experienced teachers are using their seniority to avoid assignment to inner city schools. These are only the most visible issues on which minority interests are being sacrificed for teacher or union interests; others have been noted elsewhere in this book. To some minority parents, therefore, the dumping-ground argument is not an abstract possibility to be cited as an objection to family choice proposals. It is a concrete reality that underlies their antagonism to public schools and their support of family choice proposals.

Tuition tax credits/vouchers did not create the problem but may be the way to mitigate it. The reason relates to the way schools are financed and to enrollment patterns in metropolitan areas. School districts in large urban centers tend to enroll a much larger proportion of blacks/Hispanics than surburban districts. The latter, however, spend much more per pupil than the urban districts. They are able to do so at a low cost to suburban parents because a substantial share of suburban school revenues comes from property taxes. Because of their high assessed valuation, properties in suburban districts raise adequate school funds despite a relatively low tax rate. Furthermore, suburban parents can deduct property taxes from their state and federal income taxes, whereas the inner city parents are seldom in a position to claim such deductions. The result is that the suburban parents have access to good schools at a low out-of-pocket cost, while the inner city parents have access only to poor schools that are financed from relatively high tax rates.

At the same time, suburban districts enroll only pupils from within their own boundaries. Currently, therefore, the only way inner city parents can send their children to "better" schools is to move to the suburbs. Needless to say, the vast majority of poor parents are unable to take such action.

With tuition tax credits/vouchers, however, the situation would change materially. Pupils would no longer be so confined to their neighborhood school. If parents were dissatisfied with it, they would be better able to enroll their children in a private school in or outside the neighborhood.

An interesting possibility is that tuition tax credits/vouchers might be available only for students with special needs. For example, a state could provide a tuition tax credit/voucher for handicapped pupils or for pupils who are not achieving satisfactorily. If this were done, the parents of such children would have an alternative to the public schools. If and when circumstances force teacher unions to undergo an agonizing reappraisal of the issue, it will be interesting to see whether they will be troubled by an approach that would make private schools a "dumping ground" for minorities or the handicapped or the poor.

Clearly, the teacher unions are coming under increasing pressure on family choice legislation. Governors in Colorado and Tennessee have endorsed vouchers for pupils with low achievement scores despite opposition from teacher unions. In Minnesota, Governor Rudy Perpich was elected in 1982 with strong support from the Minnesota Education Association (MEA) and the Minnesota Federation of Teachers (MFT). In 1985, Governor Perpich led an unsuccessful effort to enact legislation that would have allowed 11th and 12th graders to enroll in any public school that had space available for them. As a result of opposition to the legislation by the MEA and the MFT, the governor announced that he would not seek or accept their endorsement in 1986. Significantly, the Republican state auditor, who plans to run for governor then, announced that he was "most interested" in receiving the endorsements of the two unions. This illustrates the point that the politics of many educational issues will not necessarily reflect conventional "liberal" versus "conservative" alignments in social issues.[8]

To some extent, public opinion on the "dumping ground" issue is influenced by efforts to evade the 1954 U.S. Supreme Court decisions holding state-imposed racial segregation in public education to be unconstitutional. In an effort to maintain racially segregated schools, some Southern states enacted voucher plans. The vouchers, redeemed by the states, were made available to private schools that were racially segregated. Eventually, these voucher plans were also declared unconstitutional by the U.S. Supreme Court.

Nevertheless, the effort to use vouchers to maintain racially segregated schools is hardly a valid reason to object to tuition tax credits or vouchers. Private schools in the South reflected a greater acceptance of racial integration than public schools, both before and after the 1954 Supreme Court decisions. The efforts to use vouchers to maintain racially segregated schools were initiated by elected public officials trying to maintain racial segregation in education; they did not reflect the thinking of private schools or the supporters of family choice plans. Regardless, tuition tax credits/vouchers can be implemented in ways that do not encourage racial segregation in education. Paradoxically, one argument against their enactment is that they would facilitate "creaming" the ablest black students from predominantly black schools. It is argued that such a development would render it even more difficult to improve education in such schools.[9]

Assistance to Private Schools

The previous discussion has been devoted to public assistance for parent choice. Unquestionably, such assistance would also strengthen private schools. It would be incorrect, however, to assume that private schools do not receive public assistance in the absence of family choice legislation. Directly and indirectly, private schools received $649.2 million, or 26.4 percent of their income, from public sources of revenue in 1970-71. Of this aid, 13.8 percent was provided through indirect tax deductions and exemptions by local, state, and federal tax authorities. Another 12.6 percent was made available by direct program expenditures, such as transportation programs for the handicapped, child nutrition programs, textbooks and other instructional materials, and health and welfare services.[10] Of course, the actual amount of public support varies constantly, but the above estimate probably reflects current levels of support.

The extent to which public assistance is a benefit to parents varies a great deal. Certain types of federal aid, such as transportation services and school lunches, are a direct benefit—that is, they relieve parents of necessary expenditures in some or all schools. Of course, any program that reduces the cost of nonpublic schools has the potential for benefitting parents. Parents of children in private, independent schools seldom benefit from federal programs that are targeted for children from low-income families; in contrast, some Catholic schools enrolling large numbers of such children receive substantial assistance from such programs. The vast majority of private schools benefit from tax exemption policies of federal, state, and/or local governments, but the benefit per pupil or parent fluctuates widely. Overall, Sullivan estimated that the average per pupil subsidy from all levels of government, including both direct and indirect aid, was $123 in 1970-71.[11] In some instances, this aid seems to be based upon legislation that is at least consistent with, if it does not embrace, a family choice approach to educational funding.

In 1985, Minnesota enacted legislation that seems tantamount to a voucher plan period. The legislation provides that 11th and 12th grade pupils may enrol in 4-year liberal arts colleges or technical-vocational schools for courses that are not available in their high-school. A proportionate amount of the state aid per pupil, which normally goes entirely to local school districts, is used to pay for the out of district courses. The legislation, intended to foster academic acceleration by talented students, did not require any additional regulation of the private institutions receiving the voucherized state aid. Although proprietary colleges are not eligible to receive the funds, all nonprofit institutions are eligible without additional regulation. Thus in this case at least, the legislation does not support the argument that vouchers will lead to greater regulation of private schools. Although the legislation is not clear on several important issues, it is a significant utilization of the voucher principle.

Apparently, the fear of competition is not confined to teachers or teacher unions; the Minnesota School Boards Association as well as the two state teacher unions sought to have the legislation repealed in 1986. Such opposition suggests that other alternatives, such as contracting out instruction, may be more successful in fostering competition in the educational enterprise, at least in the short run.

Minnesota is not the only state with voucher-type legislation. Some states pay the tuition for private school students to enroll in driver education programs. Alaska and Vermont provide tuition vouchers to private high schools when no public high school is available. South Carolina and Virginia provide loans and scholarships on a competitive basis to students attending nonsectarian, private secondary schools. Technically, therefore, tuition tax credits/vouchers do not constitute a break from existing practice but an extension of it on a much larger scale. The underlying policy of vouchers—government provides the financial support for a service but the private sector provided the service—is not new. Medicare and Medicaid are only one well-established example of such a policy. Food stamps are still another. Even in education, there have been large-scale programs of this kind, such as veterans' benefits for education (the "G.I. Bill of Rights").

Family Choice: Prospects for Enactment

One objection to tuition tax credits and vouchers was based upon First Amendment considerations; inasmuch as most private schools are affiliated with a religious organization, the tax credits would allegedly constitute an unconstitutional form of assistance to religion. This objection, however, is probably no longer a factor; in 1983, the U.S. Supreme Court, in a 5-4 decision, upheld a Minnesota law that provided tax deductions for parents of public as well as private (including denominational) schools.[12] It thus appears that federal legislation can be drafted in a way that overcomes any constitutional objections. The main issue appears to be whether the legislation must be applicable to public as well as private school students. Although federal legislation that applied to both would undoubtedly be upheld, such broad applicability would probably face intense congressional opposition at this time.

Perhaps there are two basic questions to be asked about tuition tax credits/vouchers. One relates to their prospects for enactment. The other is their prospects for achieving any basic improvement in education. Let us consider these questions in this order.

As to the likelihood of enactment, the issue is not so much "if" as it is "when." After the U.S. Supreme Court decision in *Mueller* v. *Allen*, there was an upsurge of interest and activity on the subject at the state level. By March 1984, legislators in 13 states had introduced or planned to introduce tax credit or tax deductions for educational expenses. Most were patterned after the Minnesota law upheld by the U.S. Supreme Court. Inasmuch as 11 state legislatures were not in

session .at the time the survey was made, tuition tax credits will undoubtedly be introduced in more states in the near future.[13]

We can now appreciate the importance of parental/taxpayer dissatisfaction with public education, regardless of reason or validity.
Parents may wish to send their children to private schools for any one
of several reasons: Low academic standards, security problems, preference for religious indoctrination, opposition to sex education, dissatisfaction over standards of student dress, language, and/or conduct
—the list could be extended indefinitely. Parents may share nothing
in common except a mutual desire to transfer their children out of
public school. Nonetheless, public opinion polls indicate that a plural-
ity of the American people support vouchers; the 1985 Gallup Poll
of the "Public's Attitude Toward the Public Schools" indicated that
45 percent of the public supported vouchers, only 40 percent were
opposed, and 15 percent had no opinion. In 1971 only 38 percent
supported vouchers, 44 percent disapproved, and 18 percent had no
opinion.[14] Significantly, blacks show a higher link of support than
the public generally.

This situation reflects a recent increase in the level of support for
tuition tax credits/vouchers; during the 1960s and 1970s, public
opinion on the issues showed a slight majority opposed to vouchers
at least.[15] As previously noted, President Reagan has been a consistent advocate of family choice, especially tuition tax credits. Given
the enormous power of the president of the United States to generate
public support for his policy objectives, the 1984 reelection of President Reagan will probably lead to increased support for tuition tax
credits/vouchers. Although this may be an optimistic view, it is held
by some of the leading opponents as well as supporters of family
choice proposals.

Let us not, however, make the same mistake attributed to others
in this book, that is, failure to consider the obstacles to reform proposals. Despite President Reagan's support for family choice, federal
tuition tax credits face at least two major problems apart from the
customary opposition to such measures. First, the federal deficits
have generated enormous pressures on Congress and the president to
avoid legislation that would reduce federal revenues or increase federal
spending. Unquestionably, tuition tax credits would result in a significant loss of federal revenues. If Title I funds were voucherized, vouchers would not require additional federal expenditures; still, federally
sponsored vouchers would probably be unacceptable for other reasons
at this time.

Tuition tax credits would also have to survive the tax simplification movement. At a time when political and public opinion are moving toward lower tax rates tied to reducing tax deductions and tax credits, legislation that would establish another major federal tax credit will undoubtedly face strong opposition on philosophical and conceptual grounds. If the congressional proponents of tuition tax credits press for their enactment, they will encourage other interest groups to retain or establish other tax deductions or tax credits. In short, the pressures to reduce federal deficits and to simplify the federal tax structure will weaken congressional support for tuition tax credits, probably to the point of inaction on the issue. Marginal and reluctant supporters have a politically viable reason for voting against tuition tax credits without appearing to oppose them in principle. All in all, only a determined effort by President Reagan could succeed, and perhaps even such an effort would be futile unless and until the federal deficit is reduced substantially.

Needless to say, many states will be facing fiscal problems of their own. For example, the states may be forced to make up for losses in federal revenues in order to maintain various social services. Although the fiscal situation will vary widely among the states, it may be extremely difficult to enact state legislation that would intensify a state's fiscal problems. From a state point of view, the ideal solution would be to have federal tuition tax credits. In this situation, the federal government would lose the revenue because of the credits; the states, however, would benefit fiscally from lower enrollments in public schools. If, however, the states have to absorb the revenue losses resulting from the tax credits, the fiscal condition of the states becomes a critical factor.

At both the state and federal levels, we can expect intensive opposition to tuition tax credits/vouchers. Such opposition includes, but is not limited to, the organizations (including state and local affiliates) associated with public education: National Education Association, American Federation of Teachers, American Association of School Administrators, National School Boards Association, National Congress of Parents and Teachers, and so on. It also includes many religious denominations that do not operate schools, and a number of organizations, such as the American Civil Liberties Union, that are not active primarily in education but have a strong interest in it.

Where defeat of such legislation is impossible, an effort will be made to tie it to crippling conditions, such as the following:

- Tuition tax credits must be applicable only to schools with cer-tified teachers/administrators.
- The schools must meet the building and safety requirements of public schools.
- The schools must offer certain courses and/or curricula that they may not be offering when the legislation is pending.
- The schools must enroll a certain proportion of minority or handicapped or low-achieving students.
- The schools must provide certain services, such as counseling, testing, school nurses, and psychologists.

The above list can and will be extended indefinitely. What will happen in any particular state is anyone's guess. A bandwagon for en-actment is possible; more likely, guerrilla warfare will be the order of the day. The legislation will be challenged in state and federal courts; such challenges may delay implementation of the legislation for long periods of time. When legislation eventually overcomes these hurdles, opponents of it in other states will emphasize the alleged need to assess the results before enacting new state legislation. Any negative outcome will be publicized immediately and forcefully; in the absence of such, it will be contended that more time is needed to assess the results where the legislation has been enacted.

Nevertheless, the critical fact is that the politics of the issue have changed materially. When 90 percent of private schools were denomi-national, and 90 percent of the denominational schools were Catholic, the politics of the issue were unfavorable to tuition tax credits/vouch-ers. The equity argument was not persuasive to non-Catholics. Their view was: "We're providing good schools through our tax dollars. If parents want to send their children elsewhere, that's fine, but that's no reason to give them a tax break or a voucher. If you don't like the public tennis courts, we don't give you a voucher to play at a private tennis club of your choice—or a tax deduction."

The merits of the argument have not changed in recent years. What changed was the political base of support for parent choice. As more parents became dissatisfied with public schools, more have also become receptive to tuition tax credits/vouchers.

FAMILY CHOICE: PROSPECTS FOR ACHIEVING EDUCATIONAL REFORM

To what extent, if any, will tuition tax credits/vouchers generate any basic improvement in education? There is little direct evidence, especially on vouchers, to answer this question. As we have seen, many factors, such as the amount of the tax credit or voucher, could affect the consequences; at this time, therefore, predictions of great improvement or of educational disaster are premature. For that matter, it may be difficult to understand what happens if and when family choice legislation is enacted. Proponents will perceive one set of consequences, and opponents a very different set. The data and arguments of both sides are likely to be incomplete if not irrelevant to the perpetuation or extension of family choice.

The predictions that family choice measures would improve education are frequently based on the view that private schools are more effective educationally than public schools. Inasmuch as family choice measures would increase enrollments in private schools, they would presumably lead to better education for more pupils.

Although this line of reasoning can be challenged on several grounds, it dominates much popular discussion of family choice issues. It will be helpful, therefore, to review this issue briefly.

In recent years there have been two major efforts to compare student achievement in public and private schools. One, directed by James S. Coleman of the University of Chicago, was a federally financed study of 58,728 high school seniors and sophomores in 1,000 public and nonpublic schools, Catholic and non-Catholic. The major conclusion of this study was that "in general, with [family] background characteristics controlled, Catholic school sophomores perform at the highest level, sophomores in other private schools next, and sophomores in the public school lowest."[16]

The other study, conducted under the auspices of the National Assessment of Educational Progress (NAEP), was also financed federally but by a different agency. It involved 104,000 children aged nine, thirteen, and seventeen, in 1,377 schools. This study concluded that "when the data are adjusted to compensate for socioeconomic differences in the composition of private and public school student populations, national differences cease to be statistically significant."[17]

Although the Coleman and NAEP studies appear to reach inconsistent if not contradictory conclusions, the conclusions of both studies may be justified. One possibility is that the higher levels of achievement in private schools are due mainly to the effect of a peer environment more supportive of learning. To illustrate, suppose we had twins identical in every respect. One, however, attends a private school in which her classmates are talented and motivated students.

The other twin, every bit as able and motivated as her sister, attends a public school in which her classmates are much less talented and motivated than her sister's classmates.

In this situation, we would expect the twin attending private school to perform better than the twin attending public school. The difference, however, would not be attributable to the superiority of the private school as such. It would be due to the influence of a more supportive peer group. If the public school enrolled the more supportive peer group, it would achieve better results than the private school.

Another possibility is that the two studies differ because they involved different grade levels and socioeconomic types of students. For example, Catholic schools may be more effective than public schools in educating disadvantaged black elementary pupils. They may reveal no superiority or even an inferiority in educating upper middle class white high school students. In other words, the educational superiority or inferiority of public to private schools may vary according to the kind of student involved.[18]

Per pupil costs are sometimes said to be twice as high in public as in private schools. This appears to be a strong argument for family choice and private schools; the case for strengthening private schools would hardly need any additional support if private schools can achieve as much at half the cost. An automobile dealer could hardly survive if a competitor's car costing only half as much performed as well.

Although per pupil costs in private schools are commonly said to be only about half of the costs in public schools, the reasons do not always reflect any greater efficiency in private schools. Nor is the major reason the presence of members of religious orders in Catholic schools, which are now staffed largely by lay teachers. One reason is that private schools seldom conduct vocational programs, which usually cost more than academic ones. Also, private schools enroll a much smaller proportion of handicapped, retarded, and unruly pupils, hence they do not need to devote as much of their resources for such pupils. Some costs of denominational schools, such as utilities or debt service, are carried on parish or church but not school budgets. Additionally, the patrons of private schools tend to be more involved and more supportive in ways that reduce costs and generate revenues. A major factor is that some services, such as transportation and health services, are carried as expenditures by the local public schools but are not expenditures for the private schools which utilize the services.

At the same time, per pupil costs in public schools are typically understated. One reason is that the figures usually omit the costs of school land and property. Such costs do not show up on school operating budgets, except for debt service, which would typically reflect only a small fraction of the real costs to the taxpayers. Typically, school district ownership results in a loss of tax revenues from property not used commercially, but such costs are not factored in the per pupil costs of the school district. Unfunded state pension liabilities are another cost that is not included in data on per pupil costs. In short, the costs of public as well as private schools are systematically understated. Undoubtedly, the extent of understatement varies from district to district and school to school, but citizens generally are not aware of the real costs of either public or private schools.[19]

These understatements raise serious doubts about the comparisons of per pupil costs in the two sectors. They also raise questions concerning the anticipated savings from pupils who might transfer to private schools under family choice measures. In any event, since private schools typically do not offer many programs and services found in public schools, meaningful competition between public and private schools does not exist for large numbers and categories of students.

Regulation of Nonpublic Schools

From a private school standpoint, the prospect of increased regulation is the major negative associated with family choice legislation. Rightly or wrongly, most private school leaders believe that tuition tax credits would be less threatening to their independence. Unquestionably, some family choice legislation will call for increased regulation of nonpublic schools; private school leaders may be unwilling to accept such increased regulation, even if their refusal leads to legislative rejection of the legislation.

As previously noted, most private school leaders believe tuition tax credits will preserve their independence more effectively than vouchers. In theory, tuition tax credits do not require any additional regulation of private schools. The parent claims a tax credit; the regulation of private schools can remain as is. In practice, many parents are going to claim expenses for educational travel, books, supplies; some of these parents will be challenged on the issue by state and federal tax collectors. Thus although schools may avoid more regulation under tuition tax credits, some parents who claim the credit may not be so fortunate. Realistically, both public and private schools will be asked to provide or confirm liberal estimates of out-of-pocket educational expenses. When this happens, the schools may find themselves asked to confirm excessive claims to maximize the tax credit.

Voucher proponents are likewise concerned about the possibility of increased regulation. A proposed California voucher initiative would resolve this problem by prohibiting the state from adding to the regulation of private schools after the voucher initiative was adopted (see Appendix B, Section 1 [d]). This seems difficult to defend. Understandably, it would not be desirable to have a successful voucher initiative emasculated by excessive regulation of private schools. On the other hand, prohibiting any subsequent regulation of private schools is excessive protection for them; a prohibition against additional regulation for a few years would be much more defensible.

An important but widely overlooked fact is that the legislative specifics will affect the educational and fiscal outcomes of parent choice plans. At the present time, most attention is being paid to questions such as these: How large should the tax credit or voucher be? How many pupils will transfer to private schools? From what socioeconomic levels? What will be the consequences for tax revenues? Questions such as these are uppermost in the debate over tuition tax credits/vouchers. It should not be overlooked, however, that legislation implementing parent choice might not necessarily be conducive to the potential benefits of it. For instance, an interesting study by Donald Erickson indicated that a voucher plan in British Columbia actually weakened some of the positive characteristics of private schools there.[20] If parent choice legislation leads to more emphasis upon meeting government regulations than parent preferences, the virtues of parent choice may be lost.

For several reasons, enactment of tuition tax credits/vouchers is likely to lead to greater regulation of private schools. The mere fact that more pupils will be enrolled in private schools and that such schools will be receiving more public support will be conducive to this outcome. Nevertheless, in some states regulation of public schools may decrease as a result of tuition tax credits/vouchers.

To see how this might happen, consider a state where public but not private school teachers must be certified. Suppose further, as is actually the case in some states, that pupils in private schools are achieving at equal or higher levels than comparable pupils in public schools. In such a situation—and there are and will be several of this nature—it would make more sense to eliminate certification requirements in public education than to add them to nonpublic education.

The Selectivity Issue

One reason private schools can achieve higher standards of student conduct is their greater freedom to expel students. The latter must then be enrolled in public schools, which have no choice in the matter because of the compulsory attendance laws. Comparisons of pupil achievement in private schools to that in public schools are obviously unfair to the latter if the selectivity factor is ignored; any differences that favor the private schools may be due to their selectivity, not to any superiority in their teachers or their programs. This possibility points to a widespread concern among public school leaders. They fear that public opinion will favor private schools on the basis of comparisons that ignore the selectivity factor. As this happens, public education would suffer in prestige and support to the detriment of society as a whole as well as teachers.

The factual premises in this concern can be conceded. Private schools have used expulsion and the threat of expulsion to maintain discipline; they have "dumped" pupils they could not handle into the public schools; and public opinion has sometimes ignored this fact in comparing the performance of public and private schools. The extent of these things is not clear, but the underlying concern has a rational basis.

In fact, the scholarly comparisons of private and public schools are careful to use comparable groups of students. The researchers are well aware of the danger that their comparisons may reflect differences in the pupil population instead of school performance. Furthermore, the public schools have ample resources to identify and correct any inaccurate or unfair comparisons. For that matter, the public education lobby is not always circumspect in publicizing comparisons between the two systems; for example, public school leaders rarely mention the much higher per pupil costs of public schools in their comparisons. The selectivity issue would be even less important if legislation provided tuition tax credits/vouchers for handicapped pupils or pupils not performing well, thereby encouraging their transfer to private schools.

In any event, the remedy proposed (no strengthening of parent choice) constitutes a case of overkill. In the private sector, people make unfair or inaccurate comparisons of products or services every day. We do not, however, regard this as a reason to eliminate competition. On the contrary, we try to improve the competition by having consumers better informed about the competing claims. Similarly, we can deal with the problem of "unfair" competition in education without eliminating or diminishing parental choice in education.

Whether or not strengthening parent choice will lead to beneficial results, the rate at which we will move in this direction is uncertain; even with favorable legislation a large-scale shift to private schools might not occur for a long period of time.[21] It is not all that easy to start a school. Just developing the physical facilities can take years; in addition, the sponsors have to identify management, employ a teaching staff, purchase books and supplies, arrange for pupil recruitment, transportation, and so on. Any increase in private school enrollments is more likely to result from expansion or fuller utilization of existing capacity than from new schools per se.

Also, many parents who wish to send their children to private schools may live where there are none. For private schools to operate efficiently, there must be an adequate student population. Ten percent of the student population in metropolitan areas could support many private schools; 10 percent in a rural area may be unable to support one.

The rate at which existing private schools will increase their enrollments is problematical. Some are denominational and would not have any appeal outside their denomination. Others vary widely in the extent to which they can absorb more pupils. In some schools, the effect of tuition tax credits or vouchers would be to raise the charges to parents, not to increase the number of pupils.

Still, with all due consideration for the negatives in the situation, the supporters of tuition tax credits/vouchers have a stronger educational argument than they themselves realize. These supporters have always contended that more competition from private schools would be good for public education. This argument, however, was not based upon a concrete analysis of the difficulties of improving public schools. Instead, the appeal to competition has been largely a rhetorical ploy. Ironically, it was intended to wrap the mantle of the free enterprise system around nonprofit institutions.

The average parent who enrolls a child in a private school is not aware of the enormous obstacles to public school reform. The consequences of such things as tenure laws, teacher bargaining, and single salary schedules have important effects in the classroom, but most parents are not in a position to make the connections. Furthermore, they do not have the time or energy to devote to educational reform. Instead, they have their hands full just trying to obtain the best possible education for their children under the circumstances. Parents want their children to have a good education; otherwise, they neither want nor need to "participate." The parents are like the dissatisfied purchasers of a new car. What they want is a replacement without an argument. In effect, tuition tax credits/vouchers give it to them, or to more of them.

It is true that parents often criticize public schools unfairly. Nevertheless, public schools have also avoided a great deal of deserved criticism because the public is unaware of the situation. On balance, school boards, school administrators, and public school teachers probably benefit more than they suffer from public ignorance about the realities of public education.

One additional comment may be appropriate. Today, most people assume that universal, completely tax-supported public schools came about as a spontaneous reaction of the American people. This is inaccurate. As West has shown, education in the United States was virtually universal *before* it was tax supported.[22] The change to a fully tax-supported educational system was promoted by organizations of public school teachers and administrators. These groups, be it noted, stood to gain directly from the change. This does not mean the change was a mistake. Nor would it be a mistake today to change to tuition tax credits/vouchers merely because they are contrary to the interests of public school teachers.

The Role of School Boards

School board members as such do not make their livelihood from public education. For this reason, we might expect them not to be as opposed to tuition tax credits/vouchers as are public school administrators and teachers. It appears, however, that school board members and their organizations are just as opposed to family choice as their employees. My question is whether this is an effective strategy to achieve educational reform.

The critical issue is whether school boards are committed to the objective of good education, or to a particular means of achieving good education, that is, the public schools. Boards have treated the means as synonymous with the objective. At this juncture, distinguishing between them must be the top priority for boards that wish to strengthen public education as an institution.

Such a change might lead to all sorts of positive consequences. For instance, consider the reflexive way public school boards and administrators react to comparisons between public and private schools.

The reaction is: "Pupils of equal talent in private schools aren't learning more than pupils in public schools." Their reaction should be: "Inasmuch as we are spending more per pupil than private schools, why aren't our pupils learning more than private school pupils of comparable ability? What do private schools do, or what do they know, that enables them to educate as well but at a lower cost per pupil?"

Most of the time, we do not challenge our basic institutional arrangements. We establish hospitals to foster health, prisons to deter crime, and schools to facilitate learning. Sometimes, however, we have to ask: Are the means adopted impeding instead of facilitating the ends they are supposed to serve?

We are now at this stage in education: It is essential to ask ourselves whether the means are not blocking instead of facilitating the end, which is a well-educated citizenry. Intellectually, most school board members have not reached this stage yet. On the other hand, if public education is to be reformed and revived as a basic social institution, school board members should lead the way. Their strategy, however, will have to change from defending public education to criticizing it, and from avoiding public assistance to private schools at all costs to a public willingness to support such aid if it continues to be impossible to achieve educational reform in public schools.

As matters stand, state and national organizations of school board members are on record as opposed to tuition tax credits/vouchers. By taking this position, they have lost a great deal of their bargaining power with the organizations blocking reform. If a few school boards were to support tuition tax credits/vouchers because they found it impossible to achieve reform within the present system, they could have a profound effect in their districts, their states, and perhaps even the nation. Governors, legislators, political leaders, and unions, teacher and nonteacher alike, could hardly ignore such a sharp erosion of public support for public education in its present moribund state.

I realize that my suggested approach will be regarded as "hardball." Still, what is the alternative to overcome those who play hardball to block reform? In the absence of a more effective strategy than we have seen thus far, hardball may be the name of the game.

Family Choice and Entrepreneurial Schools

From the standpoint of entrepreneurial schools, the most important family choice issue is this: Will tuition tax credits/vouchers be available to parents who wish to use them in entrepreneurial schools?

As matters stand, the answer to this question in proposed state and federal legislation is negative. Because this issue is so important, and because it may be resolved more by neglect than thoughtful consideration of the consequences, some comment on it seems appropriate. Because the issue has arisen primarily in connection with voucher plans, it will be discussed largely in these terms.

Voucher supporters are divided on whether profitmaking schools should be eligible for vouchers. One point of view is that they should not be, because the danger of exploitation is too great.[23] This is not the view, however, of the leading proponents of vouchers. For instance, Milton Friedman, former president of the American Economic Association and perhaps the most prestigious academic supporter of vouchers, supported and envisaged their utilization in profit-making schools.[24] Likewise, John Coons and Stephen Sugarman, two leading advocates of vouchers in the 1970s and early 1980s, oppose the exclusion of proprietary schools from voucher plans. In their major book on vouchers, they explicitly consider whether proprietary schools should be eligible for vouchers; their answer is that it would be premature to do so.[25]

To this observer, the case for making family choice benefits available to patrons of entrepreneurial schools is a compelling one. If our objective is to strengthen family choice, why limit the choices to the establishment, public or private? On what basis can we say that parents can choose between public and private nonprofit schools, but are not capable of choosing if another option (profit-making schools) is added? Will the supporters of family choice who emphasize the benefits of competition nevertheless support legislation that stifles competition? To do so would be to destroy their credibility on the benefits of competition in the education industry.

The other major policy argument for extending family choice benefits to entrepreneurial schools is the need to avoid foreclosing significant educational policy options. Granted, we may not know enough about entrepreneurial schools to be confident that they constitute "the answer" to any major educational problem. We have even less knowledge or basis for excluding them as a part of the solutions we seek. This point is especially pertinent in view of recent trends toward utilizing private enterprise to carry out public services. We turn now to a more detailed consideration of these possibilities in the field of education—possibilities that could easily be foreclosed solely by restricting family choice to public and nonprofit schools.

NOTES

1. *President Albert Shanker's Address to the 1983 AFT Convention* (Washington, D.C.: American Federation of Teachers, n.d.), p. 3. The last sentence was included in a typewritten copy distributed separately.

2. Publications supporting family choice include: Joe C. Nathan, *Free to Teach* (Minneapolis: Winston Press, 1983); E. G. West, *The Economics of Education Tax Credits* (Washington, D.C.: Heritage Foundation, 1981); John E. Coons and Stephen D. Sugarman, *Education by Choice: The Case For Family Control* (Berkeley: University of California Press, 1978); Milton and Rose Friedman, *Tyranny of The Status Quo* (San Diego: Harcourt Brace Jovanovich, 1983); the chapters by E. G. West, Donald A. Erickson, Thomas W. Vitullo-Martin, and Roger A. Freeman in *The Public School Monopoly*, ed. Robert B. Everhart (San Francisco: Pacific Institute for Public Policy Research, 1981); and James S. Coleman, Thomas Hoffer, and Sally Kilgore, *Public and Private Schools* (Chicago: National Opinion Research Center, 1981), hereinafter "Coleman study." Significant criticisms of family choice are included in Thomas James and Henry M. Levin, eds., *Public Dollars for Private Schools* (Philadelphia: Temple University Press, 1983); Michael E. Manley-Casimir, ed., *Family Choice in Schooling* (Lexington, Mass.: Lexington Books, 1982); and the *Sociology of Education*, April and July 1982, a double issue devoted entirely to the Coleman study. These publications also include articles supporting family choice and additional references on the subject, including scores of journal articles on various issues involved in both tuition tax credits and vouchers. The Institute for Research on Educational Finance and Governance at Stanford University has published helpful monographs on family choice issues. Monographs highly critical of family choice (tuition tax credits) proposals include: James S. Catterall and Henry M. Levin, *Public and Private Schools: Evidence on Tuition Tax Credits* (February 1982); and James S. Catterall, *Tuition Tax Credits: Issues of Equity* (December 1982).

3. An excellent summary of the fiscal issues and recent federal legislation can be found in John Augenblick and C. Kent McGuire, *Tuition Tax Credits: Their Impact on the States* (Denver: Education Commission of the States, October 1982). See also David A. Longanecker, *Public Cost of Tuition Tax Credits* (Stanford, Calif.: Institute for Research on Educational Finance and Governance, Stanford University, July 1982). In some respects, the best economic analysis is Donald E. Frey, *Tuition Tax Credits for Private Education: An Economic Analysis* (Ames: Iowa State University Press, 1983).

4. Edwin G. West, "The Real Costs of Tuition Tax Credits," monograph received from Dr. West.

5. More comprehensive arguments for vouchers are set forth in the publications listed in note 2.

6. See Catterall and Levin.

7. A sympathetic analysis of the Packwood-Moynihan bill can be found in West, *The Economics of Education Tax Credits*, pp. 38-40; and E. G. West,

"Tuition Tax Credit Proposals: An Economic Analysis of the 1978 Packwood/ Moynihan Bill," *Policy Review*, Winter 1978, pp. 61-75.

8. *Education Week*, April 17, 1985, p. 8. The same page included an item about a meeting under the auspices of the National Governors Conference to explore ways in which private enterprise could become more active in the child care industry.

9. See James and Levin, Chapters 5, 12, and 13 for discussions bearing on this issue.

10. See Dennis J. Encarnation, "Public Finance and Regulation of Nonpublic Education," in James and Levin, p. 178; Daniel J. Sullivan, *Public Aid to Nonpublic Schools* (Lexington, Mass.: D.C. Heath, 1974).

11. Sullivan, p. 93.

12. *Mueller* v. *Allen*, 77 L. Ed. 26 (1983). See also Ronald M. Jensen, *Tuition Tax Credits: Has the Supreme Court Cleared the Way* (Stanford, Calif.: Institute for Research on Educational Finance and Governance, Stanford University, July 1983).

13. Cindy Currence, "Tax Credit Bills Are Advancing in Legislatures," *Education Week*, March 7, 1984, pp. 1, 18.

14. Alec M. Gallup, "The 17th Annual Gallup Poll of the Public's Attitudes Toward the Public Schools," *Phi Delta Kappan*, September 1985, p. 46.

15. Stanley M. Elam, ed., *A Decade of Gallup Polls of Attitudes Toward Education, 1969-1978*, (Bloomington, Ind.: Phi Delta Kappa, 1978), pp. 60-61, 73-74, 90-91, 104.

16. Coleman et al., p. 173.

17. *National Assessment of Education Progress, Reading and Mathematics Achievement in Public and Private Schools: Is There a Difference?* Report No. SY-RM-50 (Denver: Education Commission of the States, 1981) (hereinafter "NAEP Study"), p. 1.

18. See Richard J. Murnane, "The Uncertain Consequences of Tuition Tax Credits," in James and Levin, pp. 210-22.

19. For discussions of the difficulties of comparing public and private school costs, see Daniel J. Sullivan, *Comparing Efficiency Between Public and Private Schools* (Stanford, Calif.: Institute for Research on Educational Finance and Governance, Stanford University, February 1983); and E. G. West, "Choice or Monopoly in Education," *Policy Review*, Winter 1981, pp. 103-17.

20. Donald A. Erickson, "Disturbing Evidence About the 'One Best System,' " in Everhart, pp. 393-422.

21. See Murnane, in James and Levin, pp. 210-22.

22. West, *The Economics of Education Tax Credits*, pp. 12-13.

23. See Coons and Sugarman, p. 155.

24. See Milton Friedman, *Capitalism and Freedom* (Chicago: University of Chicago Press, 1962).

25. Coons and Sugarman, pp. 155-60.

9

ENTREPRENEURIAL SCHOOLS

Insofar as it goes, the foregoing analysis is undoubtedly a pessimistic one. Even so, I have by no means identified all the major barriers to improving American education. For instance, bilingual education has frequently degenerated into a patronage device that retards instead of fosters fluency in English. Vocational education is frequently geared more to the needs of vocational teachers than to the requirements or opportunities in the world of work. History and civics in the public schools are largely sophisticated folklore—not because the curriculum isn't prepared by "scholars" in these disciplines, but because it is. Nobody seems to know what to do about the corrosive impact of television, and perhaps nothing can be done about it. To repeat, the preceding analysis was illustrative, not comprehensive.

On the other hand, the analysis has asserted that the public education community is unable to identify, let alone to adopt the necessary reforms. In conjunction with media inability to identify the basic issues, political pressures to rely upon the appearance of reform as a substitute for actual reform, and the obstructionist role of higher education, educational reform appears to be a lost cause. We might be fortunate enough to experience some sort of technological breakthrough that would bring about large-scale improvement, but there is no way to anticipate this. Furthermore, one of the valid objections to the existing structure is its failure to foster technological progress in a field where such progress is badly needed.

Tuition tax credits/vouchers do offer some hope of improvement, but these changes face an extended legai and political struggle and are not likely to be fully effective for many years to come. Even then, their effectiveness may be limited and not deal with some of the most critical factors in the situation.

Nevertheless, the situation appears to me to be grim rather than hopeless. Without in any way softening the impact of the negatives I have mentioned, I would like to turn to a more optimistic possibility. After all, realism requires that one consider favorable as well as unfavorable possibilities as we look ahead.

Preliminarily, let me set forth a point of view about educational reform. Throughout this analysis, I have tried to avoid a mistake repeatedly attributed to others, that is, proposing solutions that would be desirable but that cannot be achieved on a broad scale for a long period of time. For this reason, I have not proclaimed a reform manifesto calling for changes in the governance structure of education, repeal of the tenure laws, abolition of most certification requirements, or a host of other changes I regard as desirable. Inasmuch as I also regard them as unattainable for a long time to come, and then only after other developments have paved the way, I do not regard these changes as a reform program, despite their importance.

At the same time, it is not true that important changes must be made incrementally, or that they necessarily require a long period of time. On the contrary, it is sometimes easier to make a major change than an incremental one. One reason is that outstanding leaders cannot be recruited for small tasks. Another is that some changes can take place only on a large scale.

For example, in eliminating racial discrimination in employment, it was often easier to do so on an industrywide instead of a business-by-business basis. Particular department stores were sometimes willing to eliminate discriminatory practices, but only if other stores also did so. Incremental change in this situation was impossible, but large-scale, institutionwide change was not.

Actually, there is no need to look outside the field of education for examples of basic change on a national scale within a relatively short period of time. The first important collective bargaining election for teachers was conducted in December 1961, in a state that had not legalized teacher bargaining. By 1965, several large states had done so; by the early 1970s, a majority. Today, 73 percent of the nation's teachers are unionized. The change from a nonunion to a union environment has had an enormous impact upon many aspects of education; it is probably the single most important change in school district operations in the past 20 years. The rapidity of the change was astonishing; even its most ardent supporters were as surprised as anyone else when their rhetoric became a reality.[1]

We should not, therefore, subscribe to the idea that educational reform necessarily has to be incremental or a long time in coming. It may be, or it may not be. I will suggest how entrepreneurial schools might achieve major improvements in a relatively short period of time. Before presenting this suggestion, let me first discuss some issues on which the distinction between private nonprofit and private profit-making schools is absolutely critical.

THE ROLE OF COMPETITION IN EDUCATIONAL REFORM

The supporters of private schools typically emphasize the benefits of competition between schools. I agree that competition from and between private schools could be a major force for educational improvement. It seems to me, however, that private nonprofit schools are inherently incapable of generating the most important benefits that could result from competition between schools. This critical point requires some elaboration.

First of all, the argument that tuition tax credits/vouchers would foster "competition" between public and nonpublic schools is severely flawed by the nature of the competition. Consider these two situations:

A.   Parents are deciding whether to send their children to denominational schools that provide religious instruction not available in public schools.

B.   Parents are deciding whether to send their children to private nonprofit schools solely on the basis of the allegedly greater secular benefits of the private school.

Obviously, the "competition" between public and nonpublic schools is very different in these situations. In situation A, the competition is very attenuated, and may not even exist. Theoretically, at least, the parents may opt for the private school even though the public school is as good or better on all of the nonreligious criteria. For example, parents may send their children to parochial schools, not because the children will read or write more effectively but because the parochial school will indoctrinate Catholicism.

In this situation, where is the competition? The parochial school provides something the public school cannot, no matter how effective it is educationally. This is not "competition" but the antithesis of it. In order for there to be "competition" in any meaningful sense, there must be, ultimately at least, striving for superiority on the basis of a common criterion.

Situation B illustrates a meaningful competitive situation. Presumably, the choice of school depends upon their comparative effectiveness on common criteria. Which school will maximize reading and writing skills? Which school will develop more appreciation of literature and the arts? Insofar as the choice of school is made on the basis of such criteria, we can say that the schools are competitive.

As previously noted, most private schools are denominational. Philosophically, many justify their existence and appeal to parents on what is essentially a noncompetitive basis, to wit, the inculcation of a religious view that could not be fostered in a public school. As a practical matter, however, the denominational schools cannot rely solely upon religious appeals for student enrollments. Literally and philosophically, they may assert that enrollment is essential to protect students from eternal misfortune. If parents really believed this claim, school effectiveness in teaching reading, writing, and arithmetic would be a secondary, even trivial, consideration. To my knowledge, however, no denominational school is content to let the issue rest at this point. On the contrary, all assert that their schools will also be better for pupils on the basis of secular educational results. For this reason, we cannot say that there is no genuine competition between denominational and public schools. What there is, however, is highly attenuated and very difficult to evaluate. At one extreme, some parents are motivated primarily by religious considerations. They send their children to denominational schools as long as such schools are not visibly inferior to public schools on secular educational criteria. At the other extreme, some parents of pupils in private schools ignore the religious appeal completely. Such parents are similar to those in situation B above; their decision illustrates the fact that the choice of public or denominational school is at least partly competitive in some situations.

In any event, the appeal to the benefits of "competition" between public and private nonprofit schools has obscured several important facts. One is that such competition has not really resulted in any significant improvement in the process of education—to quote a well-known phrase, "Where's the beef?" What are the specific improvements in educational technology or practice or content that have resulted from this competition? I know of none, not even as a plausible claim.

My point is not to denigrate the value of educational choice as it currently exists. It is an important option that should be maintained. Furthermore, I do not challenge the claim that most private schools, at least most denominational ones, bring about as much or more educational achievement at a lower average per pupil cost than public schools. My point is that this superiority, to the extent that it exists, is not due to any superior expertise or technological superiority; it is due to their social and legal advantages over public schools. Parents may be justified in paying substantial amounts so that their children can benefit from these advantages, but the latter do not include a higher level of expertise.

To achieve the benefits of competition, schools must compete on common criteria. Basically, they must generate improvements in the technology of education, in the methods and materials of instruction, and in the efficiency and usefulness of related support services, such as their evaluation procedures and communications with parents. In other words, we need the educational equivalent of automatic over manual transmission, refrigerators over ice boxes, and photocopiers over spirit duplicators. To achieve improvements of this nature, it is essential to involve the profit-making sector in education. Conceptually, profit-making firms could develop new educational technologies and sell them to public schools, just as they sell the new products mentioned above. We must bear in mind, however, that the education market was not essential to their development. In order to generate the capital required for large-scale investment in educational technology, defined to include teaching methods and processes as well as hardware, entrepreneurial leadership must be confident that the technological improvement resulting from its R and D can be marketed promptly. To use an analogy, automobile manufacturers did not have to worry about marketing automatic transmissions; they were already in the business of manufacturing and selling automobiles. By the same token, firms that are already in the education industry will not have to be concerned about the market for improvements. Instead, their concern will be not letting their competition penetrate the market first with the improvement.

For competitive reasons, entrepreneurial schools would provide a greater variety of subjects and programs and activities than either public or nonprofit schools. Public schools are limited in this respect by several factors. For example, tenure statutes may make it illegal to require a tenured teacher to direct an extracurricular activity against the teacher's wishes. Many union contracts specifically render such activities voluntary and/or require they be dropped if no teacher volunteers to direct them at the salary offered by the district.

Similarly, public schools are limited by statute or collective bargaining in hiring part-time teachers. This restricts their ability to offer courses that do not justify employment of a full-time teacher, or cannot be joined with regular courses to constitute a full-time position.

Nonprofit schools are not limited this way, but their entire program is typically even more limited than public school programs. For instance, nonprofit schools usually do not offer vocational education or special education, that is, education for the handicapped or retarded. The denominational schools may find that adding religious instruction and activities to conventional programs is often all they can or wish to offer that is not available in public schools. The independent nondenominational schools that cater largely to the very affluent often offer courses and activities not available in public schools, but their existence depends on their exclusivity. For this very reason, they have no interest, as an entrepreneurial school would, in expanding markets for courses and/or activities not available in public schools.

On the other hand, an entrepreneurial school could capitalize on several different kinds of opportunities to expand instruction. Very few public or nonprofit schools have golf or tennis coaches of professional caliber. Entrepreneurial schools could conveniently provide individual or small group instruction with payment of an additional fee. The latter, however, would be much lower than the fees normally paid for such instruction. The professionals would have access to a much larger number of paying clients, and at times when paid instruction is usually at a minimum. The opportunities to develop a clientele that would continue after school and in summer would also help to reduce the rates. From a parental/student point of view, it could only be advantageous to have such instruction available at rates far less than what they would otherwise pay.

Although the example deals with an extracurricular activity, the basic idea is not limited in this way. An entrepreneurial school could offer Chinese or Russian or whatever if ten students signed up at a specified rate. The school would make prior arrangements with a qualified teacher who would not necessarily have any other school assignment. The administrative arrangements for meeting the desires of individuals and small groups in public schools are often prohibitively time-consuming even when they are legally possible; entrepreneurial schools could act quickly and efficiently in this area.

THE BENEFITS OF PRIVATE SCHOOLS

As just noted, private schools have not but could maximize the effectiveness of competition in improving education. In addition, private schools can be expected to outperform public schools for several other reasons. Some of these reasons apply to both entrepreneurial and nonprofit schools. For example, both types would help to defuse several controversies, such as prayer in the schools, that will otherwise constitute "no-win" situations for elected officials. The more children are enrolled in schools that meet parental standards of conduct, appearance, and performance, the less divisive are the controversies over these matters.

We can also expect private schools to be more responsive to parent concerns; there should be dramatic differences between schools that depend upon paying customers and schools that rely mainly on state aid, which flows in regardless of parent satisfaction. In this connection, it is of the utmost importance that private schools, whether nonprofit or entrepreneurial, constitute a feasible alternative to public schools for more parents. This is essential to weaken the tendency for school districts and teacher unions to negotiate policies that are opposed by parents unable to modify them by political action. In short, my view is that privatizing education is necessary to democratize it. I shall amplify this paradoxical conclusion, but would certainly agree that how education is privatized is extremely important. It is also my view that privatizing education helps to develop a more realistic understanding of its costs and benefits. On this issue, entrepreneurial schools would be more effective than nonprofit schools. As long as education is supported from taxes, tax exemptions, church budgets, charitable contributions, and other relatively invisible sources, students and parents lack incentives to assess its costs and benefits carefully. Likewise, teachers and administrators are under less pressure to regard productivity as important. In fact, the naive idea that the concept of productivity does not apply to education results partly from the way it is financed. Teachers generally have difficulty accepting the idea that the concept of productivity is as applicable to education as it is to private employment.

In an era of growing concern over taxes and public deficits, it should be noted that private schools reduce public employment, hence a host of public expenditures associated with it. Public education constitutes almost half of state and local public employment. In addition, school employee retirement systems are already a severe economic burden in some states and will be in others in the near future. One way to contain these present and future tax burdens is to reduce public school employment.

It is also safe to say that the educational environment in private schools is more likely to emphasize thrift, economy, and economic realities. Administrators, teachers, parents, and pupils tend to have a more direct stake in the efficiency of private schools. Students who might otherwise waste time or school supplies, or vandalize school property, are less likely to do so if they know that their parents have paid out of their own pockets for their schooling; the existence of a tax credit would not negate this factor. On the other hand, pupils do not relate waste of public school time and resources to the taxes paid by their parents; the relationships are too remote to influence student conduct. In this connection, it would be surprising if private schools, especially entrepreneurial schools, were not more sympathetic than public schools to a market economy. Some observers may not regard this as a plus; I do.

Let me now cite some benefits of entrepreneurial schools that do not exist, or exist in a more attenuated way, in nonprofit schools. One relates to differences in their managerial incentives. The usual reason for the greater efficiency of private enterprise is that its management incentives encourage getting the work done as efficiently as possible in order to maximize profits. The important point is that managers in the private sector share in the profits or gains resulting from increased productivity. Although the managers of nonprofit schools have some incentives to be efficient, their incentives are more similar to public than to profit-making enterprises. For this reason, entrepreneurial schools would be more aggressive than nonprofit schools in identifying and utilizing more efficient educational methods and practices.

At the present time, private schools are unduly constrained as competitors with public schools. This is due partly to the denominational character of most private schools. For example, since many pupils, teachers, administrators, and public school board members are Catholics, Catholic leaders risk alienating some of their own constituents by strong criticism of public schools. As a result, the competition between public and Catholic school systems is very genteel.

This situation plays into the hands of public school educators, since they have the largest market share. Entrepreneurial schools would have fewer inhibitions about criticizing public schools. As parents begin to shop around more for the "best" school, the level of public sophistication about education would probably rise considerably.

In addition to the potential benefits just outlined, entrepreneurial schools would have the potential to increase total spending for education while maximizing parental choice. The reason is that entrepreneurial schools would enable parents to tap into personal income for a better education for their children. This point requires some elaboration.

First of all, consumer choice is a major value in our society. As income increases, citizens can buy better cars, better food, better clothes, travel, whatever. As we have seen, however, it is not ordinarily possible to buy a better education with an increase in personal income. If you want to send your child to a better public school, you have to change your residence, usually by buying up. This is simply not a practical course of action for most parents who receive a salary increase.

Let us assume, however, that a range of educational options is available to parents. Without having to change their residence, they can purchase an education at the Ford level for $1,000, or one at the Pontiac level for $3,500, or the Cadillac option for $7,000. As this happens, it becomes possible for parents to tap into an increase in personal income for a better education for their children. This would be especially pertinent if government shares the burden, either by tuition tax credits or vouchers.

For instance, black parents in an inner city area may be eager to get the best possible education for their children. They may be willing to forego better cars, better food, better housing, and so on. At present, however, they lack a mechanism to implement their willingness to give higher priority to a better education for their children.

Entrepreneurial schools could help in this situation. It might not even be necessary to have different schools at different price levels. The same school might offer a series of options above, or instead of, a standard rate available to everyone. There could be add-ons for tutoring programs, for special activities, such as sculpture, that are not normally offered in public schools, or for students not performing at grade level. An entrepreneurial school would be much more alert to these possibilities, and prepared to take advantage of them, than a conventional primary school.

The discussion thus far has emphasized entrepreneurial schools as a future development. Actually, they already exist; in fact, some have existed for almost half a century. According to Bureau of Census reports, 2,237 such schools were in existence in 1977. They averaged 11 employees per school, compared to an average of 30 in nonprofit secular schools. The average salary in for-profit schools in 1977 was $5,604, whereas it was $7,843 in nonprofit secular schools and $13,355 in public schools. Inasmuch as some schools operated for profit had owner-operators, compensation was undoubtedly distributed in the form of profits and services (meals, use of car, and so on), but no data on the profitability of K-12 schools operated for profit are available. The census reports indicated that K-12 schools operated for profit were disproportionately located in the South. This suggests that racial factors may have been operative, but systematic data on this issue are also not available.

More recent estimates by the National Independent Private School Association (NIPSA), an association of proprietary schools, indicate that the number of K-12 proprietary schools may depend largely on how "school" is defined. The founders of NIPSA conducted a national survey in 1982-83 to identify potential members. In conducting the survey, they discovered that although states list private schools, only a few states maintain separate lists of proprietary schools per se. In any event, NIPSA estimated there were approximately 500 K-12 proprietary schools in 1983; however, this figure defined "school" to refer to enterprises that included most of the grades in a conventional elementary or secondary school. On the other hand, there may be as many as 7,500 proprietary schools having at least a kindergarten or first grade.

NIPSA itself was founded on July 16, 1983. Its leadership initially was entirely from California, but has been drawn from a broader geographical base since then. Since its establishment, NIPSA has followed a typical association pattern. It has founded a journal, *Private School Owner*; conducted conferences; established accrediting mechanisms; and sponsored tours to profit-making schools in England. It has also initiated a lobbying effort on behalf of proprietary schools.

This author has not conducted an intensive study of proprietary schools. Nevertheless, visits to such schools in the San Francisco area in August 1985 resulted in two impressions that are worth mentioning. One is the enormous difference in the way school management spends its time. Specifically, because they do not have to meet frequently with school boards and secure approval for scores of management decisions, the owners/operators of proprietary schools have much more time than public school superintendents to focus upon educational matters. In this connection, it should be emphasized that public school superintendents devote an enormous amount of time outside of formal board meetings to securing board approval of their actions. For example, the preparation of board agendas and related materials can be a time-consuming task of considerable proportions.

Perhaps the most fundamental difference between proprietary and public schools is that between a market and a political system. To illustrate, one of the proprietary schools I visited required students to wear school uniforms. Parents either accepted the requirement or enrolled their children elsewhere—and that was the end of it.

In public schools, any effort to require school uniforms would be a highly controversial political decision. It would be risky legally and probably suicidal politically; even dress codes that do not require uniforms raise major legal political and practical problems in public schools. Regardless of one's attitude toward school uniforms, the advantages of resolving the decision on a market basis are evident.

Existing proprietary schools may or may not consistently reflect the hypothetical advantages of entrepreneurial schools mentioned previously. Nevertheless, even if they do not, this fact would not necessarily invalidate the analysis. Proprietary schools are still a small-scale industry, but this may change within a few years. In the case of support services, the change is already under way. For instance, Servicemaster is a service company that manages the maintenance, custodial, and groundskeeping operations for other employers, public and private. Its clients include such firms as General Motors as well as one of every seven hospitals in the United States. Servicemaster already provides such services for over 200 school districts and institutions of higher education in 34 states. It plans to expand to all 50 states, chiefly by managing school operations in its areas of expertise. Several other companies, including some in the day care business, are in various stages of entry into K-12 instruction as a market. Without endorsing any particular approach, let me speculate on how this might be done.

ENTREPRENEURIAL SCHOOLS: A SCENARIO

We will begin with an important fact. In 1983-84, our nation spent about $120 billion for elementary and secondary education. The real costs were much greater, inasmuch as the expenditures did not include the value of school district land and buildings. More importantly, the "costs" typically do not include the income students could have earned if they had gone to work instead of school. These costs, labeled "opportunity costs" by economists, may be even greater than the direct costs; they surely are at the secondary level.

Despite the size of the education market, goods and services purchased from the private sector play a relatively minor role in it. Suppose, however, one or more large corporations, such as IBM, McDonald's, or Sears decided that in view of the size of the market, it would test the waters. McDonald's, which is feeding millions of children every day outside of school, is exploring the possibilities of feeding them inside as well. Regardless, it might wish to position itself more advantageously to recruit thousands of young employees every year. Or schools, which are in the knowledge business, may be one of the bottlenecks to growth of the knowledge industries. IBM, which has an educational budget larger than the total budget of most universities, might conclude that its educational expertise can be applied profitably to K-12 education. Many other possibilities could be cited. Corporations such as those mentioned typically do not highlight their educational expertise. First, since they sell to the education market, they avoid offending educators by adopting a deferential approach to the latter's educational expertise. Second, the corporate educational expertise is proprietary information. It takes a lot of money to acquire it, and the companies need to be paid a lot to reveal it. Also, unlike professors, education and training executives in the private sector are not paid on the basis of articles in scholarly journals. For this reason, their educational expertise is not routinely publicized outside of their company roles.

Let us further suppose that in order to share research and development costs, and to avoid the danger of an adverse reaction directed against one company, a number of companies form a consortium to enter the education market. The consortium funds an extensive research and development program. Every aspect of school operations is examined carefully for potential improvements and savings. For example, is there any reason why pupils instead of custodians cannot maintain school premises? Would it not be educationally advisable as well as financially desirable to have this happen? Why are the schools paying thousands of physical education teachers to supervise classes in which students merely play the sport they play when school is dismissed? What positions are overpaid, and by how much, if market factors were considered? How much time and resources are devoted to complying with state/federal regulations that do not apply to non-public schools? Is it feasible to use part-time professionals to grade homework in their own homes? What would they have to be paid? How many qualified teachers can teach part- but not full-time? To what extent can vocational training be provided in factories or offices, thus eliminating the need to purchase sites and equipment for this purpose? Can industry personnel provide vocational training? And so on.

At the same time that school operations are being analyzed intensively, a careful study is made of various legal, economic, demographic, and educational factors that might affect the profitability of schools. What are the present and future levels of the school-age population? At what age can pupils leave school? Go to work on a part-time basis? On a full-time basis? How much could a person earn by working instead of going to college? What are state-mandated curriculum requirements? Graduation requirements?

The end product is a master document that spells out the educational benefits of entrepreneurial schools, the amount and rate of investment needed, the anticipated return, the specific savings that should result, and the legal and practical roadblocks to schools operated for profit. The research and development effort also identifies the state(s) that offer the most hospitable environment for entrepreneurial schools and why.

Using this research as a guide, the consortium identifies the school districts most likely to be receptive to a proposal for private-sector operation of the schools. The consortium's proposal, however, includes two provisions that clinch the contract and shake both the public and the private educational establishments throughout the country. First, the consortium guarantees that it will employ every graduate who meets specified criteria of performance and conduct. Such employment will be at the market rate for whatever position the graduates fill. Also, students above a certain age will be credited with seniority in a consortium company for employment and pension purposes.

In addition, the consortium agrees to provide a career path that does not rely upon diplomas, degrees, or credentials. Reliance will be on what the student employees know and can do. The career path leads to the very top echelons of management and is open to students who do not go to college. Inasmuch as the consortium companies conduct a large in-service training program as part of their ongoing operations, provision of this career path should not be a problem. Also, just as they already do, the consortium companies will provide assistance to employees who need higher education not provided by the companies themselves.

Such an initiative could have beneficial consequences, not just in education but in our society generally. In this analysis, I have not discussed the general problem of occupational licensing in the United States. In state after state, you need a piece of paper (called a "license") from the state to work in certain fields. Usually, to get the piece of paper from the state, you need another piece of paper (called a "diploma" or a "degree") from an institution of higher education. Typically, these pieces of paper are required as the result of an alliance of educational institutions and occupational groups. The alliance provides students for the former and job protection for the latter. While this quid pro quo goes on, the public pays more for the service in order to make up for the earnings lost by future practitioners who are in school.

By and large, big business has created this mess, and only big business has the leverage to clean it up. For decades, our largest business corporations routinely required a college degree for entry-level positions on the management ladder. Degrees were regarded as sorting devices. Good intelligence and work habits were presumably necessary to earn a degree.

The upshot has been a costly, destructive emphasis upon formal education and credentials, from high school through graduate school. Our educational institutions have been eager accomplices to these efforts to stifle competition through educational/credential requirements. As long as these requirements prevail, the abuses will continue; it would be unrealistic to expect individuals starting in the world of work to "buck the system." On the other hand, a clear and convincing message from some of the largest corporations that the age of the credential is behind us would have a salutary effect throughout our economy.

It is hardly to be doubted that such a consortium proposal would prevail. The minorities would be breaking down the doors to participate; with teenage unemployment among minorities about double the national average, and with an opportunity to leap into the mainstream of our economy, the minorities would have much to gain and nothing to lose by their participation. The consortium might even include a number of institutions of higher education, who would agree beforehand to admit consortium high school graduates who wanted to continue their formal education. The colleges would get students who could function academically; otherwise they would not graduate from the consortium program. The students and parents would be assured of an employment or higher education option upon graduation. And the community would receive a much larger return on its investment in education.

Whatever one's reactions to the suggestion, it is consistent with a growing interest and trend toward contracting out public services. The list of public services currently contracted out is extensive and expanding rapidly: fire and police protection, hospitals, garbage disposal, computer services, debt collection, ship repair, air travel, police services, and payment of wages and benefits. Some corporations are even managing prisons for profit, despite objections from the prison bureaucracy.

The evidence that government services can be contracted out more efficiently than they can be conducted by government is too impressive to be ignored. What is especially significant is that the benefits of contracting out public services are not confined to any particular type of service; for the most part, the reasons for the superior performance of the private sector are typically present in any public service.[2] For that matter, many school districts already contract out certain tasks, such as cafeteria services, bus transportation, or data processing. Even educational tasks are sometimes contracted out; for example, districts that do not have special services for students frequently contract with other agencies for such services. Thus some elements of our scenario do not involve new principles but the application of accepted principles to different circumstances.

School boards are typically opposed to actions that would strengthen private schools. The vast majority of boards undoubtedly will be opposed to entrepreneurial schools initially. They will view contracting out all the operations of a district as a desperate last-ditch action, feasible only in cases of dire emergency or crisis.

In my opinion, this point of view could be extremely short-sighted. School boards might function much more effectively if school operations were contracted out to a private firm. Boards typically agree in principle that they should delegate administrative matters to school administrators. In practice, however, most boards cannot and do not avoid extensive involvement in administrative matters. For most board members, the temptation to do so overcomes the academic desirability of noninvolvement. Community pressures also lead to frequent deviations from the principle of noninvolvement in administration. Thus contracting out district operations might enable boards to avoid becoming immersed in administrative issues and to concentrate on long-range policy.

NEGATIVE ASPECTS OF ENTREPRENEURIAL SCHOOLS

The discussion thus far has by no means explored or even mentioned all of the potential advantages of entrepreneurial schools. Before we get carried away any further, however, let us look at the negatives.

Undoubtedly, entrepreneurial schools will encounter many unanticipated difficulties. In any basic institutional change, emphasis is on the deficiencies of the existing arrangements and the promise of the changes. Usually, we have to wait until the changes are in place to fully appreciate their deficiencies. Partly for this reason, caution is called for in assessing the desirability and prospects of entrepreneurial schools.

Perhaps the most common objection will be that entrepreneurial schools would take advantage of children and parents to maximize profits. The specifics are not always forthcoming, but it is easy to visualize how this might happen. Poor teachers might be hired because they are inexpensive. Charges for textbooks and supplies might be padded. Meals in the school cafeteria could be of a low quality. Grades and test scores might be inflated to foster the illusion of academic achievement, and thereby encourage enrollments. Children with special needs might be ignored because of cost factors. It is also contended that entrepreneurial schools would engage in huckster-type advertising campaigns to recruit students. These campaigns would not only criticize public schools unfairly; they would also raise unrealistic hopes and expectations, and thereby lead to personal and social tragedy on a broad scale. After all, it is one thing if false advertising leads only to viewing a tasteless movie; when it leads to a substantial investment in a poor education, it is a much more serious matter. Regardless of these criticisms, however, advertising by private schools has increased dramatically in recent years and is likely to increase further. If it is effective, and it often is, more schools will resort to it.[3]

Before considering the exploitation argument directly, an assumption implicit in it needs to be challenged. The assumption is that pupils in public schools are not exploited for profit by public school teachers. The assumption survives only because popular thinking about the matter is dominated by stereotypes, not realities. For example, teachers have gone on strike for higher salaries hundreds of times in recent years. In these strikes, teachers have frequently done the following:

- Made pupil records inaccessible so substitutes cannot teach effectively.
- Told pupils not to attend school if their teachers were on strike. This, of course, is encouraging pupils to violate the compulsory attendance laws in order to increase the effectiveness of the strike.
- Refused to give credit for student work performed during the strike in some districts, and threatened to do so in others.
- Utilized children on picket lines with picket signs supporting teachers, in order to generate public support.
- Used the children of teachers and others to enter schools during a strike to lead student walkouts and student efforts to disrupt and discredit school operations during the strikes.
- Discussed actual or threatened strikes in classes, where it was not relevant to the curriculum, in ways calculated to gain student and parental support.
- Created fears among students that their opposition to a teacher strike, or even their refusal to support it, could lead to reprisals against the students.

Such conduct constitutes exploitation of students for profit, but it is by no means the only such conduct in public schools. Public school teachers frequently tutor pupils, even their own, for pay. They sometimes use their teaching positions to recruit students for their summer camps that are operated for profit. High school athletics provides many examples of exploitation of students for the welfare of their coaches; in some cases, colleges were forced to employ a high school coach in order to recruit an outstanding high school athlete.

Above and beyond all this, the most glaring and most harmful examples of exploitation of public school students is the wide range of legislation that ostensibly serves pupil interests but is actually based on teacher or union interests. Economists generally agree that our minimum wage laws serve primarily the interests of unions and unionized workers earning above minimum wage, and also that such laws are a major reason for the high incidence of teenage unemployment, especially among disadvantaged minorities. It can hardly be doubted that teacher unions support the minimum wage laws at least in part to protect the job market for teachers. Regardless, the tremendous overemphasis on staying in school, diplomas and degrees, excessive educational requirements to work at certain jobs, teacher licensing, and the legalization of teacher dismissals (even of competent or outstanding teachers) for failure to pay union dues—all suggest that public education has some exploitation problems of its own to clean up.

My point is not to characterize public school teachers as unduly self-seeking. Their pretensions to moral superiority and greater interest in the welfare of children are often insufferable. Still, as a group, they are no more self-seeking than any other in our society. The point is, however, that exploitation of pupils for profit occurs now in public education.

So does advertising, at least if my dictionary definition of it is used: "to call public attention to, especially by emphasizing desirable qualities so as to arouse a desire to buy or patronize." Let us put aside the issue of whether "advertising" means "paid advertising." For several years, the most expensive paid educational advertisement in the mass media has been a weekly column in the New York *Times* by Albert Shanker, president of the American Federation of Teachers. This paid advertisement extolls the virtues of public schools and vigorously criticizes measures to strengthen private schools.

In some ways, exploitation problems are more difficult to remedy in public education precisely because the exploitation goes on beneath a veneer of serving children. Public school personnel may sincerely believe that it is exploitation to allow children to be taught by an uncertified teacher. Nevertheless, a policy does not consciously have to disadvantage a group to constitute exploitation of it.

Most emphatically, I am not implying that private school leaders are morally or intellectually superior in this regard; no doubt they also support many policies purportedly for the welfare of children when the welfare of private schools is the motivating factor. I would have to say, however, that the restrictions on private schools originate more in the self-interest of public school teachers and administrators than out of any demonstrable relationship to the welfare of children. In any event, the problems of exploitation arise regardless of whether schools are public, private and nonprofit, or private and profit-making. Indeed, few ideas in our time have been so thoroughly refuted and discredited as the idea that an enterprise operated by government is ipso facto operated in the public interest, and not in the interest of a special interest group.

Considered objectively, the exploitation objection seems to be a knee-jerk reaction to entrepreneurial schools. Children are served by doctors, dentists, and a host of private entrepreneurs. Although these entrepreneurs can and occasionally do take advantage of children, no one proposes that only publicly funded professionals serve them. Why should entrepreneurial teachers be more of a threat to children than entrepreneurial doctors and dentists?

Parenthetically, it is a historical accident that teachers but not doctors or dentists are normally paid from public funds. Indeed, as E.G. West has ably pointed out, there was a time in the United States when education was virtually universal, but paid for privately.[4] As a matter of fact the Sophists, who were the first professional teachers in Western civilization, were fee takers; Protagoras, the best known, excused his pupils from payment of any fee if they took an oath that the instruction was worthless. One wonders what this worthy protagonist of Socrates would have thought about contemporary controversies over merit pay.

The fact is, however, that the states can and do regulate nonpublic schools now. If schools were operated for profit, the states could, if they wished to do so, set the certification standards for teachers, establish the curriculum, establish health and safety requirements, and otherwise protect pupils against exploitation by regulation. After all, government regulates thousands of businesses every day; the extent of regulation depends upon the nature of the business. There is, therefore, no reason to assume that the states cannot adequately protect children in entrepreneurial schools. What is needed, however, is not so much regulation as objective feedback about how schools and pupils are doing. At present, we overregulate education while simultaneously failing to provide usable feedback for parents and policymakers. Avoidance of this misplaced emphasis would be highly desirable with respect to both public and private schools.

THE PROFITABILITY OF ENTREPRENEURIAL SCHOOLS

The critical issue with respect to entrepreneurial schools is not their desirability, it is their profitability. It is hardly to be doubted that private enterprise could do a better job for less than we now pay for public education. This fact standing alone, however, does not mean that K-12 schools could be sufficiently profitable as a business investment.

Systematic data on profit-making K-12 schools are not available.[5] Still, in considering profitability issues, we must avoid the assumption that the factors influencing profitability will remain unchanged. At the present time, profit-making schools are a cottage industry. If such schools enjoy any demonstrable superiority over public schools, they would strengthen the movement to tuition tax credits/vouchers. The critical problem is arranging opportunities to test their feasibility as a large-scale industry, for example, as a franchise operation. What may happen is that entrepreneurial schools will prove successful at a certain cost per pupil, whether paid for by parents or by a voucher, or by some combination of the two. If and when this happens, it will become possible to provide additional public assistance that will broaden the student base of entrepreneurial schools.

The profitability of entrepreneurial schools would depend primarily upon the following factors:

- The savings inherent in private operation, for example, avoidance of state-mandated costs that add nothing to educational effectiveness.
- The extent to which educational tax credits/vouchers are available for the costs of education at entrepreneurial schools.
- The scale of operation, that is, the larger the scale, the greater the opportunities to achieve economies over public education.
- The extent, if any, to which entrepreneurial schools are burdened by special restrictions that do not apply to private schools generally.

In my view, the coming shortage of teenagers is also likely to affect the profitability of entrepreneurial schools. Indeed, this development may be a decisive factor, independent of the preceding considerations. Let me elaborate on the possibilities briefly.

ENTREPRENEURIAL SCHOOLS AND THE SHORTAGE OF TEENAGERS

As we have seen, most of the reform documents propose to increase the school day and/or the school year. Only a decade earlier, however, five major reform proposals urged substantial *reductions* in the time students spent in school.[6]

Remarkably, the amount of time students attended school in the early 1970s was not significantly different from the early 1980s, when the new wave of reform proposals urged a longer school day and extended school year. Obviously, such drastic changes among the reformers themselves does not inspire confidence in any of their recommendations, but let us reconcile the differences in the best light possible for both positions. Let us assume that less time is needed to learn what is now being learned, and also that more time in school is justified if accompanied by basic changes in the curriculum.

On this view, it would make sense to reduce substantially student time in school. Obviously, any such changes would have massive repercussions, not just in education but throughout our economy. For instance, if youth completed high school in 11 instead of 12 years (with no loss of achievement), and if they worked an additional year, and if this additional year of employment did not displace others in the labor force, the gains to our economy would be measured in tens of billions of dollars. (Of course, all of these assumptions are controversial and involve some genuine uncertainties. For example, if earlier entry into the labor force led to earlier retirement instead of a longer work life, the result would be to redistribute national income rather than to increase it.)

In fact, however, most estimates of the benefits resulting from educational acceleration err on the conservative side. This is because they are based only upon the savings resulting from the need for fewer teachers, less supplies and equipment, and other reductions in cost. Although substantial, such savings would be much less than the increase in national productivity if most of us went to school a year less and worked a year more. This is easily overlooked because the largest real cost of secondary education, student time, is typically not treated as a cost at all in educational circles. Undoubtedly, this is why so little effort is made to conserve such time.

Although the reasons why the earlier study groups concluded that secondary youth (roughly aged 14-18) were spending too much time in school vary somewhat, they can be summarized briefly as follows:

1. Studies that show secondary students learn as much even when attendance in school is reduced materially.
2. Evidence that present restrictions upon youth employment have little relevance to their educational or safety needs but are based upon labor fears of excessive competition and wage cutting from younger job seekers.
3. The widespread movement to lower the age of majority from 21 to 18. This was not just another incremental change. It was a drastic alteration of adult legal status, calling for an earlier immersion in the world of work.

4. A wide range of foreign experience in education and employment that strongly suggests that U.S. levels of educational achievement need not require so much time in school, and that youth can efficiently perform many adult jobs from which they are presently excluded.

5. The increase in programs, such as Advanced Placement and College Level Educational Placement, that make it possible to take and receive credit for advanced work in high school.

6. Studies indicating that youth capable of advanced academic work in college can usually handle more advanced studies in secondary school.

7. A significant amount of absenteeism in secondary school, especially in large cities. This was interpreted as evidence that many young people perceive little benefit in school attendance, a perception shared by some economists.

8. Evidence that physical and intellectual maturation is usually reached by age 18. There is some evidence that such maturation occurs sooner today than it did in previous generations, due to improvements in nutrition and health care. In other words, there are physiological reasons for believing students today can complete an equivalent program in less time than previous generations of students.

9. The fact that the present policies on the school day, school year, and school leaving age were formulated prior to and independently of relevant research bearing upon these matters; such research as is available is either inconsistent with present policies or can, with equal justification, be cited to support earlier school leaving and earlier participation by youth in higher education or the labor force.

10. Evidence that the alienation of youth, insofar as it constitutes a genuine problem, results largely from their sweeping isolation from responsible roles in interaction with other adults and social institutions, such as the economy and the political system. Schools cannot simulate these other institutions or successfully provide the kinds of experience they offer.

11. As more women work outside the home, the role of the family in providing meaningful interaction between youth and adults has continued to diminish.

12. Successful legal challenges (such as the celebrated case of *Griggs* v. *Duke Power Company*) to high school and/or college gradua-

tion as prerequisites for employment. Such challenges further weaken the practical value of formal education.[7]

Significantly, the reports that recommended a decrease in school time omitted a great deal of evidence that might have been cited to support their recommendations. For example, in August 1974 the New York State Board of Regents released a policy statement severely critical of overlapping high school and college programs. The statement cited 1971 studies showing that liberal arts colleges repeated 40 percent of high school social science courses, 35 percent of those in English, 24 percent of those in science, and 21 percent of those in mathematics.[8]

As we have seen, however, the educational arguments are likely to have only a marginal impact on attendance policies. Present attendance policies were not adopted on the basis of educational considerations, nor are they likely to be changed for educational reasons. The basic issues are not the educational ones relating to whether youth could learn as much or more despite less time in school. They are the economic issues relating to what youth would do if they had a shorter school day and/or graduate sooner from high school. Will there be jobs or work-study programs for those who do not want to be full-time students in higher education? Will employers be willing, even if they are legally free to do so, to employ 13-16 year olds at full-time positions? Economic issues such as these will be more important factors influencing the duration of schooling than the educational arguments on the issues.

Of course, earlier graduation from high school would necessitate some changes in higher education, especially in admissions policies. Nevertheless, these changes should not pose any major problem. Many colleges are already running short of students they would like to admit; others are running short of students of any kind. For this reason, colleges are likely to join, or even to lead, the movement toward earlier admission, even though this solution weakens the job market for teachers below the college level. Professorial complaints about unqualified students will continue, but they would be even more pro forma than they are now. The professors or the colleges who prefer no students to poorly qualified ones have yet to appear.

Needless to say, the NEA and the AFT strongly oppose lowering the age at which pupils can quit school. These unions are greatly concerned about declining enrollments. Other things being equal, a decline in enrollments results in a decline in job opportunities for teachers.

Any such decline weakens their bargaining power. To counteract this, the NEA and the AFT are urging smaller classes; they are also trying to lower the age at which children are enrolled in school. Obviously, their position would perpetuate the high unemployment rate among teenagers, especially black teenagers. About 50 percent of our high school graduates do not enter college. If high school graduates not going on to college cannot enter the labor force, many will inevitably experience a lengthy period of unemployment.

What are the chances that legislators, employers, and unions will accept earlier entry into the labor market? At the present time, the chances seem poor indeed. In April 1984, the unemployment rate among youth aged 16-19 was 19.4 percent; among black teenagers, it was 44.8 percent; among adults over 25, it was 6.0 percent. Thus, employers as such have no reason to support an earlier entry into the labor market, and unions have strong incentives to oppose it. For these reasons, legislators and policymakers are not likely to lower the school leaving age, feasible as it may be on educational grounds.

Nevertheless, the forthcoming decline in the teenage population may change the entire situation, including the prospects for entrepreneurial schools.

In 1972 the 16-19 age group in the labor force was approximately 8.4 million, or 9.4 percent of the total labor force of 89 million. By 1990 the 16-19 age group is expected to be 7.1 million, or 6.3 percent of a total labor force of approximately 112.6 million. In other words, there will be a moderate decrease in the absolute number of teenagers, and a very substantial decrease in the proportion of teenagers in the labor force and the total population. Unless we permit large-scale immigration, teenage unemployment will drop substantially; eventually, there will be severe shortages in the youth labor supply. As this happens, employers will try to weaken the complex of laws, regulations, and practices that discourage or prohibit the employment of youth in their early and middle teens.

This forthcoming change in employer attitudes should not surprise anyone. War-time employers, deprived of their traditional sources of labor, suddenly discovered that blacks and women could handle all kinds of jobs that tradition and practice had said they could not do. By the same token, employers deprived of a plentiful supply of workers aged 17-19 will suddenly discover that workers aged 13-16 can perform about as well. As full-time employment becomes a realistic alternative to full-time schooling, increasing numbers of youth will choose the work option that is not available at the present time. The pressures on a smaller labor force to support a larger number of retired workers will also force changes in legislation that prevents youth from working. In the not so distant future, the politics of the issue will differ drastically from the present situation.

Eventually, the NEA and the AFT, as well as the union movement generally, will probably lose their battle against earlier entry into the labor market. The economics of the issue will be decisive. As previously noted, the largest costs of secondary education are not to be found in school budgets. They are the "opportunity costs" of education, that is, the income that youth could have earned but did not because they were in school. This point may be critical for entrepreneurial schools, at least at the secondary level.

The economic feasibility of entrepreneurial schools may depend upon the extent to which students can perform and be paid for work currently done by the school district or by company employees. There is no reason why students cannot cook, serve food, maintain buildings and grounds, type, file, make and answer telephone calls, and do many other things currently done by regular school district employees. In addition, the parent companies operating entrepreneurial schools will have a host of other jobs that students can perform. I realize that there will be risks associated with students working for their schools or for the companies that sponsor these schools. It seems to me, however, that the risks are not prohibitive and can be managed effectively. Along with the risks, we should also consider some of the practical advantages of private-sector alternatives. For example, in New York City, the banks are among the largest trainers of the hard-core unemployed. When a bank accepts an inner city dropout for training (for example, for a position as teller), the trainee is an employee from the first day of training. Thus, unlike the school situation, there is no uncertainty about the availability of a job if the trainee is successful; the bank trainee already has what the school trainee only hopes to get. The training is conducted in the bank, on bank equipment, by bank employees; bank trainees are more likely to accept the obligations of training because they are already employees and are treated as such. With all due respect to school-based vocational education, it is readily understandable why the bank should succeed where the school did not. Exploitation of youth by the bank is, of course, a legitimate concern, but so is the possibility of exploitation by public school authorities who insist upon vocational training in public schools.

In this connection, I once asked a bank vice-president for training about the age at which youths were able to handle a job as teller. His answer was that 12-year olds could do the work efficiently, but compulsory school attendance laws, insurance requirements, and other factors unrelated to ability to do the work precluded their employment. In any case, one does not have to accept this conclusion to be convinced that our educational and labor policies overprotect our youth to their detriment as well as society's.

CLOSING THE LEADERSHIP GAP

According to the conventional wisdom, parents seeking a better education for their children should become more involved in school affairs. In a word, they should "participate" more, that is, be active in the PTA, make sure homework is assigned and performed, attend school board meetings, and so on.

In my view, this advice has just enough plausibility to conceal its basic weaknesses. Perhaps an example will help to bring this out. Suppose you buy a new car that does not function properly. When you bring it to the dealer, what is your objective? Certainly, not "involvement" or "participation" in automobile manufacturing policy or in service policy. You want the car to run properly or be replaced with no effort on your part. As far as you are concerned, the less participation the better. You "participate" only because things went wrong, and you would be happy to avoid participation if you could. If worst comes to worst, you may take your losses and buy cars elsewhere in the future.

What options exist if you are dissatisfied with your public school? For most parents, "participation" is not feasible for several reasons. They do not have the time or resources to "participate" in policy-making on textbooks, courses, teacher recruitment, and the other policies culminating in their dissatisfaction. Even if they had the time, their participation would often be futile. What can they do if they object to the textbooks? The school may have to choose from textbooks approved by a state agency that will not review them for three years. "Involvement" or "participation" is not the answer. People do not want "participation"; they want their institutions to work. "Participation" is a social goal among groups, such as professors, who have a lot to time to kill. Most of us are not in such a fortunate position.

The alternative is to enroll your child in another school. As we have seen, however, this alternative is not open to most parents, including those most dissatisfied with their public schools. Their ability "to take their business elsewhere" is too limited by their financial status and the absence of alternatives.

The question of how to accommodate dissatisfaction with public schools is ignored by the reform movement. Its premise is that certain improvements will reduce dissatisfaction to tolerable levels. It does not, however, discuss any specific changes in the ways parents now have to remove or try to remove the causes of their dissatisfaction.

This would not be so serious if it were not for the fact that the arguments against family choice are losing credibility. Its opponents shed crocodile tears for the poor while accepting an enormously expensive system of higher education financed largely by the poor for the benefit of those who are not poor. They decry the dangers of racial segregation even though the way we finance public education is a major factor in the continued existence of racially segregated schools. In this connection, it might be noted that avowed supporters of racial segregation in public education were frequently opposed to tuition tax credits/vouchers. Their intellectual heirs are the contemporary educational leaders who warn us that family choice will intensify racial segregation—even while every poll of public opinion on the subject shows that black citizens as a group are more supportive of it than the population as a whole.

The present situation reminds me of the controversies over the ultimate triumph of the proletariat. When Marxists were confronted by evidence pointing to a contrary conclusion, they responded by saying that the contrary evidence cited was true enough, but it was only short-run evidence. Ultimately it would be superseded by developments that would sustain their thesis. The argument worked for a long time, even generations. Eventually, it became obvious that the argument was an absurdity, since no conceivable evidence could discredit it. As this realization began to sink in, Marxism lost its credibility and its support.

Public education is in this situation. Setbacks, reversals, declines —all are said to be temporary. All will be superseded by developments of a more positive nature, at least if we just try harder. Personally, I don't believe it.

The mere thought of alternative systems may appear to be the crack of doom to those who earn their living or get their strokes from public education. It is, however, impossible to assess some alternatives without trying them. If parent choice legislation is always blocked because we lack actual full-scale experience with it, we will never be in a position to try it. For all intents and purposes, the reform movement resembles nothing as much as my high school basketball coach. When we came in the locker room at half-time, getting trounced, his advice was "Make those baskets." Agreed, but how in the face of vastly superior opposition? By the same token, the reform proposals have focused attention on wishes instead of the concrete barriers to meaningful reform.

From the standpoint of educational reform, entrepreneurial schools might offer unparalleled strategic advantages. Perhaps their most significant potential advantage is that they could avoid, or largely avoid, the entire political, legislative, regulatory, and structural complex of roadblocks to reform. The conventional wisdom notwithstanding, meaningful reform may not necessarily depend upon the support of governors, legislators, school boards, school administrators, teacher unions, and PTAs. It might turn out that one top executive in one of our largest corporations could do more to bring about meaningful reform than the combined efforts of the public education establishment —paradoxically, not by trying to achieve educational reform but by trying to conduct a profitable business. Granted, the legislative/regulatory framework would be extremely important; in some states at least, it would be a decisive factor, especially in the short run. Perhaps the combined opposition of both the public and private nonprofit schools will be insuperable. Nevertheless, the current legal and political obstacles, as imposing as they are, should not be regarded as dispositive.

An item that came to my attention recently bears upon this point. A friend of mine told me about an Office of Strategic Services test given during World War II to identify potential leaders. In this test, the prospective leader was assigned the task of lining up three logs to form a triangle. The logs were too heavy to be moved by one person. To carry out the task, the candidate was assigned a crew and given a certain amount of time.

Unbeknownst to the candidate, however, the aides assigned were directed to foul things up. They dropped the logs at the wrong time. They misunderstood the directions, and moved to the left instead of the right, or vice versa. The task simply could not be carried out; the logs were too heavy to be moved by an individual and the aides assigned would not carry it out.

What was the correct solution to the problem? One of the characteristics of leaders is the ability to recognize incompetence and to act promptly to get rid of incompetent subordinates. Those who fail this test do not make good leaders. Thus the "right" answer to the question was for the prospective leader to go to the person in charge and state that the task could not be performed with the aides assigned.

In my view, there is a profound lesson in this example. We cannot get the educational job done under its present governance structure. Instead of continuing the futile effort to do so, our educational leaders must be willing to say that the task, as presently assigned and managed, cannot be carried out. This is the threshold test of educational leadership. If and when it passes this test, it will find the way to get the job done.

NOTES

1. See Myron Lieberman and Michael H. Moskow, *Collective Negotiations for Teachers* (Chicago: Rand McNally, 1966).

2. See James T. Bennett and Manuel A. Johnson, *Better Government at Half the Price!* (Ossining, N.Y.: Carolina House, 1981).

3. See "Private Schools Advertise in 'Buyers Market,'" *Education Week*, May 9, 1984, pp. 1, 14.

4. E. G. West, *The Economics of Education Tax Credits* (Washington, D.C.: Heritage Foundation, 1981), pp. 9-15.

5. See Richard J. Murnane, "The Uncertain Consequences of Tuition Tax Credits: An Analysis of Student Achievement and Economic Incentives," in Thomas James and Henry M. Levin, *Public Dollars for Private Schools* (Philadelphia: Temple University Press, 1983), pp. 218-19; and U.S. Department of Commerce, Bureau of the Census, *Census of Service Industries, Other Service Industries, Parts 1-4*, Geographic Area Studies (SC77-A-53) (Washington, D.C.: U.S. Government Printing Office, 1977).

6. The five reports were: *The Greening of the High School*, Ruth Weinstock, ed. (New York: Institute for Development of Educational Activities-Educational Facilities Laboratory, March 1973); *American Youth in the Mid-Seventies*, Conference Report, National Association of Secondary School Principals, December 1972; *Youth: Transition to Adulthood*, Report of the Panel on Youth of the President's Science Advisory Committee, June 1973 (Chicago: University of Chicago Press, 1974); National Commission on the Reform of Secondary Education, *The Reform of Secondary Education* (New York: McGraw-Hill, 1973); and *Report of the National Panel on High Schools and Adolescent Education* (Washington, D.C.: U.S. Office of Education, March 1974).

7. *Griggs* v. *Duke Power Company*, 401 U.S. 424 (1971).

8. *The Articulation of Secondary and Postsecondary Education* (Albany, N.Y.: New York State Education Department, 1974), p. 7, citing B. Everard Blanchard, "Curriculum Articulation Between the College of Liberal Arts and the Secondary School," unpublished, DePaul University, School of Education, Spring, 1971.

Appendix A

MAJOR REFORM PROPOSALS AND THEIR SPONSORS

●National Commission on Excellence in Education, *A Nation At Risk: The Imperative for Educational Reform* (Washington, D.C.: U.S. Government Printing Office, April 26, 1983).

David P. Gardner (Chair), President, University of California, Former President, University of Utah, Salt Lake City, Utah

Yvonne W. Larson (Vice-Chair), Immediate Past-President, San Diego City School Board, San Diego, California

William O. Baker Chairman of the Board (Retired), Bell Telephone Laboratories, Murray Hill, New Jersey

Anne Campbell Former Commissioner of Education, State of Nebraska, Lincoln, Nebraska

Emeral A. Crosby Principal, Northern High School, Detroit, Michigan

Charles A. Foster, Jr. Immediate Past-President, Foundation for Teaching Economics, San Francisco, California

Norman C. Francis President, Xavier University of Louisiana, New Orleans, Louisiana

A. Bartlett Giamatti President, Yale University, New Haven, Connecticut

Shirley Gordon President, Highline Community College, Midway, Washington

Robert V. Haderlein Immediate Past-President, National School Boards Association, Girard, Kansas

Gerald Holton Mallinckrodt Professor of Physics, Professor of the History of Science, Harvard University, Cambridge, Massachusetts

Annette Y. Kirk Kirk Associates, Mecosta, Michigan

Margaret S. Marston Member, Virginia State Board of Education, Arlington, Virginia

Albert H. Quie Former Governor, State of Minnesota, St. Paul, Minnesota

Francisco D. Sanchez, Jr. Superintendent of Schools, Albuquerque Public Schools, Albuquerque, New Mexico

Glenn T. Seaborg University Professor of Chemistry, Nobel Laureate, University of California, Berkeley, California

Jay Sommer National Teacher of the Year, 1981-82, Foreign Language Department, New Rochelle High School, New Rochelle, New York

Richard Wallace Principal, Lutheran High School East, Cleveland Heights, Ohio

• **Ernest L. Boyer**, *High School: A Report on Secondary Education in America* (New York: Harper & Row, 1983).

The author is president of the Carnegie Foundation for the Advancement of Teaching, which funded the study. Dr. Boyer was formerly U.S. commissioner of education and was selected in 1983 as "the nation's leading educator" in a vote of leading educators. In conducting the study and writing the report, he was guided by an advisory group that included the following members:

Myron Atkin   Dean, School of Education, Stanford University

Beverly Joyce Bimes   St. Louis, Missouri

Derek Bok   President, Harvard University

Anne Campbell   Commissioner of Education, Lincoln, Nebraska

Joan Ganz Cooney   President, Children's Television Workshop

Lawrence A. Cremin   President, Teachers College, Columbia University

Alonzo Crim   Superintendent of Schools, Atlanta City Schools

Walter Cronkite   CBS News

Emeral A. Crosby   Principal, Northern High School, Detroit, Michigan

Patrick L. Daly   Vice President, American Federation of Teachers

Norman Francis   President, Xavier University of Louisiana

Mary Hatwood Futrell   Secretary/Treasurer, National Education Association

James R. Gaddy   Principal, New Rochelle High School, New Rochelle, New York

Peggy Hanrahan   Principal, Mentor High School, Mentor, Ohio

Leslie Koltai   Chancellor, Los Angeles Community College District

Marigold Linton   Professor of Psychology, University of Utah

William M. Marcussen   Vice President, Atlantic Richfield Company

Ralph McGee   Principal, New Trier East Township School, Winnetka, Illinois

James L. Olivero   Project Leadership Executive, Professional Development Program Association of California

Rayma C. Page   President, National School Boards Association, and Chairman, Lee County School Board, Fort Myers, Florida

Alan Pifer   President Emeritus, Senior Consultant, Carnegie Corporation of New York

Lauren Resnick   Co-Director, Learning Research & Development Center, University of Pittsburgh

Tomas Rivera   Chancellor, University of California, Riverside

Adele Simmons   President, Hampshire College

Virginia V. Sparling   President, National Parent & Teachers Association

Robert R. Wheeler Superintendent of Schools, Kansas City, Missouri

W. Willard Wirtz Wirtz and LaPointe

Daniel Yankelovich Yankelovich, Skelly and White, Inc.

- Task Force on Education for Economic Growth, *Action for Excellence* (Denver: Education Commission of the States, June 1983).

Chair
The Honorable Janes B. Hunt, Jr. Governor of North Carolina

Cochairs
Frank T. Cary Chairman of the Executive Committee, IBM Corporation

The Honorable Pierre S. duPont, IV Governor of Delaware

Governors
The Honorable Lamar Alexander Governor of Tennessee

The Honorable D. Robert Graham Governor of Florida

The Honorable Thomas Kean Governor of New Jersey

The Honorable Richard D. Lamm Governor of Colorado

The Honorable Scott M. Matheson Governor of Utah

The Honorable George Nigh Governor of Oklahoma

The Honorable Robert D. Orr Governor of Indiana

The Honorable Rudy Perpich Governor of Minnesota

The Honorable Charles S. Robb Governor of Virginia

The Honorable Richard L. Thornburgh Governor of Pennsylvania

The Honorable William F. Winter Governor of Mississippi

State Legislators
The Honorable Wilhelmina Delco State Representative of Texas

The Honorable Anne Linderman State Senator of Arizona

The Honorable Oliver Ocasek State Senator of Ohio

Business Leaders
Thornton F. Bradshaw Chairman, RCA Corporation, Chairman, Conference Board

J. Fred Bucy President, Texas Instruments

Philip Caldwell Chairman of the Board and Chief Executive Officer, Ford Motor Company

James Campbell President, MISSCO Corporation, Chairman, Education Employment and Training Committee, U.S. Chamber of Commerce

John H. Johnson President, Johnson Publishing Company

David T. Kearns President and Chief Executive Officer, Xerox Corporation; Member, Business Round Table

Robert W. Lundeen Chairman of the Board, The Dow Chemical Company; Trustee, Committee for Economic Development

J. Richard Munro President and Chief Executive Officer, Time, Inc.

William C. Norris Chairman of the Board and Chief Executive Officer, Control Data Corporation

Bernard J. O'Keefe Chairman and Chief Executive Officer, EG and G, Inc.; Chairman, National Association of Manufacturers

James E. Olson Vice Chairman, Board of Directors, American Telephone and Telegraph Company

John R. Purcell Chairman, Chief Executive Officer and President, SFN Companies, Inc.

Robert D. Ray President, Life Investors, Inc.

Labor
Glenn E. Watts President, Communications Workers of America

Educators
Bruce Brombacher Teacher of the Year, Jones Junior High School, Upper Arlington, Ohio

Dr. Calvin M. Frazier Commissioner of Education, Colorado

Dr. William C. Friday President, University of North Carolina

Marvin O. Koenig Principal, Southwest High School, St. Louis, Missouri

Dr. Floretta McKenzie Superintendent of Schools, District of Columbia

Judith Moyers Education Specialist, New York, New York

Organization Leaders
Ms. Joanne T. Goldsmith President, National Association of State Boards of Education

Dr. Anna J. Harrison Professor Emeritus, Chemistry, Mount Holyoke College, President, American Association for the Advancement of Science

Dr. M. Joan Parent President, National School Boards Association

Dr. Frank Press President, National Academy of Sciences

Chief Staffperson
Roy H. Forbes Associate Executive Director, Education Commission of the States

Report Preparation
Ervin S. Duggan Associates

●**Twentieth Century Fund**, Task Force on Federal Elementary and Secondary Education Policy, *Making the Grade* (New York: Twentieth Century Fund, 1983).

Robert Wood Chairman, Henry R. Luce Professor of Democratic Institutions and the Social Order, Wesleyan University; formerly Director of Urban Studies, University of Massachusetts

Brewster C. Denny Professor of Public Affairs, formerly Dean, Graduate School of Public Affairs, University of Washington

Chester E. Finn, Jr. Codirector and Professor of Education and Public Policy, Center on Education Policy, Institute for Public Policy Studies, Vanderbilt University

Patricia Albjerg Graham Dean and Charles Warren Professor of the History of Education, Graduate School of Education, Harvard University

Charles V. Hamilton Wallace S. Sayre Professor of Government, Department of Political Science, Columbia University

Carlos R. Hortas Chairman, Department of Romance Languages, Hunter College

Diane Ravitch Adjunct Associate Professor, Teachers College, Columbia University

Wilson Riles Wilson Riles & Associates, Sacramento, formerly Superintendent of Public Instruction and Director of Education, State Department of Education, Sacramento

Donald M. Stewart President, Spelman College, Atlanta

Robert Wentz Superintendent, Clark County School District, Las Vegas

Rosalyn Yalow Chairman, Department of Clinical Science, Montefiore Medical Center, New York

Rapporteur
Paul E. Peterson Professor of Political Science and Education, Department of Political Science, University of Chicago

●**John I. Goodlad**, *A Place Called School: Prospects for the Future* (New York: McGraw-Hill, 1983).

The author of this report was formerly dean, Graduate School of Education, University of California at Los Angeles, and director of the Institute for Development of Educational Activities, a division of the Charles F. Kettering Foundation. The following persons served on the advisory committee to the study:

Ralph W. Tyler Chairman, Director Emeritus, Center for Advanced Study in the Behavioral Sciences, Palo Alto, California

Gregory Anrig President, Educational Testing Service, formerly Commissioner of Education, State of Massachusetts

Stephen K. Bailey* Professor of Education and Associate Dean, Harvard Graduate School of Education

Lawrence A. Cremin* President, Teachers College, Columbia University, Pulitzer Prize Winner in History

Robert K. Merton formerly Giddings Professor of Sociology, Columbia University

Arthur Jefferson General Superintendent, Detroit Public Schools

*Also, served a term as president, National Academy of Education.

This study received financial support from the following sources:

The Danforth Foundation
The Ford Foundation
International Paper Company Foundation
The JDR 3rd Fund
Martha Holden Jennings Foundation
Charles F. Kettering Foundation
Lilly Endowment, Inc.
Charles Stewart Mott Foundation
National Institute of Education
The Needmor Fund
Pedamorphosis, Inc.
The Rockefeller Foundation
The Spencer Foundation
United States Office of Education

- **Commission on Precollege Education in Mathematics, Science, and Technology**, appointed by the National Science Board, *Educating Americans for the 21st Century* (Washington, D.C.: National Science Foundation, September 12, 1983).

William T. Coleman, Jr. Co-Chair, Senior Partner, O'Melveny and Myers, Washington, D.C., New York, N.Y., Los Angeles, California, and Paris, France; former U.S. Secretary of Transportation in the Ford Administration

Cecily Cannan Selby Co-Chair, New York, N.Y., former Dean of Academic Affairs and Chair, Board of Advisors, North Carolina School of Science and Mathematics

Lew Allen, Jr. Director, Jet Propulsion Laboratory, Vice President, California Institute of Technology; former Chief of Staff, U.S. Air Force

Victoria Bergin Associate Commissioner of Education for the State of Texas

George Burnet, Jr. Chairman, Nuclear Engineering Department, Iowa State University, former President, American Society for Engineering Education

William H. Cosby, Jr. Entertainer/Educator

Daniel J. Evans President, The Evergreen State College, former Governor of the State of Washington

Patricia Albjerg Graham Dean, Graduate School of Education, Harvard University

Robert E. Larson Chief Executive Officer, Optimization Technology, Inc.; former President, Institute of Electrical and Electronics Engineers

Gerald D. Laubach President, Pfizer Inc.

Katherine P. Layton Teacher, Mathematics Department, Beverly Hills High School

Ruth B. Love General Superintendent, The Chicago Board of Education

Arturo Madrid II Professor, Department of Spanish and Portuguese, University of Minnesota, former Director, Fund for the Improvement of Postsecondary Education, U.S. Department of Education

Frederick Mosteller Chairman, Department of Health Policy and Management, School of Public Health, Harvard University

M. Joan Parent President, National School Boards Association

Robert W. Parry Distinguished Professor of Chemistry, University of Utah, former President, American Chemical Society

Benjamin F. Payton President, Tuskegee Institute

Joseph E. Rowe Executive Vice President, Research and Defense Systems, Gould, Inc., former Provost for Science and Engineering, Case Western Reserve University

Herbert A. Simon Richard King Mellon University Professor of Computer Science and Psychology, Department of Psychology, Carnegie-Mellon University, Nobel Laureate in Economics

John B. Slaughter Chancellor, University of Maryland, College Park; former Director, National Science Foundation

●Mortimer J. Adler, *The Paideia Proposal: An Educational Manifesto* (New York: Macmillan, 1982).

Members of the Paideia Group

Mortimer J. Adler Chairman, Director, Institute for Philosophical Research; Chairman, Board of Editors, Encyclopaedia Britannica

Jacques Barzun former Provost, Columbia University; Literary Adviser, Charles Scribner's Sons

Otto Bird Former head, General Program of Liberal Studies, University of Notre Dame

Leon Botstein President, Bard College, President, Simon's Rock of Bard College

Ernest L. Boyer President, The Carnegie Foundation for the Advancement of Teaching, Washington, D.C.

Nicholas L. Caputi Principal, Skyline High School, Oakland, California

Douglass Cater Senior Fellow, Aspen Institute for Humanistic Studies

Donald Cowan former President, University of Dallas; Fellow, Dallas Institute of Humanities and Cultures

Alonzo A. Crim Superintendent, Atlanta Public Schools, Atlanta, Georgia

Clifton Fadiman Author and critic

Dennis Gray Deputy Director, Council for Basic Education, Washington, D.C.

Richard Hunt Senior Lecturer and Director of the Andrew W. Mellon Faculty Fellowships Program, Harvard University

Ruth B. Love General Superintendent of Schools, Chicago Board of Education

James Nelson Director, Wye Institute, Inc., Queenstown, Maryland

James O'Toole Professor of Management, Graduate School of Business Administration, University of Southern California

Theodore T. Puck President and Director, Eleanor Roosevelt Institute for Cancer Research, Inc., Denver; Professor of Biochemistry, Biophysics, and Genetics, University of Colorado

Adolph W. Schmidt former Chairman, Board of Visitors and Governors of St. John's College, Annapolis and Santa Fe

Adele Simmons President, Hampshire College

Theodore R. Sizer Chair, A Study of High Schools; former Headmaster, Phillips Academy, Andover

Charles Van Doren Associate Director, Institute for Philosophical Research; Vice President/Editorial, Encyclopaedia Britannica

Geraldine Van Doren Senior Fellow, Institute for Philosophical Research, Secretary, Paideia Project

John Van Doren Senior Fellow, Institute for Philosophical Research; Executive Editor, *Great Ideas Today*

- *Academic Preparation for College: What Students Need to Know and Be Able to Do* (New York: College Board, 1983).

    No specific individual is listed as the author. The preface states that "The College Board wishes to thank the hundreds of school and college educators who contributed to the deliberations that produced *Academic Preparation for College*."

- Theodore R. Sizer, *Horace's Compromise: The Dilemma of The American High School* (Boston: Houghton Mifflin, 1984). Theodore R. Sizer is currently chairman of the department of education at Brown University; formerly Dean, Graduate School of Education, Harvard University; Headmaster, Phillips Academy, Andover, Ma.; and Chairman, *A Study of High Schools*.

● **Committee for Economic Development**, Research and Policy Committee, *Investing In Our Children: Business and the Public Schools* (New York: Committee for Economic Development, 1985).

RESEARCH AND POLICY COMMITTEE

Chairman
William F. May

Vice Chairmen
William S. Edgerly   Education and Social and Urban Development
Roderick M. Hills   Government
James W. McKee, Jr.   International Economic Studies
Rocco C. Siciliano   National Economy

Roy L. Ash*   Los Angeles, California
Ralph E. Bailey   Chairman and Chief Executive Officer, Conoco Inc.
Warren L. Batts   President, Dart & Kraft, Inc.
Jack F. Bennett   Senior Vice President, Exxon Corporation
Theodore A. Burtis   Chairman of the Board, Sun Company, Inc.
Owen B. Butler   Chairman of the Board, The Procter & Gamble Company
Fletcher L. Byrom   Retired Chairman, Koppers Company, Inc.
Robert J. Carlson   Chairman, President and Chief Executive Officer, BMC Inc.
Rafael Carrion, Jr.   Chairman of the Board, Banco Popular de Puerto Rico
John B. Cave   Executive Vice President—Finance, McGraw-Hill, Inc.
Robert A. Charpie   President, Cabot Corporation
Robert Cizik   Chairman and President, Cooper Industries, Inc.
Emilio G. Collado   Executive Chairman, International Planning Corporation
D. Ronald Daniel   Managing Director, McKinsey & Company, Inc.
Ronald R. Davenport   Chairman of the Board, Sheridan Broadcasting Corporation
Peter A. Derow   President, CBS/Publishing Group
Frank P. Doyle   Senior Vice President, General Electric Company
W. D. Eberle   President, Manchester Associates, Ltd.
William S. Edgerly   Chairman of the Board and President, State Street Bank and Trust Company
Thomas J. Eyerman*   Partner, Skidmore, Owings & Merrill

---

*Voted to approve the policy statement but submitted memoranda of comment, reservation, or dissent.

---

*Voted to approve the policy statement but submitted memoranda of comment, reservation, or dissent.

Francis C. Rooney, Jr. Chairman of the Board, Melville Corporation

Henry B. Schacht Chairman of the Board and Chief Executive Officer, Cummins Engine Company, Inc.

Donna E. Shalala President, Hunter College

Philip L. Smith President and Chief Operating Officer, General Foods Corporation

Richard M. Smith Vice Chairman, Bethlehem Steel Corporation

Roger B. Smith* Chairman, General Motors Corporation

Elmer B. Staats Former Comptroller, General of the United States, Washington, D.C.

William C. Stolk Easton, Connecticut

Anthony P. Terracciano Vice Chairman, Global Banking, The Chase Manhattan Bank, N.A.

Walter N. Thayer Chairman, Whitney Communications Company

W. Bruce Thomas Vice Chairman of Administration and Chief Financial Officer, United States Steel Corporation

Sidney J. Weinberg, Jr. Partner, Goldman, Sachs & Co.

Alton W. Whitehouse, Jr. Chairman, The Standard Oil Company (Ohio)

Richard D. Wood Chairman of the Board, Eli Lilly and Company

William S. Woodside Chairman, American Can Company

SUBCOMMITTEE ON BUSINESS AND THE SCHOOLS

Chairman
Owen B. Butler Chairman of the Board, The Procter & Gamble Company

Vice Chairmen
Ronald R. Davenport Chairman of the Board, Sheridan Broadcasting Corporation

Ralph Lazarus Chairman, Executive Committee, Federated Department Stores, Inc.

James W. McKee, Jr. Chairman, CPC International Inc.

Donna E. Shalala President, Hunter College

Alfred Brittain III Chairman of the Board, Bankers Trust Company

Robert A. Charpie President, Cabot Corporation

W. Graham Claytor, Jr. Chairman and President, Amtrak

*Voted to approve the policy statement but submitted memoranda of comment, reservation, or dissent.

Martin Meyerson President Emeritus, University of Pennsylvania

Vincent Reed Vice President/Communications, The Washington Post

ADVISORS

Paul E. Barton Assessment Policy Committee Liaison, National Assessment of Educational Progress

David Bergholz President, Public Education Fund

Alan K. Campbell Vice Chairman, ARA Services, Inc.

Alonzo A. Crim Superintendent, Atlanta Public Schools

Harold Howe II Senior Lecturer, Harvard Graduate School of Education

Michael W. Kirst Professor of Education, Stanford University

Daniel H. Saks Professor of Education Policy and of Economics, Institute for Public Policy Studies, Vanderbilt University

Frank W. Schiff Vice President and Chief Economist, Committee for Economic Development

Nathaniel M. Semple Vice President and Secretary, Research and Policy Committee, Committee for Economic Development

Albert Shanker President, American Federation of Teachers

P. Michael Timpane President, Teachers College, Columbia University

Appendix B
PROPOSED CALIFORNIA VOUCHER INITIATIVE

THE INITIATIVE

The following section shall be added to Article IX of the California Constitution:

Section 17. *Purpose.* The people of California have adopted this section to improve the quality and efficiency of schools, to maximize the educational opportunities of all children, and to increase the authority of parents and teachers.

(1) Voucher Schools

(a) *Classes of Schools.* In addition to the public schools and private schools presently recognized by law, there shall be two classes of schools together known as Voucher Schools.

(b) *Private Voucher Schools.* Private Voucher Schools are private schools entitled to redeem state educational vouchers.

(c) *Public Voucher Schools.* Public Voucher Schools are schools organized as public corporations entitled to redeem such vouchers.

School districts, community colleges and public universities may establish Public Voucher Schools. Each shall be a public corporation governed by rules fixed by the organizing authority at the time of incorporation. Under this article such schools are common schools, and section 6 shall not limit their formation. Except as stated in this section, Public Voucher Schools shall operate according to the laws affecting Private Voucher Schools.

(d) *Limits on Regulation of Voucher Schools.* Voucher Schools shall be entitled to redeem the state vouchers of their students upon filing a statement indicating satisfaction of those requirements for hiring and employment, for curriculum and for facilities which applied to private schools on July 1, 1982; the Legislature may not augment such requirements. No school shall lose eligibility to redeem vouchers except upon proof of substantial violation of this section after notice and opportunity to defend.

No Voucher School may advocate unlawful behavior or expound the inferiority of either sex or of any race nor deliberately provide false or misleading information respecting the school. Each shall be subject to reasonable requirements of disclosure. The Legislature may set reasonable standards of competence for diplomas.

This initiative was drafted by John E. Coons, Professor of Law, University of California at Berkeley; he is also coauthor, with Stephen D. Sugarman, of *Education by Choice: The Case for Family Control* (Berkeley: University of California Press, 1978).

No school shall be ineligible to redeem state vouchers because it teaches moral or social values, philosophy, or religion, but religion may not be taught in public schools or Public Voucher Schools; a curriculum may be required, but no pupil shall be compelled to profess ideological belief or actively to participate in ceremony symbolic of belief.

(2) **Admissions**

(a) *Rules for Admission.* A Voucher School may set enrollment and select students by criteria valid under the federal constitution other than physical handicap, national origin, and place of residence within the state.

(b) *Protecting Low Income Families.* Each Voucher School shall reserve twenty-five percent of each year's new admissions for timely applications from families with income lower than seventy-five percent of California families. If such applications are fewer than the places reserved, all shall be admitted and the balance of reserved places selected as in paragraph (a) of this subsection; if such applications exceed the reserved places, the school may select therefrom the reserved number.

(c) *Choice Among Public Schools.* When district assignments are complete, any district with space remaining in its public schools may open such space to children irrespective of residence, giving reasonable preference to children described in (b). Children so enrolled shall be deemed residents of the receiving district for fiscal purposes.

(3) **Finance**

(a) *A Child's Right to a Voucher.* Every child of school age residing in California is entitled annually without charge to a state voucher redeemable by Voucher Schools and adequate for a thorough education as defined by law.

(b) *Limits on Tuition.* Voucher Schools shall accept vouchers from low income families as full payment for educational and related services. Charges to others shall be consistent with the family's ability to pay.

(c) *Setting the Value of Vouchers.* The average voucher shall be worth approximately ninety percent of the average public cost per pupil of pupils enrolled in public schools. Public cost here and in subsection (3) (d) shall mean every cost to state and local government of maintaining elementary and secondary education in the relevant year as determined by the Department of Finance according to law; it shall not include the costs of funding employee retirement benefits which are unfunded on July 3, 1984.

Vouchers shall be equal for every child of similar circumstance differing only by factors determined to be reasonable by the Legislature. They shall reflect the educational cost attributable to physical handicap and learning disability, and, for children of low income families, the cost of reasonable transportation. Except for schools in which parents or other relatives are principal instructors of their own children, no voucher shall be less than eighty percent of the average voucher for children of similar grade level. A nonprofit Private

Voucher School shall use income from vouchers solely for the provision of educational goods, services, and facilities for its students. The Legislature shall provide for an appropriate division of the voucher in the case of transfers. Nothing required or permitted by this section shall be deemed to repeal or conflict with section 8 of this article or section 5 of Article XVI.

(d) *Limits on Cost.* For school years 1985-86 through 1990-91 the total public cost of elementary and secondary education shall not exceed that of 1983-84 adjusted for changes in average personal income and total school age population. The Controller shall authorize no payment in violation of this sub-section.

(e) *School Building Aid.* Excess space in public schools shall be available to Voucher Schools for rental at actual cost. Where appropriate and necessary, community groups shall be assisted in the founding of Voucher Schools by guaranteed loans and similar aids.

(4) Rights

(a) *Fair Treatment of Students.* A pupil subject to compulsory education who attends a Voucher School may continue therein unless she or he is deriving no substantial academic benefit or is responsible for serious or habitual misconduct related to school. With fair notice and procedures each school may set and enforce a code of conduct and discipline and regulate its academic dismissals. No pupil enrolled in any such school shall suffer discrimination on the basis of race, religion, gender or national origin.

(b) *Consumer Information.* The Legislature shall assure provision of adequate information about Voucher Schools through sources independent of any school or school authority. Parents with special information needs shall receive a grant redeemable for the services of independent education counsellors.

(5) Transitional Provision

The Legislature shall promptly implement this section, ensuring full eligibility for vouchers of at least one-half of all pupils no later than the school year 1985-86 and all pupils in 1986-87.

INDEX

ABOUT THE AUTHOR

Dr. Myron Lieberman is Visiting Professor of Education at Ohio University, Athens, Ohio (1984-86). He is also President of Educational Employment Services, an educational consulting firm. Prior to his appointment at Ohio University, Dr. Lieberman taught at the University of Southern California, City University of New York, Rhode Island College, University of Oklahoma, and Hofstra University. He has frequently served as a consultant to federal, state, and local educational agencies as well as to numerous state and national professional and civil rights organizations.

Dr. Lieberman has authored or coauthored *Education as a Profession* (1956), *The Future of Public Education* (1961), *Collective Negotiations for Teachers* (1966), *Public Sector Bargaining* (1980), and *Bargaining: Where, When, How* (1982). In addition, he has published frequently in both professional and nonprofessional journals, including *Phi Delta Kappan, Harvard Education Review, American School Board Journal, Teachers College Record, Monthly Labor Review, Harper's, Saturday Review, Alternative,* and several newspapers and newspaper syndicates.

Dr. Lieberman holds a bachelor's degree in law, University of Minnesota; a bachelor's degree in education, University of Minnesota; an M.A. degree in education, University of Illinois; and a Ph.D. in philosophy of education, University of Illinois. He is a fellow of the Public Service Research Council and has received several academic awards and honors.